In 1986 after a stint as a burger flipper at McDonald's and a few years as a roof plumber, Rusty moved to Melbourne from his native Queensland in search of a career in entertainment. He first joined a barbershop quartet, playing festivals and shopping centres around Melbourne to great acclaim, as well as a four-month stint at Expo 88 in Brisbane. It was in this group that Rusty first met John Fleming, and together they joined another successful a capella group, the Phones. Then, in 1990, they started the musical comedy group Scared Weird Little Guys. In 2011 the Scaredies finished an incredible career which included an astonishing 4500 performances all over the world playing festivals, comedy clubs, theatres, universities, countless television and radio spots, corporate events, children's shows and everything in between. However, all good things must come to an end and Rusty and John went out on a high with a successful national farewell tour which left their legions of fans shouting for more.

This is Rusty's first book.

SCARED WEIRD FROZEN GUY

One Man's Midlife Mission from Musical Comedian to Antarctic Marathon Man

RUSTY BERTHER

The Five Mile Press

The Five Mile Press Pty Ltd
1 Centre Road, Scoresby
Victoria 3179 Australia
www.fivemile.com.au

Copyright © Rusty Berther, 2012
All rights reserved. No part of this book may be reproduced, stored in a retrieval system, or be transmitted by any form or by any means, electronic, mechanical, photocopying, recording or otherwise, without the prior written permission of the publisher.

Rusty Berther asserts his moral rights to be identified as the author of this book.

First published 2012

Printed in Australia at Griffin Press.
Only wood grown from sustainable regrowth forests is used in the manufacture of paper found in this book.

Page design and typesetting by Shaun Jury
Cover design by Phil Campbell
Cover photographs and all internal photographs, except where marked, from author's collection
Maps by Kristy Lund-White
Union Glacier map detail courtesy ANI Topographic Maps
Antarctic terrain map detail © Shutterstock

National Library of Australia Cataloguing-in-Publication entry
   Berther, Rusty.
   Scared weird frozen guy : one man's midlife mission from musical comedian to Antarctic marathon man / Rusty Berther.
   ISBN: 9781743007433 (pbk.)
   Berther, Rusty.
   Marathon running—Antarctica—Biography.
   Comedians—Australia—Biography.
   796.4252092

For Denise, Hank and Mary-Lou

CONTENTS

28 November 2011 1
What Are You Running From? 3
Look Mum, No Instruments 11
Have Sequins, Will Travel 21
Living the Dream 33
Scared Weird Little Guys Who Don't Know
 Why They Do What They Do 37
The Scaredies and the Laugh 47
'It's Only One Bomb . . .' 55
Make Me a Pizza, *Then* Follow Your Dream 65
Are Those Real Cheerleaders? 71
Yew Towk Fuhnny 85
We All Been A-Waiting On Y'alls Call 99
If It's November Here 101
Great Day for a Run 107
I'd Like to Thank 111
The Biggest Gig We Ever Done 117
That was Dudley's Sheep Rooting Joke 123
The All-Star Comedy Superband 127
Step Away from the Microphone 131
An Antique Shop, a Dog and a Pair of
 Expensive Socks 135
A Mistake You Only Make Once 143

I'm Glad I Never Have to do One of
  Those *Ever* Again 153
Eight School Mums, a Fast Lesbian and Me 155
A Marathon? In Antarctica? 159
That's it! Get Fucked! 161
Go! Where Only Hundreds Had Been Before! 165
'You Should Film It …' 169
Lock it in, Eddie 173
What if Marathon was Closer to Athens? 183
Metatarsophalangeal Articulations … 203
Stairway to Hell 209
Dodging Forklifts and Frozen Peas 217
The Most Intricate Online Scam Ever? 225
Now Just Sign Here … And Here … And Here … 229
What Kind of Shoes Do You Wear? 233
The Evil Beyond the Door 237
No Entiendo 239
Packing Expectations … and a Ukulele 241
The Flight 243
You Eat Shoe Polish? 247
Punta Arenas 255
Meeting the Other Runners 263
The Safety Briefing: Keep It Brief, Mate 269
What Does Mystery Taste Like? 273
Igor is Not a Dirty Word 281
Wow! 287
Mid Ice Crisis 297
'Are You One of This Men?' 319
7th Antarctic Ice Marathon and 100 K,
  December 2011: Results 321
Thanks 323

When people hear that I love running they often ask: 'What are you running from?'

I don't think I am running from anything.

Maybe I am running *to* something.

Maybe I am just running.

28 NOVEMBER 2011

The plane to Antarctica was leaving at 7 am. The documentary maker, Bradley, and I went back to the hotel after dinner and did some final 'night before the big event' interviews and got to bed around 11 pm. After all the planning and dreaming there was only one more sleep until my big running adventure finally began. This was getting very exciting. I felt calm and confident and ready to take on the world.

I had completed all of my training for the marathon despite the setback with my foot and I was currently fitter than I had ever been in my life. I had raised the funds for this expedition by myself and I had gathered an incredibly expensive collection of specialist clothing and gear that I would likely never use again. I had made it through hours and hours of painful gym sessions and grinding runs up mountains, along beaches, down bush tracks and through city parks and I was now ready to achieve this once-in-a-lifetime dream. I couldn't believe it was all about to finally happen.

An hour later I was lying on the bathroom floor, hallucinating and throwing my guts up with the worst bout of gastro I had ever experienced and my Antarctic dream was over.

To explain how I got to this point in my life we need to go back. Way back. I need to tell you some of the stories of my life that led me to the conclusion that running a marathon in Antarctica was some kind of good idea.

I know what you're probably thinking. A marathon? In Antarctica? Sounds like a piece of cake for such an accomplished, experienced sportsperson as Rusty from the Scared Weird Little Guys. Well, guess what my friends: the truth is I am actually not the finely honed specimen of steely-muscled man-cake that my publicist would have you believe. Nor am I a lean, sinewy runner with the physique and poise of a Kenyan Olympian.

I am actually just like you; that is if you are a 42-year-old stocky white bloke with sideburns and a slight limp. Otherwise, I am nothing like you.

But, as all runners know, you have to start your running career sometime, and it's never too late.

Have I been a runner all my life? No, I have not. Did taking up running come easily to me? No, it did not.

Will I ask myself questions and then answer them to launch into a chapter about how running has featured throughout my life? Yes, yes I will.

WHAT ARE YOU RUNNING FROM?

I ran as a child. A little bit, anyway. I was active and played plenty of sport growing up on Bribie Island. Bribie Island, or as we locals affectionately call it, 'Bribie', is a small island off the coast of Queensland, just north of Brisbane. I played Rugby League until Under-16s – when the opposition players started turning up with beards and legs like tree trunks it was time for me to stop. I played junior cricket, golf and did the general running around and exploring that was the standard thing for kids to do while growing up on an island filled with bush tracks and beaches.

My favourite sport as a teenager was squash. What the hell ever happened to squash? Squash fever gripped the world of social sport in the 1970s. It seemed that everyone was playing it. They all turned up on weeknights to puff and pant, damaging their knees by pounding on wooden floors while wearing Dunlop Volleys. We lived down the road from the Bribie squash courts and I was pretty good at squash. For a few years I even played 'comp squash', which is short for 'competition squash'.

There were four people in a team and we were a very mismatched lot. There was a bricklayer, a teacher, the bloke who ran the bike shop and me. Each Tuesday night I would be picked up by one of them – I was about fourteen at the time – and the four of us would make the hour-long drive into the northern

Brisbane suburbs to play in some social squash competition. There were many leagues around such as the SSL (Suburban Squash League) and the BSA (Brisbane Squash Association). I think our comp was called the NBASLMGBNBTDOTN – the North Brisbane Amateur Squash League for Mismatched Groups of Blokes with Nothing Better To Do On a Tuesday Night, or something like that.

It was great for fitness and it satisfied my keen competitive nature. One of the memories I retain from that time is the night I played against a fellow named Quentin Dempster. You never forget a name like that and years later he turned up on the television as an ABC political commentator. I was truly chuffed and he remains the first famous person I have ever met.

• • •

One of the few trophies I ever received in my youth was actually for running. The trophy is inscribed with the following words:

1979 BRIBIE FUN RUN – RUSSELL BERTHER – FIRST.

That's what it says. I didn't really come first. Well, I sort of came first. The run was a relay event with teams of eight people. It was part of the prestigious, inaugural Bribie Island Festival and I was part of a team from the Bribie Primary School.

The Bribie Island Festival was a big thing for us islanders and included a fete, a fun run, and a Grand Parade, which consisted of a few floats and a couple of cars containing personalities who were mostly unknown to us. I remember seeing sports commentator Billy J Smith in one car followed by a young woman waving madly from the rear window who, apparently, was 'Alice from *The Sullivans*'. It didn't take much to impress us beachy yokels back then.

The fun run was a simple affair. We each had to run a leg of the race that started at the Caboolture turn-off and finished at the school on Bribie. I had to run from the Bribie Bridge to the library – the highly important penultimate leg. It was a gruelling stretch of 2.14 kilometres (I just checked the distance on Google Earth). After waiting at one end of the bridge in the hot sun for a few hours, I finally noticed someone approaching across the bridge. Our team was in the lead! I was passed the baton by my panting, crimson-faced classmate, Peter Hampson, and though the other teams were closing fast (there was one other team), I managed to maintain our lead and pass the baton on to our anchor man, Peter Box, who powered away and crossed the finish line to bring us victory. Of course I didn't get to see the finish, it was too far away and I had just run over two kilometres for goodness' sake. So there were no triumphant slow-motion scenes of us hugging each other and jumping around in jubilation. I probably just wandered off to the milk bar to buy an icy pole and walked home.

Even with such a successful beginning to my running career, I failed to get bitten by the 'running bug'. I failed even to develop a slight 'running rash'. Running and I were still a long way from getting together. How can I put it in today's language? Running and I were not even Facebook friends, let alone swapping personal information on rsvp.com. The next time I went for a run was about 16 years later. I can safely say that I didn't run during the entire decade of the 1980s.

You know how it goes: high school comes along and sport becomes less of a priority, then you get a job, and then you're forty and unfit so you start running.

That's pretty much how it was for me anyway.

High school was the beginning of the end of sport for me. I gave up squash. (Cut to a close-up of my knees under the desk going 'Thank you, thank you, thank you!') I played a bit of tennis and golf and table tennis, but that was it. Running was something that the super-sporty types did or you were forced to do during PE.

During the high school years, different interests and priorities start to come into your life, so running and I were not destined to get together for while yet. It was around this time that I discovered music and bands.

My first band was in the year 1982 at Caboolture High School. We were called Obscure Alternatives, which was interesting as while we were certainly obscure, we were not alternative. We played songs like 'My Sharona', 'Heartache Tonight', 'My Kind of Lover' and 'Cool World'.

The band members were me on guitar, my sister Sherry on bass, and future country music star and husband of Nicole Kidman, Keith Urban on lead guitar, vocals, bass, drums, keyboards and anything else he could get his hands on. There was also a drummer called Bashy McNoRhythm or something like that. He played too loud, but he couldn't keep time. We rehearsed in the school hall and thought we were pretty good. Keith was great to play with. Even as a 14-year-old he was incredibly musically talented and had an amazing drive to succeed. He never did a scrap of schoolwork, all he ever wanted was to go to Nashville and become a country music star.

We thought he had crap taste in music, though. We would be sitting in the school music room listening to our tapes of Echo and the Bunnymen, the Stranglers and early Human League, thinking we were sooooo cool. Keith would bounce in with his *Best of Dolly Parton* tape and cheerfully try to play it for us, much to our horror. I admit I now happily own the *Best of Dolly Parton* on CD and will gladly play it any time. Keith would often come and stay over at our house and he and Sherry and I would spend hours recording ourselves on our ancient Marantz tape recorder that had speed up and slow down capabilities. We would send up ads and record chipmunk versions of pop songs and giggle hilariously as Keith would record ridiculously fast versions of the Benny Hill theme and Dire Straits songs. By the way, I still have those tapes, so if you are reading this,

What Are You Running From?

Keith, please send money in a plain, unmarked envelope via my publishers or the tapes go up on eBay.

As I mentioned before, there was pretty much no running during this stage of my life, though I can actually recall one occurrence that involved Keith and running which should be told here. During a compulsory school cross-country practice run, I found myself straggling amongst a group of kids led by Keith and his delinquently humorous cohorts, Grant Taylor and Mozzie Todd. As the run was through the expansive pine forest behind Caboolture High School, Grant suggested cutting through the trees and taking a shortcut. We all thought this sounded like a great idea and it was, apart from having to run through giant spider webs, getting scratched on broken branches, avoiding nests of tiger snakes and tripping on potholes concealed by years of fallen pine needles.

We eventually broke through the undergrowth straight into the path of Mr Gardner, the giant PE teacher, whose six-foot-four frame usually played Rugby League in the QRL state competition. He lined us up and gave us all a few whacks on the backside with an aluminium relay baton. Ah, corporal punishment, how fun it is to look back on when it was a daily part of our education system.

Of course this whole episode taught us a valuable lesson – never run in the school cross-country. I have also discovered an appropriate old West Indian proverb that sums up our experience of that day. It goes like this:

Long road draw sweat, shortcut draw blood.

Or, more accurately for us:

Long road draw sweat, shortcut draw spider webs, snakes and baton-wielding PE teachers.

• • •

I finished school and got a job with my uncles that did not involve any running. I became a roof plumber, and for two years we worked on the site of the Golden Circle pineapple canning factory in Brisbane. We were replacing the old fibro asbestos roof after it was damaged in a rather nasty hailstorm. In 1985 asbestos removal practices were a bit different than they are now. For us it involved unscrewing all the roof sheets and carrying the heavy, dusty, 30-kilogram bastards over our heads to the end of the building where we threw them into an open dump truck. No gloves, no special suits, no facemasks. As the lowest member in the pecking order of the roof plumbers, it was then my job to climb down and sweep up all the broken bits of asbestos fibro into the rather large old dump truck and drive it out of the factory. I had no driver's licence yet so this was the vehicle that I learned to drive in: an ancient 10-tonne dump truck. It was just like driving a car except everything was much larger and harder to push in – the pedals, the steering wheel, the buttons on the radio.

It never really worried me, working with the old asbestos roof sheets. We heard it was 'a bit' dangerous if you sawed it and breathed in the powder, but we weren't doing that. We were just smashing the sheets into little pieces in a truck and I was sweeping up all the leftovers. I didn't hear about asbestosis until years later and now I simply prefer not to think about it. I guess if something is lodged in my lungs, it hasn't shown itself yet and there is nothing I can do about it now. If running a marathon in Antarctica isn't going to make it show itself, then I don't know what is.

By the way, how do you know if something is made of asbestos? Sniiiiiiiiiiiiiiiff. Yep, that's asbestos ...

I worked on the roof for a couple of years while dabbling in a few local Brisbane bands. One was called Cactus Fever, which was the beginning of my life-long love affair with country music. I guess Keith Urban's Dolly Parton tapes got through to me eventually. Working on the roof was a beneficial and eye-opening time for me in many ways. I earned good money for an 18-year-old. I learnt how to use power tools and realised that not all blokes on building sites are yobbo fuckwits. I learnt that sometimes in life you have to take the blame for something that is not your fault, and other times the best thing to do in some situations is to shut your mouth and not say anything. Eventually I decided that cutting myself daily on sharpened iron roof sheets in 35-degree temperatures and getting sunburned testicles (from the sun reflecting off the roof) was not the future I wanted for myself. I had saved up some money so I packed up my 1976 Holden Kingswood with some clothes, guitars and my record collection and moved to Melbourne, arriving a week after my nineteenth birthday.

LOOK MUM, NO INSTRUMENTS

Running was still far from becoming a part of my life. All I wanted to do at this point was to become a bass player in a rock band. I immediately went on the dole – also known as the 'Paul Keating Scholarship' or the 'Fortnightly Arts Grant'. It was rather easy to get unemployment benefits in those days. You really just had to turn up to the CES office every two weeks and be polite. Each Saturday I would eagerly scour the newspaper entertainment classifieds for bass player gigs. I don't know what part of this process broke down, because six weeks after moving to Melbourne I was singing in a barbershop quartet.

If you've never seen nor heard a barbershop quartet, let me try to describe it for you. It's a group that sings music in the style of 'a capella'. A capella is an Italian term that literally means 'can't afford instruments'.

Imagine the song 'Tom's Diner' by Suzanne Vega. It's the song where she sings unaccompanied, describing all the things that go on in a diner like how she's waiting for her coffee and someone's got an umbrella and two people are talking and she's reading the zzzzzzzzzz ... Sorry, I dropped off for a moment there. Where was I? Right, so imagine there's Suzanne Vega singing with no instruments, actually imagine four Suzanne Vegas singing with no instruments, and they are all wearing stripy vests and boater hats and they've all got large black moustaches ... This is not really working, is it?

If you don't know what a barbershop quartet is, Google it.

Our barbershop quartet was called Four Chairs No Waiting. Four Chairs No Waiting is an old term often heard in turn-of-the-century barbershops that means 'can't afford instruments' or something.

We sang around Melbourne at various fetes, festivals, shopping centres and theatre restaurants. We did the floorshow at one that boasted it was 'Melbourne's only fondue theatre restaurant'. You think fondue is cheesy? You should have seen the show ...

The show wasn't *that* bad, actually, though the owner, who considered himself a bit of an 'actor', insisted on being a part of the show, and we had to write a sketch for him to 'act' in.

I remember that the theatre restaurant was located, oddly enough, between a Jewish bakery and a Christian bookstore in a strip of shops in a rather dull outer suburb and that it had a total capacity of 51 people. The three other members of the barbershop quartet were a pot-smoking, hard-drinking hippie; a John-Farnham-loving Mormon; and a fuzzy-haired, ex-operatic bass singer with a metal plate in his head. We would have made an excellent social squash team.

The hippie was the one to whom I could relate the most. Apart from being a decent singer, he was also a pretty good actor and he had a great sense of theatrics and professionalism when it came to performing. Well ... mostly. As long as the pre-performance routine involved a good bottle of red and a joint or two. I have the hippie to thank for introducing me to positive thinking and meditation, and also for teaching me how to roll three-paper joints. Though in retrospect, most of the positive thinking and meditation usually came after one of the three-paper joints. One night the hippie went onstage at the House of Cheese or the Fondue Hut, or whatever the fuck it was called, after consuming half a bottle of scotch and three or four flu tablets. In one of the all-time worst performances I have ever been involved with on any stage ever, he managed to forget his lines, fall on one of the front tables, and vomit off the back of the stage. All during the opening number.

The bass singer, who we called Big Roscoe, was an intriguing man. Due to the plate in his head, he had some memory problems that caused no end of trouble regarding rehearsals and forgotten gigs. It was frustrating as he stubbornly refused to use a diary. We were stuck between feeling sorry for him and wanting to punch him.

He drove a hotted-up 1978 XC Ford Falcon and had a fondness for Butter Menthol cough lozenges. He always had a packet of them in his top pocket and a half-sucked lozenge in his mouth. He had performed with the Australian Opera for many years and had an EXTREMELY LOUD voice and vigorous, animated arm movements, even when he was just talking. He performed with such gusto and enthusiasm that flecks of saliva would fly randomly from his mouth as he sang.

I remember one extremely windy day we were performing at the Royal Melbourne Show on an outdoor stage. We were gallantly singing one of our zingy barbershop standards like 'Coney Island Baby' or 'Sweet Adeline' or 'My Moustache is Gayer than Yours', when Big Roscoe shot a particularly large glob of spit from his mouth into the oncoming headwind. It travelled about a metre, hung suspended in the air for an instant, then blew back straight into the mouth of the hippie, who at that point was open mouthed and in full voice. He choked, grabbed his throat and started spluttering. I collapsed in a fit of laughter. The Mormon, believing the show must go on, kept singing. Big Roscoe just blasted on, completely oblivious to the fact that he had just deposited a new life form straight down the gullet of the hippie. I didn't come through the gig unscathed either. The hippie and I were standing backstage, reliving the whole frightening event, when he looked down at my chest with a strange expression on his face. I kid you not, stuck to my vest was a half-sucked Butter Menthol.

Big Roscoe didn't survive in the group for much longer. He left after a shouty two-week period of arguments and belligerent chest puffing. After we had performed a particularly average theatre restaurant gig, he ended up storming off out of our lives in a lozenge-fuelled rage. At first he was replaced by a blow-up sex doll for two gigs, the details of which I shan't go into here, but let me just say it seemed like a good idea at the time. Thankfully, Big Roscoe was eventually replaced by a human.

Our new bass singer was a stick thin, delightfully gentle ex-folk singer with a booming resonant voice. He was the only one of us with a real moustache, but that wasn't the only reason he got in the group. He immediately made a positive impression on us and for some reason he got the nickname Yogi.

Yogi, bless him, always forgot things and lost stuff. Costumes, wallets, lyrics, song parts, guitars, rhythm – he was a walking Bermuda Triangle. Yogi was also extremely fragile. Not mentally or emotionally, but physically. He once broke two ribs while sneezing. True story. I have Yogi to thank for introducing me to the fellow who I was going to share a stage with for the next 24 years.

The Mormon was moving on to greener pastures so our barbershop quartet needed a new lead singer. A few weeks of excruciating auditions later, we still had no one. Yogi had been doing some folky guitar strumming spots down at the Green Man Café in Malvern. The Green Man was Melbourne's 'folk hot spot', if there could be such a thing. Yogi mentioned to the owner, Mavis, that we were looking for a new singer. She told him about a young fellow who was a competent guitarist with a good voice called John Fleming. Yogi arranged a meeting and John came over to have a sing with us at the hippie's place in Prahran.

We sat out in the backyard in the gentle Melbourne sunshine, surrounded by a dozen or so rather large marijuana plants. The hippie had been a busy boy.

My first impressions of John were mixed. He had a strong voice and knew harmony and music theory, which excited me as I was the only one doing arrangements for the group at that stage. He was around my age (20) so I felt that at last I had an age ally, as the hippie was 40 and Yogi, a very young 44. John's dress sense, however, was something else. He was wearing an ill-fitting Daffy Duck t-shirt, short shorts and a pair of what can only be described as red leather pirate boots. Oh, how he loved those red boots! He would wear them with shorts, jeans, suits, onstage, offstage and probably to bed. They survived for years despite being nearly worn out. In fact it wouldn't surprise me if he still has them. Thankfully, though, the boots didn't influence our decision. John was by far the best person we had auditioned and his enthusiasm, musical skills and exceptional manners made him a welcome addition to our group and to the next stage of my life.

We had been rehearsing with the new line-up for a month and with the negative vibes and lozenges of the previous cast gone, Four Chairs No Waiting had a new-found enthusiasm and energy. We dropped the daggy, stripy vests and boater hats that traditional barbershop quartets wore and went for a new look which could be described as 'anything that has as many crazy colours and shapes on it as possible'. Remember this was the late 1980s. How can I describe it? Imagine if the Wiggles had 20 members with different coloured tops and a large monster ate them and the monster was chewing them all up but before it could digest all of the members it vomited them all over four guys wearing matching clothes. That's what our new look was.

Our first gig as the new, improved, funky, zany Four Chairs No Waiting was at a busking competition in the city. We didn't win. A little act you may have heard of called the Doug Anthony All Stars won. We came third ... and there were only two acts.

Unperturbed, we did some busking in the Bourke Street Mall, made about 50 bucks and went out for pancakes. This was living, baby!

We were being booked for performances through the Flim Flam singing telegram company and the gigs started to flow fairly regularly from this point. We were a little frightened when we got booked for the Black Rock Bowling Club Christmas function and they wanted two 40-minute sets. We had nowhere near that amount of material so we all had to dig deep and dust off some old solo material to flesh out the show.

Yogi sang a few folk numbers on his acoustic guitar, melting the 80-year-old ladies' hearts with the liquid gold of his rich baritone voice. The hippie broke out an old character he used to do called The Vicar. The Vicar was a dirty 'whoops! ooh er!' kind of an act except without any jokes. I had recently been on the Red Faces talent segment of the television show *Hey Hey It's Saturday* and won a trip to Tangalooma in Queensland (by bus). I had performed a ukulele version of 'I've Been Everywhere', so that's what I decided to do at Black Rock, asking John to accompany me on the guitar in what would be a precursor to our long career together as the Scared Weird Little Guys. A few years later, that song became a staple of our live set. We ended up performing it probably two or three thousand times with the Scaredies, so, counting the gig at Black Rock, it was the first and last song we ever sang together onstage.

Running entered my life again for a short moment around this time. An outdoor afternoon gig at a park in Carlton saw us getting ready in a tent about a hundred metres away from the stage. Someone (I bet it was the hippie) thought it would be a great idea to run all the way to the stage when we were introduced. I knew it was a bad idea about 20 metres into the sprint when the thought, 'Gee, I haven't run for a while,' actually entered my head. I wasn't alone, either. Before we reached the stage we were all at a rather slow jog and trying to sing the first song was a hilarious disaster.

'Good ... puff ... pant ... afternoon every ... puff ... body ... pant ... we are ... Four ... puff ... Chairs ... pant ... puff ... No ... puff ... Waiting ... puff.' [Hands on hips.]

We also scored a regular gig at another theatre restaurant in North Melbourne. We performed our show over two halves, with a magician or comedian opening the show. The standard of opening acts varied from quite good to jaw-droppingly bad. I saw a guy one night do a parody of the Elvis Presley song 'Devil in Disguise' that floored us all. It went like this:

You look like an Arab
Walk like an Arab
Talk like an Arab
But I got wise
You're just an Abo in disguise ...

Wow! I still can't believe someone would do that in the name of comedy. Sure, it was a long time ago, I hear you say. Yes, but not the 1950s.

Once again, at this theatre restaurant, the owner insisted on getting up onstage and doing a bit of 'material' at the top of the show. What is it with the owners of theatre restaurants wanting to be part of the show? Is it like they can't get work anywhere else so they have to actually buy their own venue to get a gig? I think it's possibly a case of them not wanting to pursue such a 'risky' career as entertainment but still wanting to be involved in some convoluted way that also offers them the chance to 'tread the boards' occasionally. This particular guy had a habit of turning up to the venue wearing only running shorts and a t-shirt before changing into his 'good clothes'. He would invariably get distracted and end up seating people and talking to the audience members before the show, which was great, apart from the fact he would squat down to talk and his testicles would pop out either side of his shorts. It was like, 'Welcome folks, on your table you'll find the menu. Over here is the stage, the toilets are over there and these are my balls, have a great night.'

We were doing Friday and Saturday nights, our show was really starting to come together and we were getting paid cash. I think it was the cool sum of $75 each per show. One night I did the show stoned, thanks to the hippie.

'It's not that strong,' he insisted. Oh yeah, that old one. I tell you, if I had a nickel ... Like the shows we did with the blow-up doll, it seemed like a good idea at the time but I didn't find it much fun at all. Being stoned while onstage just made everything more difficult – talking, singing, standing. We would be halfway through a song and I would be thinking, 'Whoa ... everyone's looking at me.'

My brain would say, 'It's okay, man, you're cool, you're onstage ... they're supposed to be looking at you.'

Suddenly my brain had turned into one of Cheech and Chong. Then I would start thinking about a particular word that I had just said.

Dixie. Dix ... ie ... Hmm ... Strange word. Dixie ... Is that even a real word, man?

Shut up Chong ...

Dixie, Dixie, Dixie, Dixie, Dixie, Dixie, Dixie.

Wow, I can think of the word over and over and I am still singing ... Cool.

Then I realised the song had finished and I was the only one still singing ... Not cool.

We had some fun times at that particular theatre restaurant and were starting to really hit our straps performance-wise. One night a rather theatrical-looking character approached us after a show and offered Four Chairs No Waiting a couple of seven-week engagements up at Expo 88 in Brisbane.

• • •

Expo 88 was a very memorable and significant time for me. Living in a share house with your mates and being surrounded by interesting and eccentric performers from all over the world for four months was influential, to say the least. I was single and turned 21 while I was there. There were parties and singing and musical jams and get togethers ... What a time.

It was an experience that absolutely cemented for me what I wanted to do with my life. Perform and travel.

HAVE SEQUINS, WILL TRAVEL

At the end of the year, John and I got a call for a great new musical opportunity back in Melbourne. To be honest, we'd had enough of four-part harmony. We had explored everything that four-part harmony could offer, so we jumped at the chance to do something that had nothing to do with a four-part singing group. That was to join a five-part singing group. Imagine five Suzanne Vegas in a room ...

In fact it was John who got the call from his old friend Reg Ellery to join this new group, the Phones. I was just tagging along because it seemed like a good idea. Also, at that point in time, the Phones were well established and were probably Australia's premier a capella group. When I say 'premier a capella group' I mean 'only a capella group'. Reg was the most experienced a capella singer around. I think he had been singing a capella music since the Baroque era or something like that. He was a founding member of Australia's foremost exponents of the style, Polyphony.

Polyphony had had an extraordinarily large amount of line-up changes since they started in 1978. This was mainly due to the brutal nature of Reg's vocal warm-up routines and the gruelling rock and roll lifestyle of the typical a capella singer. I believe they had had somewhere around 672 different members. Oh, if I had a dollar for each time someone came up to me after a show in some shithole backwater of Australia and goofily said, 'Hey, I used to be in Polyphony,' I would probably have about, I don't know, like five or 10 dollars. Okay, it's not that much but it seemed like it happened a lot.

In order to keep up with the heady, fast-changing world of the Australian a capella scene, Polyphony changed their name to the Phones in 1982. Five line-up changes later, in 1983, Reg decided to call it quits. It was only the begging of former members and threats from the tax department that made Reg agree to continue with the Phones. Finally, at the end of 1988, the other members had had enough and they all left, leaving Reg with the name, the pitch pipe, and a set of large pink-and-white curtains emblazoned with the Phones logo. He decided, for the fifteenth time, to give it one more go.

This is where John and I came on board. I didn't realise at the time we got the call that John, having sung with Reg in a choir before, was admitted straight into the group, whereas I would have to go through the slightly awkward process of auditioning for them. I was a confident young chap and at no time did I think I would be anything less than an automatic selection. Reg, however, had other ideas.

I had never auditioned for anything before and hadn't prepared anything special. I had my guitar with me and was going to accompany myself on an obscure, slowish, bluesy Patsy Cline song called 'Don't Ever Leave Me Again'.

I arrived at the address of the audition – the Phones' offices. It was a two-storey terrace house in Fitzroy that the group shared with a staging business. I couldn't believe this group had their own building! This was the big time, baby! In the waiting room there were quite a few poncy music-theatre types sitting around holding sheet music. We eyed each other off, smiled falsely and muttered nervous 'hellos'. I could tell they were silently scoffing to themselves when they saw me holding a guitar.

'Dammit!' I said to myself. 'What kind of idiot brings a guitar to an audition for an a capella group?'

'What kind of idiot brings a guitar to an audition for an a capella group?'

That wasn't me talking to myself again. It was the first question Reg asked me when I got into the audition room.

'Uh ...' I stammered, 'only the best damn singing idiot you'll see tonight!'

We chatted for a bit and John asked me a few loaded questions he already knew the answers to.

'Soooo [looks at sheet of paper] Rusty, is it? Do you have any previous experience in a capella groups?'

'Why, yes I do!'

'Oh good, good ... Which one?'

'Um ... the one I was in with you for the last 12 months.'

'Ah yes, yes,' he said, nodding unconvincingly, 'I remember you now ...'

So the audition went okay but Reg still wasn't convinced. I had to return a week later for a second round. Reg didn't like the song that I had done in the first audition. He wanted to see something a little more up-tempo. I didn't really want to skip down the Broadway musical path so I chose 'Viva Las Vegas' *and* I brought my guitar along again to back myself. Take that, you scoffing poncy musical theatre types!

Anyway, I guess Reg liked the song. Either that or everyone else who auditioned was crap because later that night, I was officially crowned the six-hundred-and-seventy-third member of Polyphony/the Phones.

• • •

There were five of us in the new line-up. Reg, John, me and the other two new members, Michael and Paul.

I must admit it was exciting. It felt very professional to be in an established group that had its own rehearsal space and offices. We were put on a wage and immediately started full-time rehearsals. Reg's long pink and white curtains with the Phones logo looked fabulous hanging in the front window.

By golly gosh it was fun – singing every day and learning new arrangements. Plus the Phones had one thing that Four Chairs No Waiting never had – choreography!

One day each week we would grab five microphone stands and flounce down to an empty aerobics studio with mirrored walls to practise our stylin' dance moves. We weren't actually very coordinated as a group. There was a lot of 'step-touch' and finger clicking going on, with the occasional 'box-step' thrown in for good measure.

After five weeks we had fallen into an enjoyable routine that was previously unfamiliar to me. Daily singing, weekly wage and choreographed dance steps. These three things combined to make us all very happy and excited young fellows – until the day it all fell into a stinking pile of leotards.

We arrived at the office one morning to find Reg and our personal assistant, Doris, in the front office going through the books wearing very serious expressions. They had discovered that someone within our organisation had not been as good as we thought at paying the bills and looking after the accounts. Some of the debts we uncovered were the installation of a $9000 phone system, permanent rental of *two* hire cars – you know how cheap *that* must have been – and a $5000 photocopier.

Five grand for a photocopier! And this was in 1989! What the fuck did this thing do? I could design you a photocopier that had a midget living inside it who hand sketched the copies *and* gave you a hand job while you were waiting for less than five grand.

These little financial discoveries went on all morning and by the end of the day, we discovered the Phones were a tick over $50,000 in debt.

When the smoke cleared, we decided to continue on and pay off the money that 'we' owed. There's nothing like working for six months clearing someone else's debts to make you a tad bitter. Nonetheless we were over it now. We all learned from the experience and it certainly made us a bonded unit, for a while anyway.

We had to move out of Phones Central, but we found an excellent new rehearsal space, otherwise known as 'our lounge rooms'.

A few weeks later we had about half an hour of material all ready to go, we were feeling confident and it was time for our first gig with the new line up – a twenty-first birthday party in the outer Eastern suburbs of Melbourne. We didn't have our fancy proper costumes just yet, so we decided upon black jeans with different coloured long sleeve skivvies. Sound familiar? This was a couple of years before the Wiggles started but I can't help thinking that they obviously ripped us off and we should sue them ... only joking, we were nothing like the Wiggles. Back to the party. We opened the set with 'Big Red Car' followed by 'Hot Potato' ...

Actually we opened with our peppy a capella version of 'Crazy Little Thing Called Love'. We were set up in the backyard of an enormous suburban mansion. There was a massive white marquee containing tables of food, a dance floor and a DJ. Our performance area was outside the marquee, down near the back fence, next to the pool. The partygoers were obviously not a capella aficionados and were more interested in sculling West Coast Coolers and talking than listening to us. We couldn't hear ourselves through the PA system and were singing out of tune and out of time. We forgot dialogue and dance moves, and those moves that we remembered were clunky and forced. Michael and I collided at one point and knocked a mike stand over, sending a $1500 microphone gurgling to the bottom of the pool. Risking both humiliation and electrocution, I gallantly retrieved the mike by pulling it out by the still-attached lead. I spoke into it and sounded like a cross between Charlie Brown's teacher from *Peanuts* and Optimus Prime from *Transformers*. It would have been funny except nobody was actually watching us at that point. We finished the set and retreated with our tails between our legs. It was a necessary rude awakening for us.

We worked very hard over the next few weeks and it showed. The following month we played gigs at two high schools, a TAFE college, Le Joke comedy club, three private parties, two corporate awards nights, and the Colac Pool. We had made it.

Okay, we still had a long way to go, but the show was firing and, more importantly, we were paying off our debt and were well on our way to getting paid a wage again. As we couldn't afford any hired help, we all had to shoulder the load of running the group. The organisation of the bookings and administration was taken over by Paul. Reg continued as our musical director. John and I got the job of looking after mail and the fan magazine. I can't quite remember what Michael's job was. Probably mincing around and making us laugh, as he was very good at both.

It was a rather unbalanced situation, as Paul had to do a great deal more work than the rest of us and he, rightly, asked to get paid more. Though this was absolutely fair, at the time it didn't seem so and it was the beginning of a division between Paul and the rest of us. To be honest, John and I were absolutely crap at maintaining our job. If it was a simple case of updating a website or Facebook fan page, I think we may have been better at it – maybe. Of course this was way before internet fan pages and things like Myspace.

[Cue anyone under the age of 16 –'Wot the hellz Myspace?']

In a situation that somehow still amazes me today, the Phones had established and maintained a huge mailing list of fans and even sent out a monthly newsletter ... In envelopes! With stamps! The newsletter had updates on the Phones, upcoming gigs, some badly photocopied shots of the group (despite that expensive photocopier) and a quiz or crossword. It was called some kind of poor phone-related pun like *Calling You* or *Crossed Lines* or *Hang Ups*.

The previous line-up and Doris the faithful assistant had worked very hard to maintain the compiling and distribution of the newsletter, which was an important profile-boosting tool.

John and I soon put an end to that, however. We started full of enthusiasm and zeal, answering fan mail (By hand! Using pens and paper!) and producing a couple of newsletters on John's father's computer. It was an old computer called the Commodore 64. The 64 stood for the number of words you could type into it before the memory was full. We used a program called Dinosaur or Out of Date 2.0 or something like that to produce the newsletters. After a couple of months, the glamour of the pre-Windows computer publishing world diminished and we slackened off. We received some strongly worded letters from neglected 14-year-old fans and regular verbal dressing-downs from Paul over our lack of effort. These lectures usually came at the end of a rehearsal when Paul would say, 'Is that all, Reg? Because I have a few things I would like to say.'

I would think, 'Oh God, here it comes again,' knowing full well that we really had been quite hopeless and not been pulling our weight. Then the lecture and dressing-down would begin. During the most serious parts, Michael would stand behind Paul making wanking gestures to make me laugh and make both of us seem like the immature, puerile children that we really were. Then Paul, despite his best efforts to remain serious, would crack up as well and shake his head and roll his eyes in disbelief and we would all be friends again for a while.

A major point of disagreement amongst us was costuming. Some of us (me) quite enjoyed wearing the pre-Wiggles jeans-and-coloured-tops outfits, to which we added black bomber jackets with 'The Phones' printed on the back. A few of the others (Paul) were more influenced by their – how can I put this – amateur musical theatre backgrounds. So when the time came to decide upon another set of costumes for more formal occasions, there were many heated arguments about important things like the merits of lycra versus cotton and the unitard versus the t-shirt. I think my deepest fear at the time was that if I didn't fight for my rights, we would end up wearing the sparkly vest with no shirt, bow tie and matching sequined hat combination that Paul always joked about … I am sure he was joking … I am fairly sure he was joking … We eventually reached some middle ground, which was to go with the Wiggles gear for casual shows like school performances and outdoor, daytime gigs. For the more formal gigs we bought some off-the-rack white tuxedos and had them altered to include some military-style epaulettes to jazz them up a bit. They really ended up just looking like costumes for a Sydney Mardi Gras military-style parade. They did fine for us until we unanimously decided we needed costumes that were more suited to our raging personalities.

We had a recommendation for a costume designer. His name was Glenn and his business was called Puffy Sleeve Designs or something like that. We promptly booked a meeting with him and met him at his 'design studio', as he called it, or 'small room above a Turkish restaurant', as I called it. The room had a large table with a few sewing machines attached to it and was crammed with enough shimmering fabrics and sequins to clothe a small army. A small army of what? I don't know. Let's just say you could probably see them marching from about 20 miles away.

We each decided on a costume idea that represented a little bit of our individuality or, in Reg's case, what Michael told him his individuality was. Glenn got on the case and in a few weeks we had our sparkling new costumes which contained surprisingly few sequins. Our individual looks were all quite different, thank God, though to my horror, John had got Glenn to design a new pair of red leather pirate boots for him that were even larger and more 'piratey' than the previous pair. All the costumes were based around similar colours – red, black and white, and we actually looked quite okay.

• • •

We scored a regular television gig on *The Bert Newton Show*. It was a daytime hour-and-half variety and chat show hosted by Australian television legend Bert Newton.

For those readers who have never heard of Bert, he rose to fame hosting *Countdown*, a popular Australian music show in the 1970s. Famous for his cowboy hat and mumbling speech he … Oh never mind, let's just say he is an absolute living legend in the Australian broadcasting scene and it was quite exciting for us to be part of the show.

The Phones' weekly appearances on *The Bert Newton Show* taught us a lot. We learned about the difficulty and thrill of doing live television spots and we learned just how large Bert Newton's head actually is. It is large. Really large. Really, really, really large. His television appearances when he stood next to Don Lane gave the impression that he is short. He is not. He is tall. Really tall with a really large head. I shouldn't really go on about how large Bert's head is, but one day during rehearsals I stood too close to him and I went into orbit around it. Bert is an absolute top bloke who continued to support John and I throughout our entire career.

Appearing on this show also helped to raise our public profile. That is, it raised our profile with the 163 elderly women who weren't already watching *The Midday Show with Ray Martin*.

It was an interesting experience. We did 26 appearances on Bert's show and it was a great chance to meet some quite famous people. Big names like Harry Secombe, Cliff Richard, Phyllis Diller, Joan Collins, the Leyland Brothers, Acker Bilk and Slim Dusty all happily ignored us while we were partaking of the free sandwiches on the other side of the Green Room. Meeting Rolf Harris was a highlight.

Producers Assistant: 'Hey boys, this is Rolf Harris.'

Rusty: (shaking his hand) 'Hi Rolf, I'm Rusty.'

Rolf: 'G'day Rusty.'

John: (shaking his hand) 'Ahh, the living legend.'

Rolf: 'Sorry, what's your name?'

John: (sheepishly) 'Mumble ... I was just ... mumble something something John ...'

Each week on the show we would perform a song either unaccompanied or with the excellent 12-piece house band. We would choose one of the songs from our repertoire, or a new song themed for something that was happening at the time. For example, when the Melbourne Cup was on we sang something like Abba's 'Money, Money, Money'. We would do a medley from *Les Miserables* when that musical was touring, or we would choose a song from whatever famous singer had died that week.

The *Les Miserables* medley was a cracker, despite the fact that we were dressed in French revolutionary garb (or whatever the costume department had in stock at that point) and ill-fitting wigs. My long dark sideburns poked out of my blond wig so the make-up lady spray-painted them white. I looked truly and excellently ridiculous.

No matter what the choice of song, inevitably costuming would rear its ugly, sequined head and we would have raging disagreements over what the wardrobe department had decided on.

Eventually I succumbed and realised it was not really worth all the trouble. Who was watching, anyway? Apart from our mums. By the way, if anyone needs a slightly used matching sequined vest, bowtie and bowler hat, let me know.

We got ourselves some new management, much to the relief of Paul, who I suspect was thoroughly over the inequality of taking care of the bookings and receiving little gratitude from the rest of us. The new management group was an organisation with the somewhat nondescript name of Famous Artists International. I think they put the 'International' part into the name to make it sound … well … more international. Because if you are in Australia, especially in the entertainment industry, *everything* from overseas is better than what we have here. Or so it would seem. A good example is when things are described as being 'world class'. It happens all the time with various events like festivals, concerts and biscuit-making competitions or whatever. The accompanying pamphlet will describe the event as being world class. I can tell you right now that anything that describes itself as being world class, isn't.

This doesn't happen in any other countries that I have been to. Except New Zealand. The poor Kiwis have an even bigger chip on their shoulders than we do. They actually have an event called the World Class New Zealand Awards, where they hand out awards to 'Niew Zullunders thet huv hud a but uv sucksiss ovaseas, ay'.

Famous Artists International took over managing the Phones and we continued on our merry way generally living the dream. Looking back, the different performances and venues we played were extremely varied. Universities, TAFE colleges, high schools, corporate events, fundraisers, comedy clubs, a floating stage at the Moomba festival, regional theatres, ski resorts, football ovals, supporting Phyllis Diller at the Hilton and Don McLean at the Concert Hall, and our first interstate tour, to Adelaide!

Around the middle of 1990 though, the palpable tensions and elasticised seams were at bursting point and we decided that we would finish the group at the end of the year and go our separate ways. We had to hold Reg down and make him sign a form that guaranteed he would not hold a new round of auditions to get some replacement members for yet another line up of the Phones.

Once that decision had been made, everyone was much happier and even a bit relieved. Relationships within the group returned to the happy-go-lucky times of the first five weeks before we found out about the $50,000 debt. We decided to do our final season at the prestigious Melbourne venue the Last Laugh at the end of 1990.

The decision to end the Phones left me, for the first time in a long while, wondering what the hell to do next. I immediately thought, 'I know, I'll go to Antarctica and run a marathon.' Of course I didn't think that. The idea of running a marathon in Antarctica was still far away from what I was doing or thinking at that point.

LIVING THE DREAM

During the late 1980s when I was performing with Four Chairs No Waiting, I occasionally supplemented the dole by doing some gigs with my sister Sherry in our brother-and-sister country duo. I also did some spruiking work, which means standing outside a shop with a microphone, trying to drum up excitement. That job is one of the most disheartening and humiliating of all the 'jobs' an aspiring entertainer could ever do. Also around this time, though, I had some fun doing work as an extra in films. The hippie put me in contact with his acting agent and I went and met with her in a grand-looking terrace house in Parkville. Her name was Margaret and if you were casting a film that needed a typical theatrical agent, she would have fitted the part perfectly. She was very well spoken and would always call you 'dahling' or 'dear'. Her voice sounded like Patty or Selma from *The Simpsons*, but with a British accent. She chain smoked Camel cigarettes and had two fluffy Pomeranian dogs that yapped constantly around her chair and desk. When she laughed, it would begin as a slow, descending *hmm hmm hmm* that would escalate into a violent, wheezing spasm of coughing and unladylike hoiking of phlegm that always finished with her regaining her composure and saying, 'Now, ahem, where were we, dahling?'

To be eligible to do paid extra work on television and in movies, I was informed that I had to become a member of the appropriate union – Actors Equity. In the days before the internet, joining Actors Equity was a fairly simple procedure that involved fabricating an acting career, typing it up by hand on an old typewriter and paying the required fees.

The calls for extra work came fairly steadily and I scored some pretty big roles like 'lap bell ringer' in *The Four Minute Mile*, 'camper with torch' in *Evil Angels* and 'shop assistant holding cheese' in a Coles ad. The crowning moment in my acting career came in an SBS/German television co-production of a telemovie called *Always Afternoon*. It was set in 1915 Australia and dealt with German prisoners in a regional internment camp. I had done about seven days on this movie, filling some important roles like 'Fourth woodcutter' and 'Man with bucket,' but my last day was when I really got to shine in my background role as 'Bed-ridden patient # 3' in a hospital death scene. Melbourne comedian Greg Fleet was also in this scene, but he had a genuine speaking part that involved actual acting. The scene was quite simple, featuring Fleety as a concerned German prisoner seated at the bedside of his influenza-ridden gay German woodcutter lover – this was SBS, remember. Three extras, including me, were selected to be lying sick in the other beds of the hospital.

From the end of the room we were positioned like this: camera; first bed with Fleety and dying boyfriend; second bed with me in it; third and fourth beds with extras obviously not as skilled as me as they weren't chosen to inhabit the all-important bed closest to the action.

After a few rehearsals the real actors were ready and the assistant director came over to us extras and said, 'This is really simple, guys ... you're sick, you're in bed. That's it. Don't take any notice of the actors.'

'Don't take any notice of the actors!' I thought. 'Who the hell does he think he's talking to? Amateurs?'

I proceeded to get into character and prepare myself for the scene. The director shouted '*Action*' so I started acting.

I was supposed to be sick so I did what sick people did. I tossed, I turned ... there was moaning and coughing. I'm pretty sure I accurately exhibited some of the early signs of delirium. I don't know what I was supposed to be sick with, I just know that I was pretty damn sick. I had just started hallucinating, staring horrified at my hand and trying to count the fingers when the director shouted '*Cut!*'

Damn! I didn't even get to the bit where I feign blindness and silently weep.

As the crew reset the scene, the director called his assistant over for a quiet word, occasionally looking over in my direction. He came directly over to me and said, 'For this next take, maybe just sleeping, okay?' I didn't need to be told twice.

SCARED WEIRD LITTLE GUYS WHO DON'T KNOW WHY THEY DO WHAT THEY DO

The influence of seeing so many exciting variety and vaudeville-style acts at Expo 88 had inspired me. I learnt juggling, how to ride a unicycle, and I also learnt rope and lasso tricks from a skinny, fuzzy-haired street cowboy from Oregon called David Lichtenstein. Juggling was fun but I really loved the rope tricks. I was also listening to lots of old country and bluegrass music and was teaching myself the banjo. The rope tricks seemed to fit right in.

While we were living in Brisbane during Expo, I used to walk past a hat shop that kept an enormous, 10-gallon hat in the window. It was just like the one that Hoss from *Bonanza* wore. It was large and ridiculous and fantastic. The first reaction you have when you see a hat like that is, 'What a ludicrous hat, why on earth would anyone ever buy, or wear such a preposterous hat like that?'

I had to have that hat.

I saw it every day and would stop and stare at it. It would be like a dream sequence from a movie. As I stared, misty-eyed, into the shop window, the Pina Colada song would fade in and a montage of me laughing, cavorting and having a great time while wearing a giant cowboy hat would play out in my mind.

I bought the hat.

The point is that for some time now I had been thinking about other types of performance apart from a capella singing. I still burned a small candle for the dream of the rock and roll band (who doesn't) but I also loved stunts and skills and tricks and often thought about how they could be combined with music to make an entertaining and creative performance.

Right around the time we made our decision to end the Phones, I had gone to see a Canadian musical comedy trio called Corky and the Juice Pigs. They were performing at the Prince Patrick Hotel around May 1990. I was completely stunned by these guys. Their energy and absurdity and musical insanity just blew my mind and made me realise the direction I wanted to head in. I rang John the next day and took him to see the Juice Pigs that night. He had similar feelings to me and we agreed that we should do a new act together. After three years of performing together in larger groups, we decided that it would be a good idea to downsize, if only to split the cheques in half instead of in fifths. The new group would be a duo with lots of musical gags and good harmony singing. We set a date to start writing and the Scared Weird Little Guys were born. Of course we didn't have a name or any material yet but that wasn't going to stop us.

We started writing in the lounge room of John's flat in Prahran and our influences clearly showed in the first song we ever wrote. It was called 'Nuclear Waste'. It went like this:

[Chord strum.]
[Sing slowly.] My mum cleaned her bathroom with chlorine and she couldn't use it for half an hour.

Scared Weird Little Guys Who Don't Know Why They Do What They Do

[Together.] My brother cleaned his bathroom with ammonia and he couldn't use it for a day.
But I used something stronger, and here's what happened to me.
(Count – one, two, three, four.)
I cleaned my bathroom with nuclear waste, now I can't use it for thirty thousand years. *[Repeat.]*

It was virtually identical to, and used exactly the same device as, the Corky's song 'I Used my Grandma as a Skateboard'.

[Chord strum.]
[Sing slowly.] I put a wheel in her right hand.
I put a wheel in her left hand.
I put a wheel between her legs.
(Count – one, two, three, four.)
I used my grandma as a skateboard. *Etc.*

'Nuclear Waste' was so similar it could have been a Corky and the Juice Pigs song. We didn't realise it at the time, but I guess you've got to start somewhere, right? There were other influences working on us as well. Both of us had listened to lots of Monty Python growing up. We had both seen and enjoyed the Melbourne comedy group called the Cabbage Brothers. My favourite comedy albums that I had listened to as a teenager were anything by Steve Martin, Cheech and Chong, and *439 Golden Greats* by the Heebeegeebees.

The nuclear waste song was our first day's work and we were pretty happy with ourselves. I remember the phone rang and it was our friend Elena from the new Comedy Club at the Hilton. Michael from the Phones had told her we were working on a new comedy-based act and she asked if we could do a tryout spot at the Hilton room in a few weeks' time. It took a bit of coaxing from her but we eventually agreed.

Then we thought, 'Shit, we don't even have a name, let alone any material.'

There is nothing like a deadline to help you get creative, so we met every day for the next few weeks to get ready for our first tryout spot.

We soon we came up with a device that we played around with throughout our entire career – the old 'lyrics of one song to the tune of another'. The first one we stumbled upon quite randomly. We thought the two songs would have to be well known for it to work, so we chose the ABBA song 'Fernando'. We simply started going through a songbook and tried to sing the 'Fernando' lyrics to each song we came to. After a few tries we came to 'Rawhide' and the rest is history ... Well not exactly history, but those two songs do go together extremely well and we performed that song over many years, including in our final ever show.

Much later, we also did a regular radio spot called 'Stump the Scaredies' where we would attempt listener suggestions for the lyrics of one song to the tune of another. This also became a frighteningly difficult (for us) but fun (for the audience) part of the live show. We would fail often because it's really quite hard to do, but the crowd always liked it more when we failed. It was frustrating when people accused us of ripping off the idea from the television show *Spicks and Specks*. We had being doing the routine for years before that show came around and we never had any problem with them suddenly starting to do it. It's hardly a new idea anyway. I am sure there was some guy 200 years ago doing a 'Mozart in the style of Rossini' bit and there were two more guys up the back thinking, 'I can't believe this bastard's ripping off our Beethoven/Wagner routine!'

Over a 20-year period, by far the most common question we got asked was, 'How did you get the name Scared Weird Little Guys?' The only thing we heard as often was the intro that went, 'They're scared, they're weird, they're little, they're the Scared Weird Little Guys.'

Scared Weird Little Guys Who Don't Know Why They Do What They Do

Here's how the name came about. It was the day before our tryout gig and we were really starting to feel the pressure to come up with a suitable name. 'John and Rusty' was the first idea, though I liked the catchier 'Rusty and John'. But those names were obvious and simple, if a tad unexciting. The Village People had already been used, so that was out. The Lost Marbles was a suggestion by Yogi and was on the short list. It was amended to Los Marblés, then thrown out. We still had nothing. The next day I arrived at John's house at about 10 am and he was in the middle of watching a movie, *Cruising*, starring Al Pacino. If you've never seen the movie, it is a fairly full-on story about an undercover cop who is trying to catch a serial killer in the underground gay S&M scene of New York in the 1970s. If you have seen the movie, you're probably thinking why the hell was John watching it at 10 o'clock on a weekday morning? Killing time until *The Midday Show with Ray Martin* came on? I never really thought about that. I just sat down to have a look at the movie with John – anything to distract us from the real purpose of the morning, which was to write some funny songs. A few minutes later, Al Pacino meets up with his superior, who says the line, 'There's a lot of scared, weird little guys out there who don't know why they do what they do.' We looked at each other and John actually rewound the movie (it was a video) back a bit to play the scene again so we could write the quote down.

It struck us as an unusual way to say those adjectives. It is easier to say 'scared little weird guys' in that order, so it stuck out to us. Originally we were going to call ourselves the entire quote: 'The Scared Weird Little Guys Who Don't Know Why They Do What They Do', but thought that would be harder to fit on a t-shirt.

God knows if we had our time again, we would have chosen a simpler name. Many times we were introduced as 'sacred' instead of 'scared'. MCs would get the order of the words incorrect, or simply leave out one of the words. One night Irish-Australian comedian Jimeoin simply introduced us as 'the two gay guys from the Phones'. To the absolute end of our career, people continued to get the name wrong.

'Look, it's the strange, funny-looking guys.'

'Hey, you're one of those scary, wibbly wobbly blokes, aren't you?'

One night in Mackay I heard this from a rather drunk fellow.

'Ohh maaaaate ... I love youse guys ... What are youse called again? The square queer little cunts or sumthin like that, right, *right*??'

I didn't mind those kinds of guys coming up to you after a show. They would often buy you a Bundy and Coke without asking, which you *couldn't* refuse on pain of having your sexual preferences questioned.

Later in our career we would get other backhanded compliments.

Cute young woman: 'Hi, you're one of the Scared Weird Little Guys, right?'

Rusty: (charmingly) 'Why, yes I am. Have you seen our act?'

Cute young woman: 'No, but my dad used to really like you guys.'

Ouch!

We stuck with the name Scared Weird Little Guys, thinking that once people eventually learned it correctly it would be harder for them to forget.

So, armed with a name, two guitars and 15 minutes of material, we headed off to the Comedy Club at the Hilton in East Melbourne on 17 July 1990. But what were we going to wear? We both believed in the idea of wearing costumes onstage. It must have been our previous experiences in the singing groups and Expo 88. Our barbershop hippie once said about costumes: 'Give 'em something to look at and they'll look at it.'

Scared Weird Little Guys Who Don't Know Why They Do What They Do

He could be so concise during his brief periods of clear-headedness.

Coming out of the zaniness of Four Chairs No Waiting and the sparkliness of the Phones, we wanted to wear something a little more casual and fun. One afternoon we were discussing possible costume options and John surprised me when he suggested the no shirts with matching vest, bow tie and bowler hat look. When he came to, I apologised for my overly physical reaction and he understood that it was merely instinctive and we moved on.

We went with black jeans and green t-shirts. For this new group we had decided to both play guitars. After the last three years singing a capella, we had a craving to use instruments again. Working with instruments is better than working with singing humans in a couple of ways. Instruments (mostly) do what you tell them to do, and they never chastise you for not publishing the stupid fan newsletter on time.

We arrived at the Hilton and tentatively made our way down the stairs to the Comedy Club. The MC for the evening was the tallest, skinniest, pot-smokingest comedian in all of Melbourne, Simon Rogers. He gave us a suitably mispronounced introduction and away we went. God I was nervous! We truly were scared, weird little guys. We had two extremely tall stools to sit on. I kept slowly sliding forward off the front of my stool, as my little legs didn't reach the bar at the bottom. We took a deep breath, counted in the opening song and struck the first guitar chord of the millions we were to play over the next 20 years as the Scared Weird Little Guys. The worst thing that could have possibly happened, did ... *Doingggg!* John's G string snapped ... One of his guitar strings also broke ... [Thank you, goodnight ...] This wasn't so bad, I thought. We were professionals with three years of performing experience under our belts, so I did what professionals with three years of performing under their belts do when breaking a string with the first chord of the set

– I panicked and froze. Thank God John said, 'We meant to do that,' and people laughed. Our first laugh.

With that out of the way we relaxed and got on with the spot. As John was the more accomplished guitar player of the two of us, I handed him my guitar, in what turned out to be quite a symbolic gesture. From that point onwards during Scaredies shows, I either played ukulele or just sang. John took over sole playing of the guitar. I reintroduced my guitar playing about eight years later, when we realised the strong energy of two guys with two guitars, and the value of having a spare guitar when you broke a string with the first chord of the set. John's record was breaking three strings in the first song of a show, though he was the fastest string changer that I have ever seen. As the years went by, whenever a string broke, John would simply take a step back and, with a flurry of flailing arms, strings and pliers, he would change the string and about 20 seconds later he would be ready to go again.

Looking back, this first ever Scaredies spot contained a few elements that were with us throughout our entire career. Dodgy costumes and 'nice guy' personas. We didn't plan that; we were just nice guys who liked dodgy costumes and were also maybe a bit eager to please.

We also started our long relationship with playing around with musical styles. For one of the bits in the first ever gig we chose the Split Enz song 'I See Red', doing it in reggae, country, and Russian styles. This bit morphed into us doing versions of Prince's song 'Kiss', which became the closer of our live set for many years. I also remember doing an original song about Kylie Minogue, the nuclear waste song, and we closed with the 'Fernando'–'Rawhide' combination, or 'Rawnando' as we called it. It was during this last song, and hearing the great response it got, that I first felt we were on the right track and onto a good thing.

I have the printed running sheet from that night, which lists the other comedians, the MC and our name (spelled correctly and in the correct order). I grabbed it at the last minute off the wall of the dressing room as a keepsake. My mother had been a touring country singer in the 1960s around Brisbane and always kept things like that. She has an excellent scrapbook of all her ads in the paper and booking sheets and posters, including ones with her and Billy Thorpe and the Bee Gees. I guess that rubbed off on me as, since that first Scaredies tryout spot, I have pretty much kept everything. I have boxes and boxes of flyers, interviews, reviews, posters, lanyards, stickers, magazines, set lists, booking sheets, running orders and whatnot from all over the world and from all types of shows. I don't really know what I am going to do with it, as it is a bit daunting wondering where to start. Apart from the sheer volume of material, it is mentally very taxing for me to look at. Every single item jolts a memory and it is easy to get brain overload after about 10 minutes.

THE SCAREDIES AND THE LAUGH

The Scaredies immediately started doing the rounds of the regular comedy nights that were happening in Melbourne in the early 1990s. The Star and Garter, the Tower Hotel, the Espy, Mondayitis at the Botanical and the Prince Pat, among others. We also began our long association with one of the most famous venues in Melbourne, the Last Laugh and Le Joke in Collingwood.

Towards the end of 1990, John and I were still doing shows with the Phones, who had scored a season at the legendary Melbourne venue the Last Laugh. We were in the middle of this season when the Scaredies began, and the timing couldn't have been better for us.

The Last Laugh had begun in the mid-1970s and quickly established a reputation for itself by putting on experimental and groundbreaking theatre shows. Quirky cabaret acts and innovative circus troupes would perform while patrons ate and drank ... Oh hang on ... It was actually just another theatre fucking restaurant! Why was I endlessly drawn to these places?

Of course the Last Laugh was definitely not your standard theatre restaurant. It was not like the ones that I had been used to performing in, that's for sure. The Laugh was all about the show. Well, judging by the standard of the food, it was all about the show, anyway. Only kidding! I remember eating many meals there – because they were free.

The owners were a dynamic brother and sister team called Rick McKenna and Mary Tobin. For the first time in my experience, here were some theatre restaurant owners who *didn't* want to be part of the show. They actually didn't want to star in the show, didn't want to introduce the acts and didn't even want a walk-on role. Sure, Rick would direct, set the lights, paint the set, sit in the technical box running the sound cues and give notes to the performers after the show, but that was it. Rick was all class and knew his role. Mary was obviously the brains of the organisation and is still involved in touring comedians from overseas.

The Last Laugh building housed two venues; the big room called the Last Laugh was downstairs and seated about 230 punters for dinner and show, while upstairs was the smaller Le Joke, which could cram about a hundred people in and mainly hosted stand-up comedy shows. The energy of Le Joke with a packed midnight crowd in for the late show was something pretty amazing. It still remains one of the best venues I have performed in anywhere in the world. I was part of and witnessed many absolutely killer spots in Le Joke.

The downstairs room could be incredible or atrocious to perform in, depending on what night of the week it was and how many bucks night parties were in. Fridays were typically pretty horrid – noisy groups in from the suburbs who didn't really care what the show was, though we mostly had some really nice shows in that room.

If it was particularly quiet, or your act wasn't going so well, you could hear the number 86 tram to Bundoora squeakily turning the corner into Smith Street. Between comedians, this gave rise to the expression 'being Eighty-Sixed'.

For example: 'How did you go tonight?'

'Ah, I had 'em in the palm of my hand then tried my new Pauline Hanson gag and got Eighty-Sixed ...'

The Scaredies and the Laugh

Seasons at the Laugh would typically run for six to eight weeks, Tuesday to Saturday. There would often be three or four acts as part of the show, which led to great fun in the cramped and mouldy downstairs dressing room, playing darts or the ancient pinball machine. Strong friendships and camaraderie formed in the 'us-against-them' atmosphere and I have many great friends whom I first met at the Laugh, staff included. The Laugh was known for its 'wacky and zany' staff, and it therefore attracted many interesting individuals, drama students, hopeful comedians and in-between-jobs actors.

The Laugh provided the opportunity for many acts, including us, to be able to make a living from the unreliable world of professional entertainment. With the shows running five or six nights a week, it served the double purpose of making some money and the chance to hone your act by doing it night after night. There is nothing like doing your show over and over in front of an audience to learn the skills of performing, and that's what we were doing pretty much from the word go.

The Scaredies' first actual season came with an offer from Elena at the Hilton Comedy Club. They were relocating the club to a larger venue in Carlton and had booked the insane and hilarious comedy magician The Amazing Jonathon to open the new room. She wanted us to do the support with Bruno Lucia as the MC. The six-week season opened on 17 September, exactly two months after our first tryout gig. Three weeks later, Rick and Mary asked us to be part of the Laugh show as well, so we said yes to that. We just had to scoot offstage in our costumes, instruments in hand, and drive over to the Laugh for the second half of that show. In our naivety, we didn't realise that the producers of the Comedy Club would be upset with us for doing a concurrent season at their rival club, and I got a stern phone call from producer Glenn Elston that would have put Paul from the Phones to shame. It must have made an impression on me, as I have not been able to look Glenn in the eye since, though we have crossed paths many times. I would bet he doesn't even remember it. So as well as learning some theatre-based etiquette, we were working our fresh little Scaredy arses off. In the month of October, as well as the Comedy Club and Laugh seasons, the Phones picked up a support for Phyllis Diller at the Hilton Hotel. We would begin the evening with that show, rush over to be the Amazing Jonathon support, scramble down to the Laugh and then stay around for a late Le Joke show or two. Throw in a couple of corporate gigs, two university shows and a few television and radio spots and my 1990 diary shows we did 59 shows that month.

The rest of year was finished off with the final ever Phones shows at the Laugh, doubling with the Scaredies season upstairs at Le Joke.

Some years during the busy Christmas seasons at the Last Laugh, Mary would have us performing a spot in the early show upstairs at Le Joke, then running downstairs to the Laugh to do a set in that show and finally heading back upstairs for another spot in the late show. Every December, she would bail us up somewhere in the venue and ask if we were available for the New Year's Eve shows. 'How much are you paying?' we would ask, trying to use our non-existent negotiating skills. Her exact words were always, 'Oh, we'll make it worth your while,' and she'd give us a knowing wink. In other words, 'I'll work you silly and by New Year's you will have forgotten all about this conversation.' Then sometime during the following April you would think, 'Did we ever get paid for ... ? Oh whatever.' Of course Mary would have paid us and it was so exciting to think that we were actually working as entertainers and living the dream and to be honest, as long as my meagre bills were being paid, I didn't really care that much about money. The only thing I felt I was going to need money for was travel, and that was just around the corner.

The Scaredies and the Laugh

• • •

People who aren't involved in comedy often think that behind the scenes it must be a laugh-a-minute, non-stop cavalcade of hilarity. Sure there's a bit of fun going on, but offstage many comedians are quite serious and even rather unfunny. Big egos, jealousy and competitiveness are just as much part of the scene as cracking jokes and mucking around.

On the last night of a Last Laugh season, you would often expect someone to do something out of the ordinary, and practical jokes abounded. It's just the type of wacky funsters that we were.

At the end of our first season there as the Scaredies, we were on with local funny man Tim Smith and one of Rick and Mary's overseas comedians, who they brought in from time to time. He was some typically loud American stand-up called Gags Kowalski or Shouty McPunchline or something like that.

Displaying incredible forethought, and as it was the final night of the season, John and I had brought along remote control cars. Tim was onstage doing his bit about how he used to masturbate in the shower as a young bloke, only stopping when he caught a fish in the bay that really looked like him.

We set the remote control cars behind the curtain and then remotely controlled them on to the stage, around Tim and back through the curtain. I know, aren't we hilarious! So Tim decided to get us back with the old 'burst onstage in the middle of a song and spray the Scaredies in the face with a fire extinguisher' routine. An oldie but a goodie. What Tim didn't realise as he grabbed the extinguisher was that it was not the carbon dioxide type that sprays a relatively harmless burst of CO_2, but a powder chemical fire extinguisher. One of the ones that powerfully expel a huge cloud of toxic powder that immediately travels to all parts of the room while sucking the oxygen out of the air.

John and I had just started singing our McDonald's song. Funnily enough it was our only a capella song of the set. We were about 20 seconds into the song when in burst Tim, extinguisher blazing. Of course the room immediately filled with the acrid cloud of comedy-killing powder. People were coughing and choking and running from the room with tears streaming from their eyes. John and I – either too professional or too stupid to leave the stage, kept on trying to sing the song. Trouble was when you took a breath to keep singing, your lungs filled with the powder and we were both coughing and spluttering and choking and singing. It didn't last long, though. The audience cleared the room and we cleared the stage. I have never seen a man as apologetic as Tim Smith was when we got downstairs. The management were freaking out because people were demanding refunds and threatening all kinds of lawsuits. Tim ended up shouting the whole place drinks, or at least shouting the words, '*I am so sorry ... Can I make it up to you by buying everyone drinks?*' When the smoke (and powder) cleared, we were back up on the stage packing up. The whole room was covered in a fine white powder. It was like when you're doing a drug deal and a fight breaks out over a massive bag of cocaine and someone pulls a knife and the bag gets thrown up into the ceiling fan and the shit just goes *everywhere*. That's never actually happened to me, but I imagine this was just what a room looks like when that goes down.

I remember looking down at one of the front tables and seeing a clear outline of an arm holding a drink.

Incidentally, we were recording the show that night and included this fire extinguisher version of the McDonald's song on our album *Live at 42 Walnut Crescent* – available on iTunes.

When we were performing the final season at the Laugh with the Phones, we were on the same bill as a Canadian prop and gadget comedian called Marty Putz. Yes, that is his real name. He told us about the extensive and lucrative college and university circuit in North America. He had seen early Scaredies shows up at Le Joke and said there were no acts like us doing the circuit. He had an agent in Toronto that he was happy to share with us. John and I got very excited. Here was our chance to do some overseas touring. We contacted his agent, Zoe, a chain-smoking, wild-haired Jewish woman with a drawling monotone voice, and set up some trial gigs for the following year.

'IT'S ONLY ONE BOMB ...'

It was around this time that we started our long association with the medium of radio. We started by going on the excellent local independent radio station 3RRR. We had met one of the presenters, Bruce Berryman, at a party and he invited us onto his show each week to perform a frivolous original song. We had continued our writing sessions at John's house and were working up a decent whack of original material. After about a month, though, we were 'poached' by the RRR breakfast show – imaginatively called *The Breakfasters.*

We would come on their show on a Thursday morning and talk about some news items of the day. Once Chris or Richard, the presenters, had decided on our topic for that week, we would run out of the studio and write some absurd and twee song *in 25 minutes*, then sprint back in and perform it. Frequently we would run out of time and be literally scribbling down the final lines as we got into the studio, and having to ask, 'What rhymes with Vizard?' or some such thing.

Topical humorous songs about things in the news have been around forever, but I believe this was the first time that a song like this was attempted in such a short amount of time. It didn't make them any funnier, but it sure helped hone our songwriting skills.

ABC regional radio also contacted us around this time for a topical song of the week, but unlike poor old community station 3RRR, the ABC were going to pay us! We got $30 for each song. Not each person. Thirty dollars between us. In those days the ABC building was in the city and while we were in there singing the song, we would often get a parking fine that was more than what we got paid.

The humorous topical song can be simultaneously the best friend and the worst enemy of the musical comedy performer.

These spots can be great for exposure to a wider audience, but on the other hand you have to actually spend a fair few hours writing the fucking things. Some weeks it would be a piece of cake. Shane Warne, Brendan Fevola or John Howard would do something in the news and the song would be half written before you even started. Other times there would be a tsunami, a mass murder or the tragic death of someone famous dominating the news and it would really be a struggle to come up with a comical perspective.

We were pretty much self-editing, meaning that we were usually trusted by whoever was producing that we would not cross the line of bad taste and say something that would offend listeners. Of course you can never please everyone, nor should you ever try, and we had our fair share of complaints about topics or certain jokes. Mostly the producers would keep the complaints to themselves and merely offer a few subtle words of guidance.

'Ah guys,' they would say, 'just a quick word, maybe next time not so hard on the transsexual thing, or the alzheimers patients, or the Bible jokes … we've had a few calls …'

Topical song writing devours a fair amount of creative juice and sometimes our self-editing would get out of whack. We would think that something was funny merely because it was in the news and we would forgo cleverness for mere topicality.

'It's Only One Bomb...'

You see and hear this every day in the voraciously joke-hungry world of commercial radio.

In the early 2000s we appeared simultaneously on the commercial Austereo network nationally as well as on local ABC radio around the country. We would go in twice a week to Austereo and cross to Perth, Brisbane, Sydney and Adelaide, and then sing our spot for Melbourne live in the studio. We would do Stump the Scaredies on a Tuesday for Austereo and the topical song of the week for both Austereo and the ABC on a Friday. This was our first taste of regular commercial radio and we had seen and heard from friends about the soulless, money-driven nature of this industry. From when we first started, we quickly learned of the high turnover rate of staff, from on-air personnel to the techs and sales team. Every time you went in there, someone would have left. They had such a high turnover rate that I think three-quarters of the world's population must have worked in commercial radio at some time. When one of the on-air team was 'moved on', they never got to say goodbye to the listeners. A show would come back on the next day and there would be no mention of the previous person at all. We would turn up and the producer would quietly call us aside and say, 'Oh yes, so-and-so is not with us any more, so don't mention them, okay?'

'Good morning, you're listening to KGB-FM. Who? No, they never worked here, I've never heard of them.'

One song that I regret doing followed a news story of a boy who had swung on a basketball hoop, which broke. As a result of the accident, he lost both his hands. Now, there is obviously nothing funny about that, right? Somehow, in our insular topical-joke world, we took that as a challenge and wrote in that week's song something along the lines of '... and ironically just before the accident he shouted, "Look mum, no hands ..."' I can still hear the audible gasp of horror as we performed that down the line to the breakfast radio show in Brisbane that morning. We dropped that line from the song for the rest of the morning.

You can also find yourself saying quite nasty things about people in the name of a joke that you would never say if you met them in person.

In the first series of the renovation show *The Block*, one of the contestants, Amity Dry, used the show to try to boost her singing career and had a song called 'The Lighthouse'. As it was the biggest thing on telly at the time, we of course used it as fodder for the weekly song. We changed 'lighthouse' to 'shitehouse', as in, 'this song is shitehouse' and said things like, 'Amity Dry? I'd rather listen to paint dry.' I am pretty sure we rhymed 'worst song I've heard' with 'polishing a turd'. She was apparently quite upset about it and contacted the Sydney radio station we appeared on with all kinds of threats. While we were writing the song we had discussed this possible reaction but decided that if you go on a television renovation show and use it to help your singing career, you really open yourself up to jokes being made about it. Besides, we truly felt it was a shit song. Still, it never sat well with us when we found out someone was upset with our jokes.

In order to have the song ready for breakfast radio on a Friday morning, we would have to get it written on Thursday afternoon. That would sometimes mean that an event would occur Thursday night that overshadowed our already-written song, or something would happen to make it redundant. For example, one Thursday night we were up in Sydney appearing on *The Footy Show* and took advantage of the time we had together to write a song for the next morning. It had just been announced that London would be hosting the 2012 Olympics. What perfect timing! As topical songs go, England is a fairly easy target. There were plenty of references to them being terrible at all the sports they have invented – rugby, cricket, tennis, soccer, etc. I might as well list some of the verses here. It's sung to the tune of 'Rule Britannia':

'It's Only One Bomb...'

Historically England are very good at things like war and conquering.
They're also good at digging up peat and having citizens die of the plague.
Finding unexplored countries and sending their prisoners there.
They're also internationally acclaimed at hooliganism, dreariness and whinging.

Rule Britannia, Britannia rules the waves.
But when it comes to most things, they're actually quite crap.

When London had the Olympics back in nineteen hundred and eight,
They had events like chimney sweeping and the urchin toss.
England won gold medals for scurvy and tuberculosis.
The Games were funded by a team of pick-pocketing orphans.

Forty years and two wars later the Olympics were in London again.
We're not quite sure who opened those games but we're pretty sure it wasn't Hitler.
There were power blackouts; food rationing and all were gloomy.
Now it's 2005 and nothing's really changed...

We would often feel the pressure of working to a deadline each week, so whenever we had a song with a few decent gags in it all written and prepared, it was a nice feeling indeed. We were sitting in our dressing room at *The Footy Show*, flicking around the television monitor. Being in a television station, the monitor often showed a stream direct from the studio as well as feeds from studios in other cities. As the show had not started yet, it was quite entertaining watching the goons 'rehearsing' in the studio. By 'goons' I don't mean *The Goon Show* with Sellers, Milligan et al. I mean 'goons'.

I always thought that in broadcasting there is an unwritten rule: the camera or microphone is always on.

Thankfully this didn't seem to stop us hearing all about who got sacked, who's stuck up and who got sucked off. Maybe if Channel Nine made that into a show, they wouldn't be so in the shit.

Anyhow, we flicked around the telly some more, basking in the glow of our newly finished London Olympics song. On the next channel the headline screamed 'breaking newsflash'. A bomb had just been detonated in London.

I questioned whether this affected the tone of our freshly written song.

John confidently said, 'It's okay; it's only one bomb. The song is still good.'

Three more bombs later we realised that sticking the boot into London and England probably wasn't the topic that was going to get us many laughs the next day.

'Oh great, now we have to write another song,' we said almost in unison, expressing great sympathy for those who had died in the bomb blasts.

Another time, in June 2009, we were departing Brisbane on a morning flight and were due to perform a topical song on the Lindy Burns drive program on the ABC in Melbourne that afternoon. A two-hour flight is usually a perfect time to get one of these songs done if you have a good topic and the tune of the song already decided. We had read the papers and online news stories and this is what we had to choose from: Kevin Rudd's 'ute gate' scandal – a story involving the then Prime Minister being accused of giving favourable treatment to a Brisbane car dealer (massive story that one); the Wimbledon tennis tournament;

'It's Only One Bomb...'

AFL club Carlton's players being involved in a drunken incident; and the opening of a museum display of artefacts from Pompeii. See what we had to deal with some weeks. As we were about to board the flight, John saw a scrolling news flash at the bottom of the television screen say: 'Michael Jackson taken to hospital after suspected drug overdose.'

John suggested that maybe we could work that into the song.

'Nah,' I scoffed 'It will probably turn out to be nothing.'

So we got on the plane and during the flight we happily worked away and scraped together a song about politicians name-calling and tennis players grunting and what not. Done to the tune of 'Down Under' by Men At Work for some reason that was clear to us then, but not to me now.

Well, by the time the flight landed in Melbourne, Jacko was dead and all hell had broken loose. Facebook and Twitter were already full of more (and funnier) jokes than we could have come up with. Most of them completely unsuitable for broadcast in a friendly little topical song on the ABC.

In the end it turned out fine, as I don't think there is any kind of topical song that you could possibly write about the death of Michael Jackson and do it justice. We performed our other song and it was actually a perfect escape from the domination of the Michael Jackson-related news of that day.

The September 11 attack on the World Trade Centre was another example of a tricky topical song. Now there's an understatement if you ever want to hear one. Four days of non-stop 24-hour coverage on virtually every radio station and television channel. But we had a contract to fulfil and, dammit, we loved a challenge. This was the mother of all challenges. We obviously couldn't sing about the attacks, but then again, nothing else was in the news. Think harder.

Nude photographer Spencer Tunick had been in Melbourne that week doing a shoot. That's something. Hmm, spring is here. Let's do a happy song about springtime! Actually, singing this song to a bright and happy original tune was quite a surreal experience at the time, though reading back the lyrics now it seems ever so innocuous. I will include a couple of verses from our song 'Springtime's Here Again' performed on Friday 14 September 2001:

Springtime brings such a pleasant scene,
The flowers are blooming and the grass is green.
My pockets are full of antihistamine,
Springtime's here again.

A mass nude photo shoot by Spencer Tunick
It was so cold you felt like you were a eunuch.
Ironically you couldn't wear a spencer nor a tunic.
Springtime's here again.

By the way, the contract that I speak of at that point in time was a verbal contract we had with Virginia Trioli's drive program on ABC 774. I am sure I can now reveal the gritty details of our agreement. What are they gonna do, sack us? We had started back on ABC radio a couple of years before, in 1999, and we received $100 a week to write and perform the song. This was about nine years after our original $30 a week ABC payment. That's a pay rise of $7.77 per year. Not bad for the ABC. Things obviously soon got tough for them though, because at the end of that year they had to halve our pay to $50 a week.

Six months later Virginia Trioli herself called me and said, 'Sorry guys, we have to let you go.'

'What? It's the ABC! You can't let anyone go! You're not allowed to,' I protested.

'We just can't find room for you in the budget.'

'Budget? It's $50 for fucksake! That's not a budget! It's a ... it's a ...' I was trying to find the word that means the opposite of budget 'it's a ... non-spendy-thingy!'

'It's Only One Bomb...'

I find it's always good when talking to one of Australia's most erudite, intelligent and well-spoken journalists, to swear and use terms like 'spendy thingy'.

I continued.

'That's it!' I screamed. 'Fuck you Virginia! And *fuck the ABC!*'

I didn't really scream that ... I *thought* that I should have screamed it – about three hours later.

What I actually said to Virginia, in a nice, slightly apologetic tone, was, 'Oh well, that's okay then. Thanks for having us.'

John and I discussed it and agreed that we should continue to do the songs for no payment as it was good exposure and we mostly enjoyed it, and that's how it happily stayed for the next 10 years.

Interestingly, the next time we walked into the plush ABC radio building in Southbank, we noticed seven (!) extremely large flat screen televisions being hung as part of the extensive foyer renovations.

Budget ... hmph.

There was no danger of crossover between the ABC and commercial radio as the stations were not up for the same audience. In six years, I only heard of one instance where someone heard the song on Triple M in the morning, and again on the ABC that afternoon. Most of the time we would use the same song on both stations and it wouldn't matter. We would maybe change a couple of the references to be a little more high brow for the ABC audience. Although we learned that when it comes down to it, your average ABC listener likes a well rhymed fart joke as much as your regular Triple M-listening tradesman.

I am happy to say we had a suitably low-key exit from the Austereo gig. We merely didn't return one week after being away on tour. A phone call from our extremely sorry producer gave us the news and of course we didn't get to say goodbye to the listeners on air.

MAKE ME A PIZZA, THEN FOLLOW YOUR DREAM

It was 1991. The Phones were a distant, sparkly memory for us. We had been working consistently throughout the first half of the year. Television spots were becoming regular for us. Our first ever TV spot as the Scaredies was on the ABC's *Big Gig*. Exciting! We were introduced by Wendy Harmer. ('They're scared ... they're weird ... they're little ...' etc.) We did our intergalactic surfing song called 'Seven Foot, Eight-Eyed, Four-Breasted Beach Slut from Outer Space'.

Wendy cornered us after the rehearsal and wanted us to drop the word 'slut' and replace it with 'chick'.

'No way, man!' I thought. 'This is our art, man.'

John and I discussed our newly found principles for ages in the dressing room.

'I haven't given the whole last three months of my life to compromise now, man ... having the word slut in the chorus was what the whole song was built around, man,' I spouted with self-righteous conviction.

John said, 'I think we should drop it, and please stop calling me "man".'

After another hour or so, we obediently agreed to drop the word slut. On the actual (live) broadcast, when we got to the first chorus, I said 'chick' and John said 'slut' anyway. So it turned out just fine, man.

We also did *Tonight Live with Steve Vizard* and our first of 16 appearances on *Hey Hey It's Saturday*. I guess all the new exposure started working for us, because we received our first booking for an interstate gig.

Actually flying interstate! This was the realisation of our dreams! Flying to a gig and *someone else was paying for the flights*! We were really living the dream. We didn't realise it at the time but we were also about to unknowingly influence a Tasmanian pizza maker.

Oh, how we were excited! Did I mention that *they were paying for the flights*? May I remind you that this was in the days before budget airlines and mass air travel. Interstate flights were the domain of grey-suited businessmen, the wealthy, and competition winners. Travelling by bus was still an accepted form of transport between capital cities for God's sake. No buses for high flying entertainers like us, though. On top of the *free flights*, we were going to get paid ... $400!

A good indication of how excited we were was the location of the gig. Sydney? No ... The Gold Coast? No ... Burnie, Tasmania? Yes! And we were still excited! Now Burnie may not sound like the most glamorous interstate destination for your first gig, but to us it sounded fantastic! The event that we were going to perform at was a fundraiser for the Tasmanian Youth Orchestra. I think they were trying to get new music stands or raise enough money to leave Tasmania or something.

We arrived in Burnie and were picked up by Bernice, a stern-looking elderly woman with unusually high plucked eyebrows.

I said, 'You pluck your eyebrows very high.'

She looked surprised.

Bernice was in charge of the orchestra, which was based in Burnie. Bernice from Burnie. Yep. John wittily pointed out the similarity between her name and where she lived.

Make Me a Pizza, *Then* Follow Your Dream

'Hmph,' she responded, with the stony face of someone reacting to something they have heard at least 10,000 times. 'Everyone always says that. For the last 20 years that's all I've ever heard. Here comes Bernice from Burnie. Hey everyone, it's Burnie Bernice! I've had a gutful of it. I'm so sick of hearing that, Burnie, Burnie, Burnie. I am thinking of moving.'

'Oh, where would you go?' John politely asked.

'Bunbury seems nice ...' she said.

There was a strange burning smell in the car and we noticed that Bernice was driving with one foot on the accelerator and the other foot on the brake, often pressing both pedals at the same time. We survived the trip from the airport and she dropped us off at the motel. I think it was called the Folded Towel Motor Inn or something like that. It was about 4 pm. This being our first time in Tasmania, we thought we'd head out and see the sights of Burnie. We were back in the room about 10 past four for a quick rest and shower, then it was off to get some dinner before the big show. We wandered into town and found that the only place open was the Burnie pizza shop.

I remember it well. We ordered the Hawaiian pizza. Or was it the Capricciosa with pineapple? Ah, the Capriwaiian. Or was it the Hawaiicciosa? Okay, I don't remember it so well.

We ordered the Hawaiian pizza and started chatting to the friendly youngish bloke behind the counter.

'So what are you guys doing here in Burnie?' he asked.

'How do you know we're not from Burnie?' said John.

'Well, you've got all your teeth, your eyes point in the same direction and you know how to pronounce Caprich ... capreech ... capricciosa.' (He didn't really say that last bit.)

John actually said, 'We are a musical comedy duo from Melbourne. We've been flown over here to do a show tonight ...' He quickly and breathlessly added, 'And *they* paid for our flights!'

'No kidding!' said the pizza man. 'That sounds incredible! You're entertainers and you get to travel round the country doing gigs. That's just great. Is this what you've always wanted to do?'

'Sure is,' we nodded.

'Wow! You guys are very lucky, doing what you love.' He shook his head thoughtfully. 'I've been in Burnie my whole life. I've been making pizzas since I left school.'

'Well mate,' I said with the worldly, experienced attitude of someone who has just taken a flight *paid for by someone else*, 'anyone can follow their dream, you just have to decide what you want to do and go for it. What have you always wanted to do?'

'I dunno,' he paused, thinking. 'Travel up north I guess ... and root chicks.'

'Well, it's good to have some clear goals, mate,' I offered.

John added, 'And you know there's nothing stopping you from achieving them.'

The pizza was ready and we ate it in thoughtful silence at a table near the front window. I am happy to say that this was possibly the *best* pizza I had ever eaten ... in Burnie. Just kidding. This was a seriously delicious pizza. What made this pizza so damn good? I don't know if it was the comforting glow of our impending first interstate gig, the highly skilled pizza making, or the view. Probably not the view, which was of a run-down panel beating shop across the road. More likely it was the excellent pizza maker.

The ham was sliced off the bone, the cheese perfectly melted and blended with the pineapple on top of a freshly made, thin and crusty base. We thanked our new pizza friend and scurried off to do the gig, which in itself was quite unremarkable. I remember they had an auction of celebrity items to help raise funds. I did my bit by purchasing an autographed photo of comedian Lucky Grills for two dollars.

The show completed, we returned to the motel to indulge in some typical post gig, rock and roll activities, which for us usually

Make Me a Pizza, *Then* Follow Your Dream

meant playing gin rummy or Game Boy Tetris. After a couple of tepid beers from the motel mini bar, we started getting hungry and as the memories of the excellent pizza were still with us, I rang up the Burnie pizza shop to order another one.

A familiar voice answered the phone.

'Hello Burnie Pizza,' he said.

'Oh can you please not burnie the pizza and just cookie it?' I said in a post-gig-inspired rush of humour.

'What?'

'Never mind. It's your comedian mates here. Just wondering if we may order another one of your delicious pizzas?'

'Oh g'day there!' he said. 'Listen, I've been thinking about what you guys said about following dreams and I want to thank you both. You really made an impression on me.'

'No worries mate, good luck with that. So it's one large Hawaiicciossa please. We're staying at the Folded Towel.'

Ninety minutes later our pizza had still not arrived.

I was halfway through calling them up and was trying to think of another play on words I could do with 'Burnie' and 'pizza' when there was a knock on the door.

I opened the door to see a flustered, slightly dishevelled-looking man holding a pizza box.

'Oh sorry about the wait, mate,' he said. 'We are completely under the pump down there tonight. You'll never believe it. My pizza maker just got up and walked out on me about two hours ago! He muttered something about following his dream ... and rooting chicks, and then off he went, gone, right out the door!'

'Oh, really?'

John and I looked at each other open mouthed. We had inadvertently caused a guy to follow his dream and we thought that was just great.

I am happy to say the pizza was the *worst* pizza I have ever tasted.

ARE THOSE REAL CHEERLEADERS?

After our triumphant interstate trip was over, we slotted back into another season at the Last Laugh and got on with the planning of our first overseas trip. Marty Putz's booking agent, Zoe, was on the phone with us from Toronto every few days, telling us what gigs were being booked, and what was needed to get Canadian work permits.

She had a voice like George Costanza's mother from *Seinfeld*, but slowed down to half speed.

'Hiiiii guuyyyssss, dooo yoouu haaave yoour woork paappeerrs yeeeet?' she would drawl, while taking a drag on a cigarette. Then her two dogs would start barking in the background and she would scream at them but somehow also scream into the phone receiver at the same time.

'*Bennnyyy!!!! Jaaaake!!!! Shuuutt uuuuuppp!!!* Soooo, Ruussttyy, wheeere weeeere weeeee?'

Zoe was remarkably similar to my old acting agent, Margaret. What was it about booking gigs that attracted chain smoking, gravelly voiced, middle-aged women with dogs?

We had sent over a videotape of our act to Zoe (expensively converted into the NTSC format) and, thanks to Marty's recommendation, she had booked us six weeks of college and comedy club gigs around Ontario in Canada. When the first few gigs started coming through, it sounded ever-so exciting:

University of Toronto.
The Comedy Nest, Montreal.
Wilfred Laurier University, Waterloo.
Carleton University, Ottawa.
Zaks Sports Bar, Wolverton
University of Western Ontario, London.
Humber College, Toronto.
The Laugh Resort, Toronto.

I had wanted to do some of this overseas touring stuff for a long time. When I was still in the Phones I was living in a big share house with lots of music industry hopefuls. There was talented songwriter Charles Jenkins, radio announcer Tony Biggs, and Bob, the monitor guy for the Angels. Another person living in the house was Triple R's Denise Hylands, my future wife. One of the other housemates had just got back from being the roadie and driver for Australian band the Go-Betweens on their tour of Europe and the USA. I was completely enthralled by his stories of driving around 30 states of America in a crappy van, playing in all sorts of venues, good and bad. At the time, it sounded to me like just about the best thing you could ever think of doing.

So, with the work permits attained and the costumes packed, off we went. Denise and I departed first and had a few months travelling around the United States. We then met up with John in Toronto in late September 1991 for the start of the tour.

The three of us all lived together in a small, sparsely furnished flat on the lower west side of Toronto. The gigs were an eclectic mix of colleges and universities, comedy clubs, nightclubs and band support spots. Zoe also managed a couple of reggae bands and a few times we found ourselves on the bill supporting acts with names like Dread Serious, and Ganjah Pahtay. The first show we did in Canada was a real initiation into North American culture for us. It was part of Orientation Week, the first week back for the schools. We were part of a 'pep rally' at Wilfred

Are Those Real Cheerleaders?

Laurier University, about an hour's drive outside of Toronto. Crammed into the expansive gymnasium were 600 very excited new students, fresh out of high school and ready to take on the challenges and beer of college life. The first gig you ever do in a foreign country is a pretty intimidating experience, and this particular gig posed a few serious questions for us.

Are they going to think we are funny?

Will they understand us?

Are those *real* cheerleaders?

Yes, they were real cheerleaders, and we had to do our performance right after them. We even got changed in a bona fide North American college locker room, like a real pair of jocks. Bad analogy that ... pair of jocks in a locker room. As we were peeking out of the locker room door watching the cheerleaders doing their act, I felt we were risking being beaten up by a real pair of jocks. It was like we were in an episode of *Glee*, except without the bullying or the auto-tuning on our voices.

Due to me going over early, the Scaredies had not done a gig in nearly three months and we were feeling a tad underdone. We had a discussion about what they might understand or not, did a quick run-through of some songs, then went out and smacked their little maple-leaf-loving asses. Boy, were they ever excited! I don't know if it was that they were away from home for the first time or drunk or that they were still gobsmacked from the cheerleaders. Maybe it was a combination of all three, because they went freaking nuts. We came off dazed and speechless. John eventually said, 'What just happened?'

I couldn't answer. We had never experienced such a loud and enthusiastic reaction.

During the drive home we were filled with excitement and anticipation. We were also filled with Tim Horton's delicious donuts and coffee. Wherever you are in Canada, it seems like you are never more than 100 metres from the closest Tim Horton's Donut Shop. I think it must actually be a law there.

Scared Weird Frozen Guy

We became quite partial to a post-gig donut or six, washed down with a hot coffee served in the 20-ounce 'Super Tim' travel mug. It may have taken me 20 years, but I reckon I finally lost the last of my Tim Horton's extra kilos during the training for the Ice Marathon.

The first gig had been a raging success and as the warm glow from the cheering crowd and the cheerleaders' thighs subsided, we were on top of the world and couldn't wait to see what the next six weeks had in store for us. However, we were about to come crashing back to earth in startling fashion.

The next day we were up reasonably early, as we had an 11 am show at a local community college. These schools are quite similar to TAFE colleges in Australia. For some reason, lots of these colleges seem to think that programming a 'Morning Comedy Hour' in the non-theatrical, neon-lit setting of a cafeteria is a good idea. They would usually book a stand-up comedian and this was the kind of spot they thought would suit our act.

Our info sheet for the gig seemed rather innocuous. It listed the school (George Brown College), the address in Toronto, where the show was (the cafeteria), the name of the person we had to meet there, the length of the show, etc. We had a trusty fold-out street map so we looked up the address and off we went.

Once we found a carpark, we made our way inside and located our contact for the day, a friendly young student named Brian. I don't know what it is, but we met a hell of a lot of Canadians named Brian, some of them were even men. Brian showed us the stage and performing area, which was really just the floor in a corner of the cafeteria, right next to the video games. Once we had rearranged the fake pot plants, we had quite a nice little space to perform in.

Now we just had to organise the sound.

'Hey Brian, can we set up the sound system to do a little sound check?' I naively asked.

Are Those Real Cheerleaders?

'Sound system?' he looked at me like I was a girl named Brian.

'We don't have a sound system. Normally when we have comedy shows in here, we just plug a mike into the wall socket right there and use the speakers that are built into the ceiling.'

'But there are two of us,' I explained, 'and we also have a guitar.'

'Hmm, yeah,' he pondered. 'I'll have to go and see what the audio visual department have got in the way of sound systems.'

And so began the farcical routine that we were to confront over and over again when doing these types of gigs. Faced with no sound system, we would scramble off to an under-resourced AV department to scrounge up some semblance of amplification.

Brian returned five minutes later wheeling a trolley loaded with a couple of very dodgy-looking microphones, a cassette deck with built-in amp, and two home stereo speakers. This was going to be a challenge. We tried in vain to get all the 'equipment' to work for us. Eventually we had the two mikes going into the stereo inputs on the tape player. The play, record and pause buttons had to be pressed in for the mikes to work, while the other microphone was gaffer taped to John's guitar and was played through the overhead speakers in the ceiling. Our voices were distorted but at least the guitar was too loud. In between every song, the pinball machine next to us would bellow in a demonic voice, 'I am Gorgar! *Challenge me!*' Oddly, Gorgar's voice was more understandable than ours. The only redeeming feature of this gig was that there were only about 11 people in the audience to witness the ludicrous carnage that we were producing in the name of entertainment. If by 'audience', you mean '11 people more interested in reading textbooks or eating, who happen to be in a room while two guys in a corner make inaudible noise', then it definitely was an audience.

We should have told Brian to stick it and that if we didn't have decent sound then we were not going on, but John and

I were way too polite or scared to actually follow through on a threat like that.

Of course, Zoe should have told every person running these shows what our technical requirements were and I think she mostly did. A lot of these colleges simply didn't have the equipment, or they would bring out some kind of ancient, dinky speaker set-up that even the Beatles would have refused to use. We ended up travelling with our own microphones, a dozen cables of varying lengths and a box filled with every type of adaptor plug imaginable.

We had RCA to phono, XLR female to male RCA, quarter-inch mono female to dual right angle stereo mini plug, dual phono to single RCA, etc. We were a portable Dick Smith shop.

One of these absurd technical set-ups for a college gig had the AV guy in a room directly behind the stage. We were onstage plugging leads and adaptors randomly into a junction box. We could see the AV guy through a triple-paned window of soundproof (and probably bulletproof) glass and were desperately trying to communicate with him through an intricate array of hand and finger signals, while holding up various adaptors. The only way to enter his room, of course, was by walking off the stage to the other side of the venue, going through two classrooms, up and down some stairs and down a long hallway. We ended up writing signs to each other and reading them through the window. I can understand why the glass was so thick as, by the end of it, we wanted to shoot him.

This peculiar gig also gave us one of the most inappropriate introductions for a comedy act I have ever known.

The room was full of a couple of hundred students anticipating a lunchtime comedy show. They were quiet and the scene was set for a good gig. The student activities officer checked that we were ready and walked onstage to introduce us. I noticed that he was holding a bucket.

Are Those Real Cheerleaders?

He began, 'Hello everyone and welcome to today's comedy show. Many of you know one of our popular photography students from last year named Robert Lees. We have many fond memories of his time here at the college. This year, Robert has been working as a photojournalist covering the war in Bosnia and we have just received the unfortunate news that he has been killed. We will now be passing around this bucket, to take donations to help his wife and young child. On a lighter note, please welcome the Scared Weird Little Guys.'

We certainly learned a hell of a lot about performing in those days. We faced just about every experience onstage that you could imagine. Power blackouts, music coming on in the middle of a show, people walking onstage, weird introductions, sound cutting out, stuff being thrown at us, four-hour drives to a gig with no crowd.

There was only one time, though, that a brawl started in the middle of the audience, and it was all our fault.

It was in a small town in northern Ontario called Kirkland Lake. Kirkland Lake is an eight-hour drive directly north of Toronto, though the last four hours of the drive are through spectacular, unchanging scenery of beaver-dammed lakes, wild moose and autumn coloured trees of unimaginable beauty. Then you arrive in Kirkland Lake. It is a smallish ex-mining town and its claim to fame is that it is the birthplace of Alan Thicke, the actor from *Growing Pains*. How do we know that? It's written on the sign as you drive into town, of course. Kirkland Lake doesn't have a lake any more, nor do they have a mine. The lake drained into the mine and closed it down.

We were playing a gig that night (hurrah, a night-time gig, we thought) in the bar of the local college. I remember it had an intrinsically northern Canadian name like Beaver College or the Moose Fucker Institute or something like that. We were about halfway through the set when we saw through the windows next to the stage that it was starting to snow. It was early October and this was the first snowfall of the upcoming winter. To two Australians who are halfway around the world, the first snowfall brings feelings of excitement and wonder. To a room full of northern Canadians, the first snowfall brings a reminder that the next seven months will be freezing cold, inconvenient and difficult to drive in. We were feeling happy and fascinated. They were feeling depressed and grumpy. Not the best setting for a hilarious comedy show. John and I started talking about Skidoos, which is what we thought all snowmobiles were called.

'Hey!' we chirped. 'Who's got a Skidoo? This will be great weather for bringing the old Skidoo out and zooming around on the snow.' It was inconceivable to us that anyone there could be anything less than excited about the snow falling.

We were all Skidoo this and Skidoo that when someone called out, 'Skidoo sucks! Yamaha rules!'

'What's this?' I thought. 'There is another type of Skidoo?'

A voice on the other side of the room yelled out to the 'Yamaha rules' person.

'You suck! Skidoo rules, man!'

Holy shit, this was a whole new level of the Ford versus Holden thing. Others in the room now started to join in.

'Fuck you, Skidoo asshole!'

'Yamaha can kiss my sweet Skidoo ass!'

They were getting creative now. Then it quickly started to get ugly. I guess it was a combination of their God-given right to stick up for their chosen brand of snowmobile and the first snowfall. A chair was kicked across the floor towards a rival snowmobile table and it quickly escalated into standing, pushing and then punching. There were many involved and John and I didn't need any coaxing to get the hell off the stage and run to the relative safety of the dressing room.

Ever the concerned professionals, we both agreed that the person who had booked us, I think his name was Brian, wouldn't mind that we cut the set a few minutes short.

Are Those Real Cheerleaders?

• • •

A few days after we returned to Toronto, John started feeling a little under the weather. He had a headache, a fever and, for want of a better description, he began expelling bodily fluids from all major orifices. Luckily there were no gigs scheduled that day, so I said maybe he should just get some rest and see how he felt in the morning. When John woke next day, he felt no better and his eyes had turned extremely red. They were so red I couldn't believe it. How can I describe the redness of his eyes? If there was a redheaded guy with a red hat on, named Redmund, and he was on his way to a Simply Red concert, even *he* would have been impressed at how red John's eyes were.

I asked him how he was feeling and he said, 'Well, Rusty, I am not feeling very well and I believe that we should endeavour to make our way to see a doctor.'

Actually what he really said was 'Errmmnngghhh ...' which I accurately interpreted as, 'Well, Rusty, I am not feeling very well and I believe that we should endeavour to make our way to see a doctor.'

So I said, 'I will take you there, John, as I am a caring and supportive friend.' That's me. The kind of caring and supportive friend who realised that if John didn't get better we wouldn't be doing any gigs and we really needed the money.

I thought, hmm, how do I find a doctor? We didn't have the *Yellow Pages*, the internet or even a phone for that matter, so I simply got the street map and looked up the location of the nearest hospital to take him to Emergency. There was one located quite close by, so Denise and I led John down to the car and headed straight there. Denise drove and I sat in the back seat with John, giving him, in no particular order, moral support, pats on the back and tissues. I remember thinking at this time thank God we had travel insurance. We had been warned about, and heard horror stories of, travellers being injured in North

America, going to hospital and being left with bills for tens of thousands of dollars.

John was looking fairly shabby at this point. His skin was patchy and his eyes were now so red he was starting to resemble Darth Maul. We pulled into the Emergency section of the hospital and I said to John, 'You just wait in the car, mate. I'll go in and we'll get a doctor to see you real soon.'

Anyone who knows us will probably be doubting this story now, because in the 24 years I have known John, we have never called each other 'mate'. The story, however, is true. So there is Darth John waiting in the car while caring, capable and confident Rusty makes his way inside the hospital in search of a doctor. There were the usual chaotic scenes of a hospital emergency waiting room playing out around me as I took my place in the queue for admissions. Various groups of people were sitting or standing around; each group had at least one person suffering some form of injury that I guessed had caused them to be there. A man walked past with a crazed look in his eye and his hands down his pants shouting, 'I'm Wayne Gretzky! I'm Wayne Gretzky!' Two middle-aged women were trying to calm down a younger woman who seemed very upset. I don't know if it's because she was in pain or because she wasn't a Wayne Gretzky fan.

After about 20 minutes I got to the front of the line. It was my time to shine and get some much-needed help for my sick friend.

'Can I help you?' the admissions nurse asked.

In a confident, clear voice I answered, 'Yes, my friend needs to see a doctor.'

She looked at me a little strangely and said, 'What are his symptoms?'

I proceeded to describe them, and to help her understand, I tried to put my description into official medical speak.

'Yeah, we're looking at uh … major liquid expulsion from

most orifii ... um ... extreme reddity of the eye-ial area ... um there seems to be some slight patchinisation of the facial skin.'

'Does your friend have any history of mental illness?' she asked.

'Ahhh, not that I know of,' I said. 'Why do you ask?'

'Because this is a psychiatric hospital,' she said drily. 'You want St Mary's, just down the road.'

I paused. This was my big chance. I could put John away for a long, long time, but I decided I needed him around for the next 20 years or so. I turned and walked from the admissions window with the poise of someone who is suffering a level of embarrassment that would make Darth Maul turn red. On my way out through the door, I briefly locked eyes with the Wayne Gretzky man. For a fleeting moment we looked at each other and he gave me a barely perceptible nod of acknowledgement, like he'd been putting on an act and I was in on the joke. As I left, two white-coated men descended upon him, injected a clear liquid into his arm and escorted him away.

I finally got out to John, who was waiting patiently in the car like a child at a casino car park. He looked at me hopefully with his bloodshot puppy dog eyes. I said, 'Uh, sorry, John, this hospital is full. We're going to try another one down the road.'

We got to the next hospital, this time an actual hospital that doesn't see people who think they are famous ice hockey players. John and I walked in, leaving Denise to mind the car to avoid paying the exorbitant parking fees that Toronto is world famous for. This time the attempt to see a doctor went more smoothly. John was signed in and taken away and I was told that I should wait. However, I wasn't told what I was actually waiting for. A receipt? A doctor? To sign the death certificate? I took the least stained seat in the waiting area and proceeded to play the games I used to play in waiting rooms before they invented solitaire on mobile phones. You know the games I'm talking about.

Find the oldest magazine. Count the square tiles on the ceiling. Add up how much money it would take to buy every single item in the vending machine. Make up names and backstories for the other people in the waiting room ... That's Jeannette and Vernon McAlpine over there, from Cornfield, Ontario. Vernon's a retired watchmaker and Jeannette likes cribbage and vermouth. Vernon has an inflamed goitre on his right testicle and Jeannette has a fetish for wearing Tim Horton's donuts over her nipples ... Oh, God ... *How much longer??*

After three hours I asked the nurse if there was any news. She told me John had had some tests, they would keep him in overnight for observation and that I could go now. I said, 'That's great news. By the way, how fucking long have you known this news and when the fuck were you going to tell me about it?' Actually I said, 'Okay, thanks.' I said my goodbyes to Jeannette and Vernon, walked out and suddenly thought, shit! Denise had been in the car all this time. She was too afraid to leave for fear of getting a parking ticket and I hoped she wasn't too pissed off. I got back to the car but it was too late. Denise was dead ... dead fucking angry with me is what she was. I simply played the 'John's on his deathbed and I have been holding his hand and caringly bathing his forehead for the past three hours' card and we were on our way.

We went back the next day to see how he was going. I am happy to say he was looking much better and he was allowed to leave the hospital. I know what you're waiting to hear – the official diagnosis. Well, after a lumber puncture, two blood tests, stool, saliva and urine samples it turns out that John had got pneumonia ... or diabetes ... or something, I wasn't really taking any notice of what he was saying, but I am sure it was rather serious.

And what of the medical costs? John received the bill in the mail, about a month after we had returned home to Melbourne. He braced himself for the total, even though he was happily aware that the travel insurance was going to take care of the entire sum. It came to the grand total of $19.58. You've got to love the Canadian health system.

John recovered very quickly from his lumbago or scurvy or whatever it was that he had. We actually only missed one gig due to him being ill and that one missed gig remained the only show we ever missed due to illness during our entire career. In over 4000 shows over a 20-year period, that was not a bad strike rate.

• • •

We returned home and had two weeks off, then started another Last Laugh Christmas season in mid-November. The year 1992 was going to be just about the busiest year of our career. Looking at the diary for that year, I notice we played continuously at the Last Laugh from November 1991 to the end of July 1992. The only breaks were ten days at the Adelaide Fringe in March, and two weeks back in Canada for a college showcase in June.

The extended run at the Laugh was an invaluable experience for us. As I mentioned before, it helped us hone our performing skills no end. The run took in shows with Marty Putz, an Argentinian foot-juggling family, an array of local comedians and the final-ever season of the excellent trio, the Found Objects. They were known for their wonderful slapstick, silly songs like 'The Tim Tam Song' and 'Punt Road' and general daggy farting around. This was the group that Frank Woodley and Colin Lane were in before they formed Lano and Woodley. We were on the bill with them for the final-ever show and in another inspired act of final night hilarity, John and I jumped in on their act from the raised band shell that was set about five feet above the stage. I really cracked my ankle as we landed and the injury stayed with me for about the next 10 years. It was like an old war wound. When the weather would turn cold

Scared Weird Frozen Guy

I could feel it in my ankle again. For some reason I would put on the voice of an old Welshman and say to myself, 'Ah, me old Found Objects ankle is playing up again ... the weather ... she's a gonna change ...'

YEW TOWK FUHN.

The June break from this marathon season at the Last Laugh was for the Scaredies to go over to Canada and perform at a showcase for an organisation called COCA.

The Canadian Organization of Campus Activities, and in the USA, the National Association of Campus Activities (NACA), are organisations that put on annual showcases of bands and comedians and variety acts. There are around 11,000 colleges and universities in the US alone and the people who book the entertainment for individual colleges come along to these showcases to see what's on offer and then book the acts for their school. You can perform one 20-minute showcase spot and then quite easily book a three-month tour on the back of it, so this is what we started to do. Over the following five years we did 11 more tours around North America, visiting every province of Canada and 32 states of the USA.

The tours around the USA would usually involve John and me flying into a particular large city like Chicago or Atlanta, then picking up a hire car and driving around the surrounding states for a few weeks of shows. Then we would fly to another city and do the same thing all over again. The tours would last two to three months. We travelled to all parts of the mid-west and central and eastern America, but the south-east was particularly exciting for me, being a fan of bluegrass and country music. I got to visit many places that I had only heard of in songs: Mobile, Jackson, Memphis, Little Rock, Chattanooga, Charleston and

...tless more. We travelled extensively throughout the states of Georgia, Alabama, Kentucky, North and South Carolina, Florida, Virginia and West Virginia. I actually thought bluegrass music would be on the radio all the time and everyone would be into it. It's like Americans coming to Australia and expecting to see kangaroos hopping down the main street. I went to North Carolina expecting everyone to be walking down the street pickin' banjos and sipping moonshine. It was a genuine surprise to find it was not like that, but we did have a very authentic experience one night in a little town called Ferrum, Virginia.

Ferrum is located in the Blue Ridge Mountains, near the border of North Carolina, and is surrounded by other small towns with names like Bent Mountain, Redeye and Horse Pasture. We played an early evening gig in the local college and while driving back to the motel, stopped for supplies at the local gas station. My attention was drawn to a hand painted sign leaning against one of the petrol bowsers – 'BLUEGRASS HERE TONIGHT 9 PM'.

It was about 8 o'clock and I looked around but could see no space for a bluegrass concert. Maybe it was here next to the bowsers? I went and asked the gas station attendant inside.

'Is there bluegrass here tonight?' I asked.

'Heh heh ... yew towk fuhny,' he drooled. 'N y'all gut a purdy mowth ...' or words to that effect.

I took it as a 'yes' and John and I agreed we should come back later and check it out.

Around 9.15 we drove up but couldn't see any movement happening outside the gas station. I pictured the drooling attendant peering out from behind the curtains in the shop thinking, 'Ah caint buhlieve mah trayup wurked!' and we were about to become the victims in an elaborate hillbilly murder/abduction scheme that used bluegrass music as bait. But as we got out of the car, we heard the muffled sound of some stringed instruments being plucked and realised that the show was on in the mechanics' workshop. We made our way through the front entrance of the gas station into the workshop and thankfully saw some other people already in there. All of the mechanics' tools and equipment had been pushed over to one side, so the room was mostly clear and resembled a venue, but it still had that strong mechanics smell that was part oil, part petrol and part body odour. There was a table with a keg of beer on it and probably about 30 or so people standing around in groups while some danced. We felt a little overdressed, as we were wearing shoes. What made us stand out even more was that we weren't wearing overalls. It was actually quite a mixed group of young and old people and I could tell there were even a few students from the local college there.

The 'band' of musicians were standing in a corner sort of facing each other, it was kind of hard to tell which way they were facing as their eyes all looked in different directions. You know when you see a painting that seems to be looking at you no matter where you are standing in a room? That's what it was like watching this band. There were five members in the band and all the classic bluegrass instruments were being played: guitar, double bass, fiddle, banjo and air compressor, though the guy on the air compressor may have been playing the mandolin – it was difficult to tell from where I was standing. Strangely, each time he finished a solo there was a loud whooshing sound and a rush of air. He was wearing overalls with no shirt and a trucker cap and his face looked like he was permanently sucking on a Fisherman's Friend. Our old friend Drooly the gas station attendant was on bass and the fiddle player stood perfectly still and must have been at least 105 years old.

Musically, they were very intriguing. They played in time with each other, there was just no way to tell where one bar ended and the next one began. There were no dynamics to the music, it was a 'one in all in' vibe with one or two of them sort of wailing vocally over the top of the instruments. As far as bluegrass music went, I've certainly heard better, but I've never seen it in such an authentic setting. After a few songs some of the students came over to chat with John and me. They were very friendly and said they could tell we 'weren't from around here' and that we 'stuck out like a diamond in a goat's ass', which I took as a good thing. They asked us if we wanted to go to a party that they were headed to and we said sure. What did we have to lose apart from our money, our dignity and possibly our lives? We followed them in our car about five miles out of town to a rather large and run-down-looking wooden house situated almost under the state highway overpass. It was a student share house and a noisy party was in full swing. Us being newcomers in a town where they don't get too many newcomers, let alone Australian comedy duos, made us a welcome novelty. We were instantly ushered into the kitchen where someone extracted from the freezer a large, frosty glass jar filled with half a dozen peach halves floating in a clear liquid. We were knowledgably informed that the drink was authentic peach moonshine and we were both obliged to take a swig straight from the jar as part of some sort of welcoming ceremony. I took a large guzzle and immediately thought someone had kicked me in the balls ... Let's just say it cleared out the sinuses. John had a turn next. I don't know if it hit him like it did me, but I did notice that soon after he had a drink, he put on his glasses and left them on for the rest of the night. I remember wandering around from room to room, someone brought out a banjo at one point and I had a bit of a bash on it and sang a few bluegrass standards, harmonising randomly with some strangers – God I love the South. In the lounge room I came across the longest bong I ever saw and was enthusiastically offered a go. It was a very, very long bong. I literally had to stand on the couch to make it work. I remember one of the guys there saying in an excellent Southern accent, 'Hell boy, that thar bong is tall as y'all!' which made me cough uncontrollably for about 15 minutes. Those college kids loved their pot, that's for sure. I never really chased down pot on the road in the US, but sometimes it would come our way.

A popular post-gig question was 'Do you guys party?' which simply means 'Do you smoke pot?' When I first heard that phrase, in Grand Forks, North Dakota, I politely answered, 'Oh you know, we like to have the occasional drink but we're not big partiers.' The two young guys could tell I didn't understand them, so they persisted, 'Yeah, but do you *"party"* ?'

'Oh no,' I thought, 'these two nice young gay students want to know if John and I want to "partay" with them ... Not that there's anything wrong with that ... um ... Hey John! Come over here for a second will you?'

We weren't really that into having many huge nights while on tour, but sometimes, like in Ferrum, they just happened.

I remember talking to a motel owner named Wilbur in a small town after a show one night.

'So, Wilbur,' I asked him, 'what do you do for fun in this town?'

'Fer fun?' he said, as if he could remember what fun was but hadn't actually had any for quite a while.

'Yeah, you know, if you want to go out with some friends and have a good time,' I said.

Wilbur stared in thought at a point just beyond my left ear.

'Hmm, fun ... well, ah, I know. You get a box of beer and head on down to the river bank and drink it.'

There followed an awkward pause of about five seconds, where we stared at each other, both of us waiting for the other person to say something.

'Sure that sounds fun,' I eventually said. 'But what about if you're in for a really big night and want to have a big celebration?'

He thought for a while on this one, then finally said, 'Well ... you get two boxes of beer and head on down to the river.'

One thing I did chase down whenever we were in the States was fireworks. Oh, fireworks. In most US states fireworks were illegal except around the Fourth of July, when they were available exclusively in safe places like every supermarket and liquor store. In a few states though, giant barns of fireworks were sold year-round. States like Tennessee, Kentucky and South Carolina just decided 'Fuck it! If our citizens want to blow up their fingers and eyes year-round, it's their God-given right!' What was it about these multi-coloured paper and cardboard explosives with badly translated English instructions that made them so damn attractive to travelling Australians? Boredom, for one. We could roll into a new town just after lunch, check in to the motel, and be shooting bottle rockets at each other by the middle of the afternoon. We used to buy way more than we could possibly let off in one tour. I even used to send them home in the post. I know, I know, but this was in the days before 2001 and I don't think anyone ever checked, besides what are the fireworks going to do? Light themselves? I don't think so.

One place we stopped at in South Carolina was called Wild Bill's Fireworks and the proprietor was a hippie-looking Vietnam veteran who I struck up a conversation with. In between facial tics, he said how he met lots of Aussies when he was in Nam and had lots of good friends from there still. Inevitably, the conversation soon turned to marijuana and he asked about the drug laws in Australia compared to the US. Before I knew it I walked out of there with some kickass fireworks and a bag of pot for good measure. That was all fine; I just had to remember to get rid of the pot before we left to fly home two weeks later. The night before we departed, I was packing up a box of shopping goodies to send home in the post like I usually did. I always bought any *Simpsons* memorabilia I could find, and would buy silly little American trinkets and chocolate bars, as well as toys and souvenirs that interested me. I always had too much to fit in my bags, so would pack up a box or two and send it home in the post. This particular box was a good haul: books, t-shirts, souvenirs, CDs and plenty of fireworks.

When everything was packed and taped up and addressed, I couldn't find the bag of pot anywhere and thought it must have been lost along the way.

Two months later the box arrived at home, as always, addressed to my girlfriend (I wasn't taking any chances). We opened it up and there was the bag of pot sitting right at the top of the box. Denise was not happy. I said, 'Hey, it's okay. It's just my way of saying I love you.'

Yeah ... I love you, honey, and here are some drugs and explosives.

• • •

During the years we toured North America we spent an awfully large amount of time driving around in cars. Actually we spent an awfully large amount of time in hotels, flying in planes and waiting around as well. From 1991–98 we took 387 flights covering over 800,000 kilometres. We drove roughly 75,000 kilometres in that time as well, which equates to about 1250 hours of driving, or 52 days of sitting next to the same person, trying to decide where to stop for lunch, what route to take, how warm or cold the air should be, how fast we should drive and where I could hide John's body after I murdered him. Actually, I can honestly and quite boringly say that we got on extremely well considering the difficult circumstances. We both realised early on that it's no fun for either person if one of us cracks the shits and stays in a bad mood. Sure, we had our silent periods. They say that a sign of a healthy relationship is when you can enjoy comfortable silence with each other. Going by that rule, we were in good shape, because we would often go for days without talking to each other ...

While John and I are quite different people, we obviously share some common interests. This would help us immeasurably in passing the time on long drives. Apart from music and performing, we both love good books and well-told stories, and would often take the time during a drive to recount to each other, with as much detail as possible, the plots of books we had read or movies we had seen. We both have good brains and a keen interest in science (John actually has a Bachelor of Science, whom he keeps locked in a trunk in his basement) and would spend many happy hours discussing wild theories on things like:

'How fast would you have to drive to keep the shadow of the car constant?'

'If you drove around Australia clockwise instead of counter-clockwise, how much further would you travel?'

The old 'how many times does a car wheel spin in a minute/mile/journey' and many others. Those things kept us busy during our travels and I recall that many times after a gig I would be about to mention something interesting to John then would think, 'No, I'll save that for the trip tomorrow, I think we'll get a good few hours out of that.'

We would also play games to pass the time and our 'Stump the Scaredies' routine developed during these travels. We started challenging each other to combine television themes. For example, sing *The Brady Bunch* theme to the tune of the *Gilligan's Island* theme. Try it. Now do *Bewitched* with the words of *F Troop*. Ha!

We couldn't really even listen to music to help pass the time while we were driving. IPods didn't exist. None of the rental cars had CD players in them, just cassettes. We used to buy books on tape, but only the cheapest ones we could find, so we would have some schlocky novel like *Beast* – Peter Benchley's follow-up to *Jaws*, read by Paul Sorvino – or some war story we'd never heard of like *The Annoyed Squadron* read by Jamie Farr or *The Eagle and the Hitler* read by Alan Thicke. We also bought some *Learn Spanish – The Easy Way* cassettes and would start the day learning our Spanish numbers and nouns. Little did I know that this would help me prepare for the Antarctic trip years later.

The South of the US continued to fascinate and amaze us. The place names of some of the towns were very weird and we would sometimes pass the time by scouring the Rand McNally road atlas trying to find the rudest-sounding names. I found this list in my 1994 diary (I knew it would come in handy one day). These are actual towns from all over the United States:

Hooker, Fannie, Beaver, Weiner, Jigger, Dickey, Mashpee, Yellow Water, Square Butt, Colon, Big Lick, Porkey, Kickapoo, Bumpass, Oral, Needmore, Threeway, Intercourse and Climax.

Kentucky was quite fruitful in the weird town name department and all of the following towns are from that state: Bugtussle, Slapneck, Oddville, Monkey's Eyebrow, Possum Trot, Drip Rock and Lick Fork.

You could travel all around the world and never leave the USA if you visit these towns: Paris, Moscow, Vienna, London, Rome, China, Earth, Mars, Moon and Jupiter.

Or you could live in a town that's also an adjective, such as: Difficult, Eclectic, Strong, Normal, Happy, Humble, Smiley, Friendly or Carefree.

The logistics of booking our shows into a feasible travel schedule was a nightmare. Most of the time it went fairly smoothly thanks to the experienced skills of our excellent US booking agents, Lee in Orlando and Susan in Chicago. However, sometimes they just couldn't get the dates to match up and keep the gigs within a three- or four-hour drive of one another. One itinerary had us doing a show at Kennesaw State University, just outside of Atlanta, Georgia. We had performed in Mobile, Alabama the previous night and done a six-hour drive to make the show in Kennesaw. The next morning we were off on another six-hour drive to Rock Hill, South Carolina, for a show that night, and here's where it got a little sticky. The next morning we were due at an 11 am Sunday morning show in Morgantown, West Virginia. Why so early on a Sunday? It was homecoming weekend and we were playing before the big homecoming football game. Homecoming is a time when ex-students flock to their alma mater to watch football and catch up with their college buddies who have been too stupid to graduate yet. This plan to do a Sunday morning show sounded fine, but Morgantown is an eight-hour drive from Rock Hill. We decided to do the show in Rock Hill and leave straight away to get two or three hours driving under our belts, find a motel along the way, get up early and arrive in time for the 11 am show. Sounded like a good idea. We did the show for our great friend Boyd from Winthrop University in Rock Hill, who insisted that he take us out for catfish and dumplings after the show. We tried to tell him we were tired and had a big drive ahead of us, but when it comes to socialising and dumplings, Boyd just won't take no for an answer. With full stomachs and sore hands from Boyd's ridiculously painful high fives, we set out on our drive to Morgantown, West Virginia – 720 kilometres away. It was just after 10 pm. Remember we had already done a six-hour drive that day just to get to Rock Hill. We started well, heading north on I-77 and crossed the state line into Virginia around midnight.

We were both starting to feel the effects of the long day and agreed we should find the nearest motel, grab five hours sleep and do the rest of the trip in the morning. If you have ever done any driving around the USA, you will know the familiar sight as you approach any town on the interstate highway. About 20 kilometres before the town, the billboards start appearing that list the dozen or so hotel chains, gas stations and fast food restaurants that you will find there. We knew this would be the case so there would be no need to call ahead to book a room; we just had to roll up and check in. When the first hotel we stopped at was full, we didn't think anything of it – it was a Saturday night after all. When the third, fourth and fifth hotels we tried were all full, we started getting a little bit concerned. The hotel clerk at the fifth hotel informed us, like we were complete idiots, that: 'This is homecoming weekend! Y'all are not gonna find a room for miles!' and laughed. Then I stabbed him. Not so funny now is it, you hillbilly fucker? Of course I didn't stab him. I was just getting delirious from tiredness, plus there were witnesses.

We had no choice but to climb back into the car and keep driving. We took short shifts behind the wheel to try to keep fresh and tried a few more out-of-the-way motels with no luck.

Two hours later, just after 2 am, we were in the Blue Ridge Mountains. I was driving and John was dozing. The dual lane interstate was quite straight and reasonably safe. We were doing about 80 mph (125 kmh) when a large deer ran onto the road, straight in front of the car. I now understand when people describe an automobile accident as happening in slow motion. The whole moment would have taken less than a second but to me it unfolded like this:

I was driving and I noticed something moving just to the side of the reach of the car's headlights. 'Oh, that looks like a deer,' I thought, as it made its way onto the very side of the road and stopped momentarily. I said to myself: 'I sure hope it doesn't make its way onto the road in front of our ca–' The deer then sprang out in front of the car and actually nearly made it across our path. The car hit the rear half of the deer, spinning it all the way down the driver's side of the vehicle. As the deer sprang, I tried to shout, *'John, wake up there's a deer and it's about to run in front of the car and we're going to hit it!'* But it just came out as a very short 'aaAAGGHH!' followed by the very loud sound of a deer hitting every part of the side of our car. I didn't even have time to slam on the brakes, but managed to maintain control of the car. John woke up shouting *'What the fuck?'* and all I could say was *'Deer, deer, deer!* We just hit a deer!' We slowed right down and eventually pulled over to assess the damage. The initial impact with the deer had smashed the front right-hand-side lights, then, as it spun down the side of the car, it dented the front panel, both the driver's and rear passenger doors and the rear panel, leaving blood and deer hair smeared along the length of the car. I don't know what became of the poor deer. It was pitch black all around us so I couldn't see it, but I didn't hold high hopes for its welfare. I withheld the impulse to say, 'Dear oh dear oh dear.' The car was driving okay so we continued on. My heart was beating wildly and with all the adrenalin flowing through my veins, there was no danger of feeling sleepy so I kept on driving, reliving the incident over and over in my mind. Just before 4 am, we finally found a hotel with a vacancy and fell onto our beds for a ridiculously inadequate three-hour sleep, before continuing on to the Morgantown show. The question you may ask is, 'Was the gig worth all that driving and almost dying in a bizarre deer collision?'

We arrived at the West Virginia University in Morgantown about 20 minutes before we were due to start our performance. There were many people arriving for the big football game and we were directed to a field behind the stadium where the organisers had thought the spectators might gather for some picnics and entertainment before the game. We set up on the back of a truck and performed a 40-minute show in front of maybe 20 people. It was such a bizarre situation after everything we had been through in the previous 24 hours that about halfway through the set we both got the giggles to the point where we couldn't even speak. It was spectacularly ridiculous and a great example of the old line 'What? And give up showbiz?' We finished the show, packed up and treated ourselves to a slap-up breakfast, but it didn't end there.

Yew Towk Fuhnny

In the last two and a half days, we had done three shows, driven for 20 hours and 1600 kilometres through five states, hit a deer and wrecked our hire car. Now all we had to do was complete the final show of the tour that night – a five-hour drive away in Lynchburg, Virginia.

WE ALL BEEN A-WAITING ON Y'ALLS CALL

It goes without saying that we toured with no mobile phone, no internet and no GPS. We literally were on our own. Before each tour, a folder would get mailed to us that would have most of our info printed on various sheets of paper. It would list the date, the college, the town and a phone number. Sometimes there would be a map of the college included. We would have to call ahead to each college to get specific information regarding our hotel, exactly where the gig was and who we should meet. We would always save our change and carry a huge bag of quarters with us just for phone calls. Every few days we would stop at a gas station with our information folder and call the next week's colleges. Most of the time you would get an answering machine and of course they couldn't call us back so we would have to try again the next day. The conversations would go something like this:

'Hi, can I speak to Vernon please?'

'Who may ah say is spaykin'?'

'It's Rusty from the Scared Weird Little Guys.'

'The hwat?'

We found that while talking to people in the south of the United States, especially on the phone, they can have real trouble understanding an Australian accent. We would often resort to putting on accents simply to be understood. It's fairly straightforward doing an accent that they can understand – just add the extra syllable 'ay' into every word.

'The Scayerred Wayerred Layittle Gahze.'

'Oh hey thayere! We all been a-waiting on y'alls call!'

'Oh great, well hello to all … y'all … of you all there. We just need some quick directions to the college and where the hotel is that we are staying at please?' And I would add for good measure, 'if'n all y'all don't mind.'

'Okay, here's how y'all get to the hotayel.'

There would follow an extremely long description of unnecessarily complicated directions involving turnpikes, crosswalks and stoplights. The only geographical features used were fast food restaurants:

'Take exit 24601 off the turnpike 85 B North. Take a right at the stoplights and then you come to another stoplight. There's an Oily Joe's on the left and a Jimmy McFatass Burger on the right. Just keep going straight ahead until you come to another stoplight. There's a Tacky Taco on one side and a Chicken Pit on the other side, now the Chicken Pit *used* to be a Custard Shack but it burnt down, okay now go straight ahead until you come to a Bob's Biscuit World, then take a left at the Something Fishy and you'll see your hotel – the Super-Econo-Value-Inn-Suites.'

IF IT'S NOVEMBER HERE ...

During the early 1990s if you were an Australian travelling in North America you had to put up with a lot of *Crocodile Dundee* references. At first it surprised me just how little most Americans knew about Australia, or about the rest of the world for that matter. As we travelled more extensively and got in to the backwoods and met the locals, it didn't surprise me any more. Many Americans have never left their own county, let alone the state that they live in or their country. They are also brought up with a patriotism that we foreigners can barely comprehend, and they do love to bang on about the whole 'freedom' thing. We would meet people who just naturally assumed that we would want to move to the United States.

'So you live here now, of course ...'

'Uh ... no, we live in Australia.'

'Oh,' they would answer, almost sympathetically.

Many Americans just assume that they live in the best country in the world, and everyone else lives in dark, dirty holes under the regime of a brutal dictator. I mean, sure, I grew up under Jeff Kennett, but the hole we lived in was quite clean and not even that dark.

Most people we met would ask, 'Do you like America?'

'Of course!' we would chime.

'So what is it you like the most? Is it the freedom?'

The first time I heard someone say that, I was bewildered. Freedom? What does that even mean? Being able to live the life that you choose, within the law and pursue your dreams without fear of oppression? If so, I live in one of the 'freest' countries in the world, though Australians tend to take it for granted. In Australia, we just don't have the 'freedom' thing shoved down our throats by the government or media, like in the United States.

Growing up in Australia, we are bombarded with American culture and accents through movies, music and television, so it's really not that difficult to understand most Americans that you meet. It doesn't work the other way, though. On our early tours, we had terrible trouble being understood by the locals. They just were not used to hearing our accents. The only Australian accents the poor Americans had as a reference to that point were *Crocodile Dundee*, Yahoo Serious and Olivia Newton-John's weird accent in *Grease*.

When we first went over, we wondered why parts of the show weren't working as well as they should have been, then we realised the audience simply couldn't understand us. We had to slow our talking down to what seemed a ludicrously deliberate pace. They could understand us easily when we sang, but our talking in between songs was always difficult for them. Talking to the audience like they were small children made it easier for them to understand, and not just because of the accent.

I still owned the large cowboy hat that I had acquired during Expo 88 and introduced it into our act by doing an unintelligible routine about a cowboy with a lasso, who we called Bubba. Bubba started out as a fairly tame cowboy with a mild Southern accent who did a couple of rope tricks, but with the first-hand experience of talking to some authentic Kentucky and North Carolinian old-timers, he grew over the years into an insane, incomprehensible, ranting maniac – but with a heart.

I remember the first time we were to perform in Georgia, and I was shitting myself about doing Bubba, thinking that the crowd would be offended. They lapped it up because they thought that it was about everyone in Alabama; and when we did Bubba in Alabama, it killed because they all thought it was about people from Mississippi. When we did Bubba in Mississippi they all just went: 'Ah yup, that's us!'

The Americans generally love Australians, albeit in a quaint, ever so slightly condescending way. Most meetings I had with Americans could pretty much be summed up by the following:

'Oh I love your accent! Are you from England?'

'Australia.'

'I love that movie *Crocodile Dundee* ... uz thut a knoife? Yuk yuk yuk.'

'Ah yes ... the "knife" thing ... We all say that down under. Actually that's not a knife, *but this is!*' Then I would pull out a huge, sharpened hunting knife and plunge it repeatedly into their stupid, fat chests. At least that's what I always felt like doing whenever I was asked about *Crocodile Dundee*.

Once on a bus from Chicago airport I struck up a conversation with a man after he overheard John and I talking to each other.

'Where are you boys from?' he asked.

'Australia,' I said.

He frowned for a moment, then said, 'Wait a minute. Did you say Australia or Austria?'

'Oh, Australia,' I repeated, smiling.

'Australia! Damn! Yeah I seen that movie y'all made down there ...'

'Here we go,' I thought.

He continued, '... yeah, what was it called? *The Sound of Music*, that's it. Man y'all got some beautiful scenery and castles and shit down there.'

'Well, you'll never believe it, I actually live in a castle,' I said, reaching for my hunting knife.

Americans often had trouble with the whole time zone/

opposite seasons in the other hemisphere thing, which would usually lead to some entertaining questions.

'When do you have Christmas in Australia?'

'Is morning in the night time in Australia?'

But the best I ever heard was, 'If it's November here, what month is it in Australia?'

Trouble understanding the accent led to me having the following exchange with one of the extremely cheerful American Customs and Immigration agents that you encounter when you first arrive in Los Angeles, and when I say cheerful, I mean not cheerful at all. His name was Carson or Dwayne or Horace or something like that and his hair was styled in a classic buzz-cut flattop. He looked like Forrest Gump, except smarter and meaner.

'What is your occupation, sir?' he asked.

'I'm a comedian,' I replied, somewhat optimistically.

Unfortunately Forrest thought I'd said, 'I'm a Canadian,' so he said, 'Yes, but what do you do for a living?'

Of course I took this the wrong way and thought to myself, 'What's this? The flipping Immigration bloke is doing gags now?'

So I repeated: 'I'm a comedian.'

He got serious then: 'I need to see your ID, sir.'

He wanted me to prove that I was a comedian? What bit should I do? I haven't got my costume, oh no. I was starting to panic.

'Okay then,' I said. 'How many customs and immigration agents does it take to screw in a light bulb?'

'Are you being smart, sir?'

'You haven't even heard the punchline yet.'

'Give me your passport, sir'

'Do you want to hear this joke or not?'

I gave him my passport.

'You're Australian, not Canadian,' he said.

'And you're an idiot,' I said. Actually I said, 'Yes, sir.'

If It's November Here...

The penny dropped.

'Ohhh,' I said. 'Canadian ... comedian ... I'm sorry, I thought that you thought that I thought tha ...'

'Sir, stop talking.'

It all got sorted out eventually and we both had a big laugh about it and we promised to stay in touch. At least, he didn't arrest and detain me so I think I came out of it all right, and he had an amusing story to tell at the customs and immigration agents Christmas party.

We never had as much trouble with the accents in Canada. Canadians in general just seemed to be a bit more aware of everything else in the world than their southern neighbours were. Until I first went to Canada, I never really thought they were any different to Americans. (Canadians *really* love it if you say that to them.) To our untrained ears, their accents were basically the same, except for that 'eh' thing. We knew they loved maple leaves, and ice hockey, and that the Queen of England was somehow involved, though I wasn't quite sure how she was involved. Even today, I don't think the Canadians are quite sure how she is involved. She's on their currency, yet not on the flag, but they do compete in the Commonwealth Games ... hmm. Now after having spent so much time there I must say I have the utmost respect for and many fond memories of Canada.

Canadians are really just Australians with different accents. We have a lot in common. Like Australia, they were populated by England and European nations. They love ice hockey, while we love footy. We both love drinking beer and have a weird love/hate relationship with England. They've got Newfoundland and we've got Tasmania. We both live with extremes in weather and we have both pretty much destroyed the societies of our original inhabitants.

Canada does have that weird French thing going on with Quebec and Australia doesn't really have an equivalent to that, and where does New Zealand fit in to all of this?

GREAT DAY FOR A RUN

On one particularly slack (fitness wise) Scaredies tour of the USA in 1995, the seemingly endless cycle of gig/sleep/drive/buffet started to take its toll and I actually decided to start running.

I remember exactly where we were – Greenville, Pennsylvania – a smallish, rather dull town in the eastern part of the state, near the border of Ohio. It was early February, pretty much smack bang in the middle of a long and cold winter. I don't remember what the gig was that we were playing, most likely it was at some undersized, cringe-worthy community college.

The (memorable) gig was completed. After a late night bean burrito we retired for the night back to the luxurious surrounds of the Red Rash Inn or wherever we were staying.

I meticulously set the alarm in the room for 6 am, laid out some 'suitable' running gear, watched an episode or three of *Star Trek: The Next Generation* and went to bed.

Holy shit it was cold the next morning! The weather lady on the television cheerfully said it was a 'chilly' 23 degrees, which didn't sound too bad until I did the rough conversion into Celsius. Minus five. Ouch!

I prepared myself physically and mentally for the experience that I was about to undergo, which means I clumsily pulled on my clothes and was too sleepy to realise the stupidity of what I was about to do. I did a few token stretches, took a deep breath and opened the door. Wham! The cold air smacked me in the face. I sure was awake now.

I braced myself and took off down the road. Arms pumping back and forth, legs moving one in front of the other.

'I can still do this running thing,' I told myself, recalling the glory days of the Bribie Island Festival Fun Run of 1979.

But the cold was getting to me.

'Wow! It actually hurts to breathe,' I thought.

'Yes, it actually hurts to breathe, Rusty, because you are an unfit slob,' countered my brain.

I continued to 'run' down the road. Notice I say down the road instead of down the footpath because the USA doesn't generally seem to think that anyone might want to not fucking drive everywhere and actually want to proceed on foot occasionally. There ... I said it.

I continued down the side of the road until, about four minutes into the run, I realised that I was hopelessly underdressed for winter running.

I had on my blue cotton long johns, a pair of rugby shorts, a long-sleeved cotton t-shirt and a beanie. I couldn't feel my chin and my fingers had started to really hurt. This was not fun.

I didn't know where the hell I was going. This was in the days before the internet and Google Earth. Now, if you want to go on a run while travelling, you can scope out the potential route online before you go. You can measure the exact distance and even street view any potential hazards like hills, fences and dangerous dogs, etc. I was running alongside a rather busy peak hour road, breathing in the exhaust fumes from the traffic. I could self-consciously feel the stationary drivers sniggering at the inappropriately dressed, shuffling weirdo ambling along next to their heated cars. I had had enough and couldn't take it any more. I turned around and before long was back in the warmth and privacy of the motel room.

I had been gone just under 11 minutes.

I'D LIKE TO THANK ...

The time that we spent touring in North America is filled with fond memories for me.

I am extremely grateful that I had the opportunity to experience so much of North America in a way that few people have. We got to visit so many of the famous cities and small towns and back roads and each day would be a new adventure, good or bad, with a fresh group of people to meet. Our one constant during that time was the hour that we spent onstage.

It was an exciting, fun, eye-opening, amazing and sometimes lonely experience.

The audiences seemed to like us and we received awards from COCA for 'Best Variety Act 1994 and 1995' and NACA for 'Best Comedy Act 1995' and were nominated for NACA 'Entertainers of the Year 1995' for the entire United States.

In between all of the North American tours we would come back to Australia and try to keep some semblance of a career going here. With all the time spent out of the country, it was difficult to keep any sort of momentum going back at home. During the 1990s, we never had the luxury of a regular television or radio spot, which would have made it much easier, so we continued the back and forth routine and, while we were home, regularly travelled interstate to the capital cities and started doing our own Melbourne Comedy Festival shows. We also started recording some of our songs and released a cassette called *Scared Weird Little Guys – Volume 1* that we sold off the stage. The 17 people that bought a copy must be sitting pretty with that little collector's item. If you're interested, I have a few hundred I could sell you at a good price. We also recorded our first EP – *Bloody Jeff* – and our first full-length album, entitled *Scared*.

During our first trip to Perth in 1994, we were sitting backstage in the small theatre of the University of WA tuning up our guitars and discussing the set list when there was a polite knock on the door. Two very young-looking fellows were standing there. One had wild, fuzzy hair and an equally wild look in his eye, while the other was more preppy-looking and seemed to be the spokesperson.

'Oh hi guys,' he squeaked enthusiastically, 'we are two local comedians just starting out and we want to know if you would let us do five minutes before you go on?'

John and I looked at each other, shrugged our shoulders and said, 'Sure, why not?' It meant five minutes less that we had to do. They virtually bounced off the walls with excitement and we made some small talk with them before the show started. We felt ever so experienced and important answering all of their questions about showbiz and comedy and Melbourne and the like. About three years later, we were standing backstage at the Cheese Shop comedy night at the Prince Patrick hotel in Melbourne and a new young stand-up comedian called Rove McManus came up and said, 'Hi guys, I just wanted to thank you for giving me and my mate Duff our first-ever spot over in Perth three years ago.'

You're welcome ...

Please don't hold us responsible for Rove's subsequent career; I am sure you would've done the same had you been in our position.

• • •

I'd Like to Thank

It's actually not the entire recording industry that is eligible to win an ARIA; you have to be a registered (and paid up) member of the Australian Recording Industry Association to nominate a recording. That generally restricts nominations to artists associated with major labels, and excludes hundreds of talented, independent music-makers. Regardless, it is nice to be nominated and as Polygram had released our album *Scared*, we were nominated for Best Comedy Release in the 1995 awards. That was the year that Silverchair exploded on to the scene, winning five ARIAs. The other nominees in our category were comedy big hitters Kevin Bloody Wilson, Jimeoin, Austen Tayshus and The Twelfth Man, who won, and also picked up highest-selling single of the year.

We were happy just to be there, though due to five hours of plane delays trying to get up to Sydney, instead of arriving at 4 pm, we got there just as Silverchair took the stage, near the end of the ceremony. It was still fun to be at the party and pretend we were an important and integral part of the music scene in Australia.

Nine years later we were nominated for an ARIA again, for our album *Bits and Pieces*. On the date of the awards show, John had a prior engagement, so I made the trip up to Sydney by myself to enjoy the glamour of the Australian music industry's night of nights ...

To tell you the truth, I didn't hold much hope of us winning the Best Adult Contemporary Album that year, as we weren't nominated in that category. We were up for Best Comedy Release again and I didn't think we were a chance for that award, either. Musical trio Tripod had two nominations in our category, those greedy bastards, and they were riding high on weekly national television and radio exposure that we surely couldn't compete with. They were a shoo-in to win for sure. I wouldn't have to be making any thank-you speeches that night, I thought. Which is why I started hitting the free drinks fairly early and fairly hard. By the time the telecast started, I was feeling comfortably numb. I was seated at the Shock Records table with people like Dan Kelly and members of TISM, writer Patrick Donovan and Bruce Milne from Au Go Go records. I was having a great time, chatting away, sharing opinions about the host, our old mate Rove. Jesus! Hadn't he kicked on! All I had to do was sit back and enjoy the night, watching Jet pick up ARIA after ARIA. These nights do tend to drag on a bit though, so when someone at the table suggested nicking outside for some 'fresh air' I thought I'd go for a walk too. Meandering through the tables at the function, I was a bit wobbly and realised the drinks had been going down quite easily and I probably should slow down a bit. I then learned that when someone at the ARIAs says 'go outside for some fresh air' they of course mean 'go outside to smoke a joint', so when I returned to the table, let's just say that things were moving a little differently and I knew something strange was happening because I laughed at one of Rove's jokes. The room had grown quite noisy and it was around this point that I heard the name Scared Weird Little Guys being read out. We had won! I stood with my arms raised and yelled, 'Yes! Fuck you, Tripod!' then Bruce tugged on my sleeve and said, 'Rusty! You haven't won, they're just reading out the nominations.'

'Oh ... I knew that,' I mumbled and sat back down.

As the Best Comedy Release award is held in such high esteem at the ARIAs, it is announced during a commercial break in the main broadcast, which explains why the room was a little distracted and noisy. I started to feel a bit of panic and thought, 'Oh shit, what if we do win? What will I say?' Then, through the fog of the smoke machine, and the fog of my mind I heard, this time for real: 'And the ARIA goes to – Scared Weird Little Guys for *Bits and Pieces*.'

A mighty cheer went up around our table, then I realised it was mostly coming from me, so I stood up and starting heading towards the stage. As our table was one of the important ones,

I'd Like to Thank

we were located right up the back, near the sound desk, so it took me a while to get down to the front. I could hear someone on the microphone saying, 'Is anyone here from the Scared Weird Little Guys?' I tried to shout and wave but somehow I had gone the wrong way and ended up in front of the stage, in the rent-a-crowd mosh pit that they place there for atmosphere.

'Here he is!' someone shouted and the mosh pit magically and respectfully parted for me. For a moment I felt like a rock and roll Moses as two burly members of the rent-a-crowd lifted me up onto the stage to accept the award. What an entrance! Luckily, no one was really taking any notice, as it was still the commercial break. With my muddled head, I garbled out a few thank-yous and was directed backstage to the waiting press conference. Before I reached the back of the stage, I was chased down by the girl giving out the awards. She grabbed the ARIA back off me, informing me that I couldn't keep that one, it was the only one they had (!) The real awards were sent out a month later. Visions of me triumphantly stepping off a plane to greet the cheering masses while holding my shiny ARIA award evaporated in an instant. Still, it was a very cool feeling, having just won an ARIA. I was led to another room backstage where there was a small stage containing a couch and a microphone. Seated in front of the stage were about 20 members of the press who now had the opportunity to ask questions of the award winners. I was introduced as the recipient of the Best Comedy Release ARIA and I must say that the questions from the press weren't exactly flying thick and fast. That was probably a good thing, too, given the state I was in. I answered the first question with a rambling diatribe about the validity of awards in comedy and/or music and the changing role of social media in today's music industry. I also somehow managed to include references to John, Jet, Rove, the dessert, the Little River Band and Guy Sebastian. After a couple more polite questions from the gallery, I was discreetly led away for some photos.

THE BIGGEST GIG WE EVER DONE

We've played some fairly small crowds in our time. Apart from the gigs where hardly anyone turns up, like some of the daytime college gigs or the deer accident show in West Virginia, some gigs are booked for a small audience on purpose. There have been a fair number of private parties, with 20 to 30 people, but the smallest ever was a dinner party at a swanky mansion in Toorak. There were seven people around a large dining table, including two big-time Hollywood producers who had just made the movie *Terminator 2*. To be fair, they told us there were supposed to be eight people at the dinner party, but the eighth guest, Robert De Niro, was feeling sick and stayed at his hotel.

We've also played some fairly large crowds in our time.

In 1998 a good friend, who we had worked with on various projects since the Phones, called up and asked about the Scaredies doing some shows with an orchestra, and we said yes.

The shows with the orchestra were a highlight of my performing experience, no doubt about it. We did the orchestral arrangements ourselves and worked closely with a conductor to get them just right. The show was a combination of Scaredies songs with lush orchestral arrangements, the orchestra playing pieces by themselves and John and me getting to take the piss and play around with them like a giant, living toy. We wrote the show with our good friend, Fred, who was an experienced classical music producer and Mahler fiend. Fred organised the first orchestra we worked with – the community-based Malvern Symphony, who were really quite amazing and great fun to work with. We performed the first shows, called *Score*, at the Melbourne Town Hall for the Comedy Festival in 1998.

What fun! A 70-piece orchestra to play around with! Over the next few years we toured this show around Australia and worked with professional symphony orchestras in Tasmania (including our triumphant return to Burnie), Adelaide and New Zealand, culminating in a couple of sold-out shows at the Concert Hall in Melbourne with the State Orchestra of Victoria and a 200-voice choir in front of 2500 people. That is quite a large crowd of humans to come out to one place to see your act, and those shows will remain fondly in my memory forever. When you play a version of 'Duelling Banjos' with yourself on banjo versus 70 professional classical musicians in front of a few thousand people, it is not something that you will easily forget.

The Scaredies once played the halftime break in the Australian National Basketball League grand final, which was in front of 15,000 people, though if you count all the ones who were out at the toilet or purchasing overpriced hotdogs, there were more like 6000. That was a fairly big show.

Four Chairs No Waiting got to sing a song at the final-night concert of Expo 88 – there were 20,000 people in the crowd that night. With the Phones, we played on a floating stage on the Yarra River during Moomba, where we mimed to three songs as the stage, built on a barge, slowly moved down the muddy waters of Melbourne's main watercourse. They say up to 30,000 people were seated along the banks of the Yarra that night, waiting to be dazzled by a fireworks show and the equally bright sequins of the Phones costumes.

The Scaredies once performed before an AFL game between Collingwood and North Melbourne. Perched on the back of a truck facing the Southern stand, filled with 50,000 people.

The Biggest Gig We Ever Done

But the biggest gig we ever did would have to have been the closing ceremony of the 2006 Commonwealth Games at the MCG in Melbourne. They needed an act to warm up the crowd of 90,000 people before the 'real entertainment' of the main ceremony began. We had to teach the crowd three 'dance moves' and keep everyone entertained while waiting for Prince Edward to arrive to officially start the proceedings. Why did the closing ceremony organisers choose us? Because we could handle the high-stakes pressure and use our exceptional talents and professional performing skills to get the job done? No, actually. It was because Lano and Woodley turned the gig down and recommended that we would be more suited to making fools of ourselves in front of 90,000 people than they would. Thanks guys!

It didn't matter to us how we got the gig, we relished the idea of playing to an audience that size. Usually when a crowd that big is in the MCG, all the lights are on to watch the sporting spectacle on offer. This was different, though; everyone would be in the dark, which offered many possibilities for fun.

We had to do 40 minutes and we were warned that the end of our act depended on when Prince Edward was ready to make his entrance into the stadium. When we were introduced and took to the large, circular podium in the exact centre of the MCG, it was one of the more surreal onstage experiences I have had. To enable us to hear ourselves and keep in time with each other, we had small ear-pieces jammed into both of our ears, which blocked out all other sounds. All I could hear was my voice, John's voice, his guitar and a bloke in the control room, who was timing the set. He would burst into our ears at the end of a song and say in a distorted voice, 'Okay guys, that's 18 minutes ...'

We started with a few simple, energy-laden songs from our set – there was no room for any subtlety when your audience is in the dark and at least 100 metres away from you. The bizarre thing about it was that we couldn't even hear the crowd, or see them. I remember at the end of songs I could hear the very faint dull roar of many thousands of people cheering and clapping, but we may as well have been standing by ourselves in the middle of an empty field with very strong spotlights shining on us. Apart from teaching the crowd their arm movements, to be done later during the actual televised ceremony, we had some other tricks up our sleeves. You know that 'pop' sound you make by pulling your finger out of one side of your mouth?

We had a giant imaginary game of 'mouth ping pong,' where it was one side of the MCG versus the other side, with 40,000 people simultaneously making that 'pop' to hit the 'ball' back to the other side. As most people there had cameras, we tried to coordinate a synchronised massive single camera flash, which actually looked quite spectacular. But the most successful thing we did was to direct what I believe was the world's largest ever flash bulb Mexican wave. Starting at the city end of the Southern Stand of the MCG, we got people to take a flash photo as the wave went around the stadium in total darkness. It took just over a minute for it to travel the circumference of the ground and thankfully included boos as it travelled through the members' section. Many people have come up to us after shows and said they were there for that experience, and many have put their footage of the flash wave up on YouTube.

During our last scheduled song, the mysterious timekeeper in our ears came on, shouting, 'The Prince is here! The Prince is here! Finish up after this song!' I thought, 'Oh my God! Prince is here! I wonder if he knows they've booked Prince Edward as well, how awkward.' But it was actually just Prince Edward arriving. We thought, 'That's it, we did it! We got through it!' As the song was finishing, however, the guy was back in our ears saying, 'He's been held up! Stretch it for another seven minutes.'

Seven minutes! That's easy for you to say, faceless distorted voice guy, but what the hell do we do now? That was the worst possible thing that we could have heard at that point. Our initial 40-minute set had been timed to within an inch of its life, and now we had to fill for another seven minutes? We had been thrown off our guard, and we were about to die onstage in front of 90,000 people. In our career up to that point, we would have written hundreds of songs and had literally hours of material to choose from. Do you think we could think of even *one* appropriate bit to do? Every possible song that I thought of had swearing in it. As you can imagine, one of the strict directions from the organisers of the event was that there was to be no offensive language. John started pulling out some of our old, lame one-liners that we hadn't touched in years, which filled in about 20 seconds. Of course, the slightest feeling of panic is magnified immeasurably because you are standing in front of 90,000 people and a second feels like a minute. Then, just as I was about to say, 'We've been Lano and Woodley, thank you good night!', John had a musical epiphany and started the familiar chords of 'Cleaning Out My Tuckerbag', our Eminem-does-Waltzing Matilda song. Ah! Thank you, comedy gods! I joined in on the song and realised why we had left this song out of the set in the first place. In the third verse I was going to have to say, *'What's in the bag with your tucker, motherfucker?'* Thankfully, we got about 40 seconds into this song when the guy came back in our ears, 'Prince Edward is in position, guys, finish up the song immediately!'

We had just completed what would have to be the biggest show we had ever done. What a rush! I didn't sleep for hours, though it may have been from 90,000 camera flashes imprinted on my eyeballs.

THAT WAS DUDLEY'S SHEEP ROOTING JOKE

We did get to do some interesting support spots along the way. There was Phyllis Diller, Don McLean and Harry Secombe, Lenny Henry and Alexei Sayle among others. These support spots for famous overseas (world class) artists were usually a pretty sweet spot to do, even though the audience was obviously just there to see the main act. The shows were always in beautiful big theatres and the audience arrived ready to laugh. They'd paid big money so subconsciously they wanted to get their money's worth by laughing, plus once any audience gets over about 800 people, it turned into a lovely, giant, amorphous thing that fed itself on laughter. With audiences like that, if people thought you were funny and you did something that sounded like a joke, they laughed. I've seen it time and time again with famous people. So to be the opening act was usually great, as long as you didn't wear out your welcome by staying on too long.

We were very excited when the Scaredies were asked to be the support act on the national tour for Dudley Moore. This was big. We would be getting extensive national exposure, as the tour was going to every capital city and playing in huge venues in front of large audiences. The first show of the tour was in the Royal Theatre in Canberra in front of 2000 people. We turned up backstage to meet the promoters and were excited to see that we were assigned our very own assistant to look after us – just us. She was a nice girl named Rachael who was studying personal assistantry or slavery or something at the local university and I guess she wanted to gain some real showbiz experience by fetching bottles of water for Dudley Moore's support act. Rachael showed us to our dressing room, which we could hardly fit into due to the enormous bunch of flowers that sat on the table in the middle of the room. We were so impressed! This was not just any large bouquet of flowers, it was like someone had chopped out half a greenhouse of the most exquisite orchids and colourful blooms you could imagine, then placed it in a vase so big I could have bathed in it, which was good, because after the long flight to Canberra I felt like freshening up. However, I considerately restricted myself to just splashing some of the scented water from the vase behind my ears and we continued looking around the expansive backstage area.

In the dressing room next to us was Dudley Moore's pianist and close friend, Rena Fruchter, with whom we had a nice chat. I noticed there were no beautiful flowers in her room. So, Rena, you may be Dudley's friend but *we* got the flowers. We got to meet Dudley before the show and John and I both commented later that he seemed 'affected'. His speech was slurry and he was a little unsteady. Much later we found out that he wasn't drunk or affected by drugs but in the early stages of Progressive Supranuclear Palsy (PSP), the disease that eventually claimed his life 10 years later. We returned to our dressing room to prepare for our performance but we had to get changed in the hallway as, due to the flowers, there was simply not enough room.

We went onstage for our 25-minute spot and I can happily say that we killed. We hit them squarely between the eyes with a powerful set of our best energetic material. That's the nice thing about doing such a short set. Dudley's audience were a bit older than we were used to, but they seemed to really enjoy our highbrow musical gags cunningly mixed with toilet humour. We were later described as 'mindless stupidity for the thinking person'.

Rachael was dutifully waiting for us with more bottles of water when we got back to the room. She was very keen and had been so efficient, but we just had nothing for her to do. After a quick consultation with John, we told her that as we were flying out the next morning, she should keep the enormous bunch of flowers from our dressing room as a gift. Well, you should have seen her face. She looked as if she was about to cry. I don't know if it was because she had never received flowers before, or she was wondering how much it was going to cost her to ship the bastards home. She thanked us over and over but it wasn't like we had done very much. It wasn't like we had called ahead to organise a bouquet for her or anything. Lets face it, if she didn't take the flowers, the cleaners probably would have thrown them out, but that didn't matter. To Rachael, we were generous showbiz gods and we felt all warm and fuzzy to have done a good deed for her.

After the interval, and still glowing with kindness, John and I snuck out to the rear of the venue to watch Dudley Moore's show. His performance was a mix of stand up, characters and songs, either backed by himself or Rena on piano. Unfortunately he was not on song this night. He slurred words and repeated jokes and some of the material was fairly dodgy. I remember John and I looking at each other when he did a particularly lame sheep rooting joke. He made mistakes when he played the piano and it was actually a bit sad to watch. Dudley ended the concert with an energetic piano duo with Rena, who was presented with a huge bunch of flowers onstage as they took their bows. 'Ah, she did get flowers after all,' I thought.

We made our way back to the dressing room and I noticed that Rachael was looking a little down. Then I noticed that our dressing room was quite empty and it dawned on me that the flowers that had been in our room were the very same flowers that had been presented onstage to Rena, and they now sat happily crowding her dressing room. What the hell were those stingy promoters trying to pull here? Getting double the emotional value for the one bunch of flowers? Making us think we were so special and then giving Rena the same feeling with the very same blooms. Actually we didn't really care, as now that the flowers were gone from our dressing room, we could finally access the fridge containing the free drinks.

The next morning at the airport, we spoke on the phone to our manager, Michelle. She had bad news.

'Sorry boys, you've been kicked off the tour!'

'What!'

'I just spoke to the promoter,' she said. 'He explained that you guys don't really fit the energy of Dudley.'

'It was the flowers, wasn't it?' I said.

'He also said that there were complaints about you.'

'Complaints about us?' I was shocked 'What complaints?' We never got complaints.

'He said there were complaints about your sheep rooting joke.'

'We don't even do a sheep rooting joke!' I shouted, getting some strange looks from the people around us. 'That was Dudley's sheep rooting joke!'

Our protests were to no avail. We were off the tour virtually before it began. It was very disappointing for us, but I felt a bit better a few weeks later when we were up in Brisbane doing some shows. I saw a review in the paper of Dudley Moore's Brisbane show which began: 'The evening started badly when it was announced that the advertised support act, the Scared Weird Little Guys, would not be performing. It proceeded to get worse from that point ...'

THE ALL-STAR COMEDY SUPERBAND

People often would say to us, 'Oh, you have such lovely voices, you should do some real singing.' We always knew that the last thing people want to hear from a comedy group is a 'serious' album and we resisted that.

We loved singing in harmony and our voices blended well, but we weren't trying to be Simon and Garfunkel. I believe you have to know what your act is, and stick with it. If you want to try something different, start a new act under a different name.

We could get away with roughly one song per show that didn't have jokes in it, but was a nice song to listen to, without people losing interest. It's all about the expectation of the audience. Go and see Billy Connolly and you expect to hear some jokes and some swearing and maybe a bit of banjo and everyone's happy. If he came out onstage and said, 'Here's a little song I wrote about the plight of the West Highland Woodgrouse,' the audience would politely listen to one song, but then be, 'Get on with the jokes.'

Nevertheless, there came a time when John and I felt we needed to satisfy our cravings to be rock stars. After all, in my experience, most people in bands like to think they are comedians and most comedians just want to be rock stars. What better way to help all concerned than form a rock band with some of our musician friends, play the best 1970s and 1980s cover songs, and get comedians to sing them?

We humbly called it the Scared Weird Little Guys All-Star Comedy Superband, though due to a printing error, the bands' skivvies just had the word SUPERBRAND misspelled on the front. We didn't mind, it looked funny and it was kind of apt.

In 1999, we approached the Melbourne Comedy Festival with the idea. They were hesitant at first, giving us a Thursday night downstairs at the Melbourne Town Hall. It went quite well. Tripod did a fantastic version of 'YMCA'. Rove was great, bringing the house down singing 'Footloose'. Adam Hills did 'Antmusic' in full costume, and there was plenty of dancing and fun. It went well enough that the Comedy Festival offered us the prestigious Saturday night late spot at the festival club in the HiFi Bar for the following year. It was not that prestigious really, we couldn't start until the late comedy show had finished and, as is the tendency of most comedians, they just can't drag their ego-driven arses off a stage when it's a good audience. We would often start after 2 am, doing a two-hour set while living out our rock and roll fantasies in front of an enthusiastic audience of drunken comedians and a few sad comedy groupies trying to crack on to any visiting overseas comedians. John and I gave ourselves about five songs each to sing. My favourites were 'What I like About You' and 'Bad Case of Loving You', but the highlight was doing 'Eye of the Tiger' which we always closed the set with.

We did the Superband at the Comedy Festival for the next eight years and the highlights were many: Frank Woodley wearing a beanie and tight jeans doing 'You Shook me All Night Long', The 3 Canadians destroying the room with 'Fight For Your Right to Party', Lawrence Mooney pashing Damian Callinan while dressed as New Romantics and singing 'Tainted Love', Jason Byrne wearing only a sock over his privates doing the Chili Peppers 'Give it Away', the Bedroom Philosopher stripping naked during an inspired version of 'Anarchy in the UK', Tim Minchin doing 'Little Less Conversation', Dave Gorman stage diving and crowd surfing during 'Song 2', and many, many more.

It was great to take these confident comedians out of their comfort zones to sing in front of a rock band.

I remember walking into the dressing room just before we were about to go on one night and there were Jimeoin, Frank Woodley, Lee Mack and Ross Noble all sitting there absolutely shitting themselves with nerves. What a sight. The Superband ran its course and was a heck of a lot of fun for all concerned. The festival has never really been able to match the energy of those years when we rocked the late night HiFi Bar crowd, though they have tried. People seemed to think it just magically came together and was a bit easy to do. They don't realise just how hard we worked on getting it right.

STEP AWAY FROM THE MICROPHONE

For any Australian comedy act, it seemed inevitable that at some point you should save up some money, head over to the Edinburgh Fringe Festival and lose it. Lose the money that is, though I know of quite a few acts that have lost more than just money at the Edinburgh Fringe: band members, self-esteem, partners, the will to live. No matter how you came out of it, though, the Edinburgh Fringe Festival was an incredible experience. It could be fun, exciting, competitive, inspiring, depressing, challenging and exhausting, usually all in the one day. We first went to Edinburgh in 1997 to play in the Assembly Rooms, then followed up in 1998 and 2001 at the Famous Spiegeltent. The festival ran for four weeks and the first time we went over, we played every single night. It was relentless. As well as your own show, there were numerous other guest spots, television appearances, radio interviews and photo opportunities that you could and should do. There were over 1200 other shows on that first year, all competing for audiences. It was a rude awakening indeed for any act that considered itself 'established' in its own country to come to Edinburgh and fight for an audience, put up posters themselves and hand out flyers for their show. It was hard work but don't get me wrong, we loved it. Some of the toughest gigs you could ever play were in Edinburgh.

The *Late'n'Live* show at the Gilded Balloon was the toughest. Usually starting around 1 am and finishing after 4 am, it featured an MC host and three acts, often stand-ups or variety acts like the Scaredies.

Comedian Johnny Vegas described *Late'n'Live* as 'the performing equivalent of self-harm'. It was scary. The mostly drunken, mostly Scottish crowd came along to see some late night comedy and felt it was their right to offer 'advice' to the comedians onstage. I saw some horrific treatment of comedians who weren't going so well. The Scaredies always did quite well there, though. We were fairly bulletproof as we would do some of our fail-safe, high-energy songs and keep the talking to a minimum, cunningly leaving no room for the scary drunk Scottish people to abuse us. There were some great heckle lines thrown around. I heard this said to one stand up who was not going so well:

Heckler: 'Knock knock.'

Comedian: (foolishly answers) 'Who's there?'

Heckler: 'Fuck off!'

Later in his set it was a bit quiet and a voice from the back of the room said, 'Step away from the microphone ...'

Another time the MC, whom the crowd hated, refused to introduce the next act unless the audience applauded but, as a group, they refused to applaud while he was still physically on the stage – brilliant!

In 2001, I saw a pre-famous Russell Brand there and he took special pleasure in baiting the crowd. He was not really doing any jokes or material, just abusing people, but he seemed to be somehow enjoying it. He was the only one who was. At one point he smashed a glass and pretended to cut himself with it – he had a fake blood capsule under his shirt. People were booing and shouting 'fuck off!' and as he went off through the door at the back of the stage a glass was thrown at him from the audience. It missed Brand but shattered on the wall in the corridor behind the stage, showering glass over Australian comedian Fiona O'Loughlin, who was waiting to come on next. As she was being introduced by the host, Adam Hills, she was literally pulling glass out of her leg and went on with blood streaming down it. The next day a rumour spread around Edinburgh that Fiona had been stabbed at *Late'n'Live*. The crazy thing is not that the rumour spread, but that people could accept that getting stabbed at *Late'n'Live* was a realistic possibility.

Above: Obscure Alternatives perform at the 1982 Bribie Island Festival. From left: my sister, Sherry, Keith Urban and me.

Left: Cactus Fever, Brisbane, 1985. From left: Sherry, me, Scott Austin and Stephen Mee.

Below left: Four Chairs No Waiting in early 1987. Finger clickin' fun at the 'Fondue Hut'.

Below right: At least 50 per cent wackier and zanier than before. The new Four Chairs No Waiting 1988 line-up, with the first appearance of John (top left).

Above left: The official 128th and final line-up of The Phones in 1989.

Above right: The first ever Scared Weird Little Guys publicity photo, 1990.

Left: The Phones complete one of Reg's gruelling vocal warm-ups downstairs at the Last Laugh in 1990. Standing left to right John, Paul, Rusty, Michael. Reg seated.

Below left: The fire extinguisher incident at the Last Laugh, 1990.

Below right: Scaredies onstage at the Laugh in 1990 performing our version of 'Duelling Banjos'.

Scaredies, circa 2003.
Courtesy of James Penlidis

Left: The running gear I took to wear in the Ice Marathon, ready for inspection.

Below: Dodging boxes of frozen peas and forklifts while running in a giant industrial freezer.

Lock it in, Eddie! Just after going on *Hotseat Millionaire*.

A Chilean *Hairy Maclary* gang. Don't be fooled by their cute appearance.

Up a hill in Santiago with Bradley the cameraman.

Punta Arenas … or is it Geelong?.

Left: Exhibit A – The Misterios.

Below: The Ilyushin jet that took us to Antarctica.

Courtesy of Mike King

Above: The interior of the Ilyushin, with Igor in position.

Left: The main buildings of the Union Glacier Camp, with the dining tent in the foreground.

Below left: The accommodation tents.

Our tent.

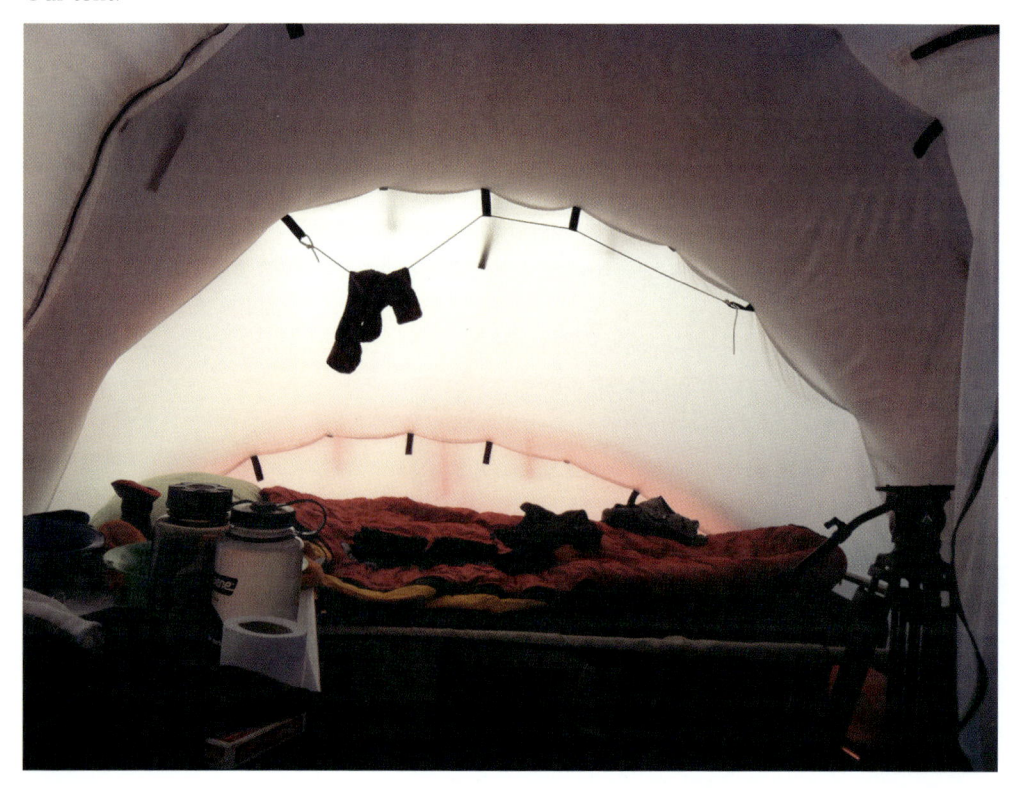

The luxurious interior.

The interior of the dining tent – participants could sit here and read, write, play games or quietly sob to themselves.

The toilets at Union Glacier. Everything had to be taken back to Chile, and I mean everything.

The author on the track.

Inset: Being taken away to our impending doom . . . I mean the starting line.
Both pictures courtesy of Mike King

All of the participants of the Ice Marathon.
Courtesy of Mike King

Just after the start of the race. Clement already taking the lead, followed by Emer, Matthew and Yvonne.
Courtesy of Mike King

At the one-kilometre mark.
Courtesy of Mike King

A long way from anywhere.
Courtesy of Mike King

Left: The long straight section approaching final drink station.

Below: Crossing the finish line.
Courtesy of Mike King

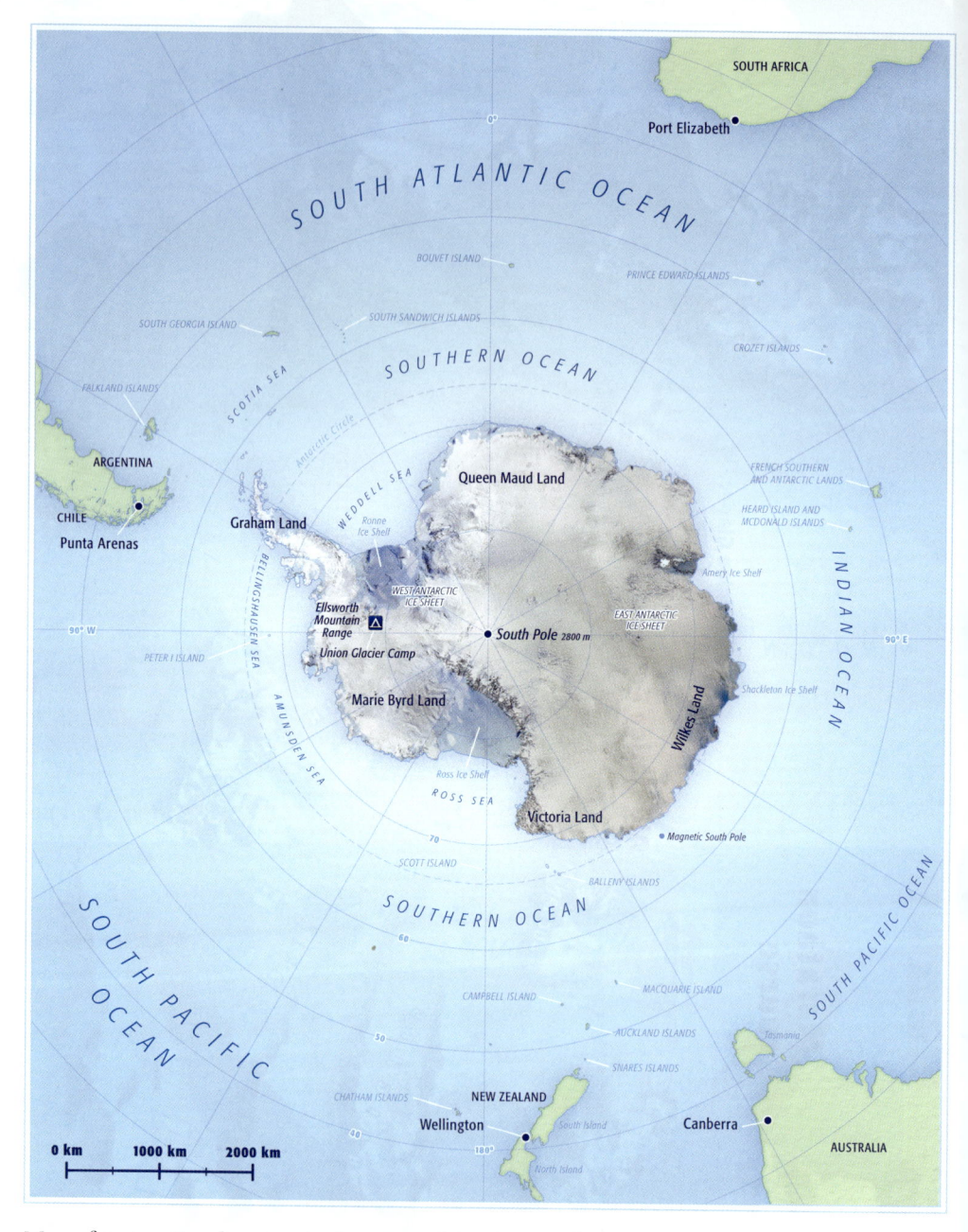

Map of Antarctica showing the location of the Union Glacier Camp in relation to Punta Arenas, Australia and the South Pole.

AN ANTIQUE SHOP, A DOG AND A PAIR OF EXPENSIVE SOCKS

I have one person and a dog to thank for getting me into running – one is named Bernadette, she's a person, and the other is named Dolly, she's a dog.

The Scaredies had been renting a room above Bernadette's shop in South Melbourne to use as an 'office'. When I say 'office' I really mean 'room with a desk and two chairs that was not in either of our houses where we could store all sorts of accumulated crap like old costumes, CDs, broken microphone stands, props from old shows, LP records, instruments we never played, old photos, and boxes and boxes of VHS cassettes. It was always our plan to go through the old videos and convert them to digital format so we could throw out the bulky cassettes, but we would start and get easily distracted. Most of the videos had our old TV appearances on them that had been diligently recorded by our mothers from shows like *Hey Hey It's Saturday*, *The Midday Show* and *Sale of the Century* (we appeared on the gift shop once). Each video would have a cryptic handwritten note on the side saying something like 'Phone Book Midday', 'Bloody Jeff 7.30 Report', 'Chairs Red Faces', which was supposed to let us know which song was on what tape. It usually meant we had to fast forward through a three-hour tape just to find a couple of songs, or to discover the video had been subsequently taped over with an episode of *The Young Ones*. The office was a good place to go and write and pretend that we had real jobs. We mostly worked well at the office, but were easily distracted. When the creative juices weren't flowing, or one of the whiteboard markers was running a little dry, we would enthusiastically take an excursion to the milk bar, or down to OfficeWorks to stock up.

Bernadette's shop, which tolerated having the Scaredies office above it, sold something called 'Belgian brocante' which is really just a fancy way to say it sold 'old stuff from Belgium'. The name of the shop was Izzi and Popo, which is a difficult name to remember and confused people who came to visit us. They would pop their head in the door and tentatively ask, 'I'm looking for a shop called Fonzie and Potsie?' or some other mispronounced version of Izzi and Popo which, I believe, is a Belgian term meaning 'those termite holes add character'.

I had known Bernadette and her audiophile husband, Harry, for a while, and when they asked me if I knew anyone who wanted to rent a spare room, the timing was perfect and the Scaredies had a new headquarters.

Some days during our intense (ahem) creative writing sessions in the office, I would often wander downstairs to the shop for a coffee and a chat and it was during these times I learnt of Bernadette's love of running. Like most non-runners, I didn't get it. Why on earth would you get up before dawn in winter and go out to puff and pant around a park? What on earth would make thousands of humans line up with numbers pinned to their shirts, then run around the city in something called a 'fun' run?

Whenever I knew Bern had completed a fun run the previous day, I would politely ask, 'So, how did you go in your run yesterday?' She would begin to answer, then my eyes would glaze over in exactly the same way I have now seen other people's eyes glaze over when I answer that same question.

'Well, I was aiming for a sub 45, but I started too fast and my legs felt heavy from all the fartlek training, then at the 7 k mark, I knew that a negative split was out of the question and then, hey, you're not listening ...'

So I know what it's like to have a runner around when you yourself are not into running. Runners can just seem so bloody smug sometimes, like they're in this little club with all their special talk about shoes and gels and pronation. I am happy to say, though, that Bern wasn't one of those smug types of runners that are always trying to convince you that you should take up running. Well, she wasn't until she convinced me to take up running, that is. Then, of course, we started having our own smug little running conversations about sore joints and ice and runner's high. There's a joke there somewhere ... with all that ice and joints, no wonder they were experiencing 'runner's high' ... Continuing on ...

Bern didn't actually tell me I should start running, but being around her and listening to her talk about it certainly planted the seed in my mind. I still knew nothing about running and remember asking her one day when she was off to do a 14-kilometre run, 'Is that like half a marathon?' How embarrassing. A friend has since asked me exactly that same question and my response was to scoff while shaking my head dismissively.

'Ugh, these runners can be so bloody smug sometimes,' they must have been thinking.

I really started running because of Dolly. That's Dolly the dog I am talking about, not Dolly Parton. I don't know how Dolly Parton could make you start running. Unless you really hated her music ... or really liked it. Or you were a teenage Keith Urban and you were trying to force your Dolly Parton tape onto people and they got so sick of it they chased you around the school. That might work.

Dolly the dog is our family pet. We got her from the Lost Dogs' Home. Denise and I had always had dogs but we had been without dogs for a couple of years since our previous canine friends had gone to doggy heaven.

Dolly is a greyhound crossed with a Staffordshire bull terrier. I don't know exactly how that worked but I am guessing that the greyhound was probably the father. With that kind of pedigree, it's no surprise that Dolly loves to run, so when I started taking her out for her daily walks, I guess it was a combination of her running, seeing other people running and Bern talking about running that made me spontaneously break into a slow shuffle one morning during a lap around the park. I would self-consciously slow down to a walk when I saw another runner coming my way, as if I had been doing it without permission and they would be able to tell I wasn't really a runner. I imagined them stopping suddenly and demanding to see my running licence like a ticket inspector asking for your train ticket. 'What do you think this is, mate? Free running for everybody?'

When the experienced runner passed by and it was safe, I would shuffle off again, like I was involved in some sort of secret mission comprising shuffling, walking and intermittent stops to collect samples of dog poo in little plastic bags. I hadn't been doing any regular exercise for a while, so it felt good to be moving and using muscles and breathing. When babies and children became part of our life, routines changed, and exercise was one of the things that got put up on a shelf, along with the fancy knick-knacks that break when toddlers touch them. I needed to get into some form of physical activity again as I still hadn't lost the baby weight from the birth of our son six years before. I returned home from that first run/shuffle a little tired and sore, but also feeling that lovely post-exercise mental and physical satisfaction that is sometimes mistaken for smugness.

I completed this 30-minute routine three or four times a week over the next month. Walk to the park, jog around a bit and walk home again, and as the weeks passed, it was gradually getting easier. The big moment came down at the park when I didn't slow to a walk as one of the runners approached. I just kept my slow jog going and was happy to see that they barely noticed me. There was just a slight knowing nod to each other as we passed. I could tell he didn't even think about asking me for my runner's licence. After six weeks of this routine, I felt happy that I hadn't given up yet, and was actually enjoying the early mornings and knowing nods to the other runners in the park. I wondered how long you have to do it before you can call yourself a runner. Hanging around in Izzi and Popo one morning, I gathered up the courage to tell Bern that I had been running.

'Uh, Bern ... I've got something to tell you.'

It felt like I was about to admit to her that I had been stealing Belgian chocolates from the shop fridge for the past six weeks (which I had been).

'Yeah, ah, for the past month or so, since we got our new dog, I've been doing some running.' There, I said it out loud.

She was very excited. 'That's great!' she said. 'Now you have to come and do some fun runs. Let's sign you up for the Run for the Kids. It's only 14 ks!'

We jumped on the computer and signed us both up and my running career was launched. There was only one problem. The Run for the Kids was only six weeks away and I had never run further than about seven kilometres.

'Oh, you'll be fine,' insisted Bern, then she proceeded to work out a training plan for me involving things I had never heard of, like 'repeats' and 'strides' and 'training plan'.

As any runners reading this will attest, there is nothing like a goal to help you get out the door in the morning and get running, especially if that goal involves some sort of monetary entrance fee that you have to pay in advance. I didn't even know how far I had been running around my park until Bern pointed out that you could measure distances on Google Earth. Using the excellent ruler function on that site, I planned out little courses around my suburb, through parks and down bicycle tracks. I bought some new shoes and hit the track, always with my constant canine companion Dolly at my side. I didn't know at what point I could officially call myself a runner, but the term was certainly starting to sit more comfortably with me. I was really starting to enjoy running. Let's face it, at 40 years of age, it felt great to just be able to get out and move around for an hour.

I was not a runner yet, of course. Surely you couldn't call yourself a runner until you'd woken up before dawn, rubbed paw paw ointment between your thighs, and then caught a train into the city for your first organised running event. Just three months after my first, secretive shuffles around the park, that was where I found myself; surrounded by drunks still coming home from a big night out and fit-looking people wearing no natural fibres. The fairly limited training I had done for this 14-kilometre race was completed, and had included my regular trips to the park, as well as two 12-k runs on the previous two weekends before the fun run.

Dolly and I were virtually part of the scenery down at our park, as we had been running five days a week for the past month and a half, which brings up the interesting topic of 'running in a park etiquette'. Our local park has a nice gravel track that weaves around the perimeter, with an extra little loop around the tennis courts. There are two pedestrian bridges that cross a picturesque streamlet filled with storm water and effluent from a sheep carcass processing plant somewhere upstream, which explains why Dolly and most of the other neighbourhood dogs like to jump in it at any opportunity. One complete loop of the track is a tick under 2 ks and, despite the creek, it is quite a nice little place to run. As you jog around the park, you will often see runners coming in the other direction and as you pass each other, I always like to do a quick raise of the eyebrows and say 'G'morning.' Usually people respond the same way and we happily continue on, though sometimes people give such a startled look upon hearing you speak, you would think I had drawn a knife and said, 'Give me your money' or 'Show me your runner's licence.' Usually it all works out nice and easy because there aren't so many other people running at our park – you might see three or four other runners throughout the morning.

But if you go to a busier track, or to a park in the city, and there's more than 20 or 30 people running, then everybody just ignores each other because you would never be able to keep breathing what with all the 'mornings' and 'g'days' going on. When I first ran along the busy St Kilda beach track, I just thought that everyone was up themselves. Well, most of them are up themselves of course, but usually the runners will take part in the inane morning greeting routine that I like to enforce on anyone unlucky enough to cross my path. It doesn't stop there, either. As you run around the park and you've said your good mornings to the other four runners who are out that day, what happens when you see them again in five minutes time?

I think the second time you pass each other, just a knowing raise of the eyebrows with the 'pursed lips smile' should do it. For any third or subsequent passing, it is acceptable to not even have any eye contact. I think everything that needed to be said between you both was summed up earlier with the mumbled 'morning'.

With many of these previously unknown running secrets being slowly revealed to me, I guess I was starting to feel a bit like a runner, though up to this point, I had resisted buying a light and breathable nylon running shirt. I'm just a natural fibre kind of guy and have always been happier not 'running with the pack' as it were. Bern did buy me some fancy $25 running socks as a present for my first race. I can accurately say that in my entire life, I had never spent even half that amount on a pair of socks until I started running. While stocking up for the

Ice Marathon in Antarctica, I happily shelled out $150 on four pairs of special socks that now sit in a drawer as, despite being very comfy, they are way too warm for me to wear on runs in Australia.

A MISTAKE YOU ONLY MAKE ONCE

Wearing a black cotton Hank Williams t-shirt, football shorts, new runners and $25 socks, I was ready for my first fun run. The 2008 Run for the Kids had over 30,000 entrants, most of them, it seemed, needing to use the Port-a-loos at the same time, judging by the lengthy lines that greeted me as I approached the starting area. Organising that many people to simultaneously drop bags off, pick up race bibs, meet friends and go to the toilet before 7.30 on a Sunday morning must be a logistical nightmare, but it seemed to be working rather smoothly, so well done to whoever was responsible. I had arrived early at the pre-determined meeting place where I was to catch up with Bern – a rotunda in the Botanical Gardens. We had chosen the meeting spot well, as there were only about 4000 other people who had decided to meet their friends there too. As there were still 45 minutes until the start of the race, I commenced a complicated muscle stretching routine, as that's what everybody else who was waiting there was doing. After all this preparation, I didn't want to stand out and get asked for my runner's licence even before the race had started. The fact that I had never attempted *any* stretches before that morning didn't stop me from copying the seasoned runners around me, who were arranged in complex yoga-like positions along the fence of the rotunda. I imagined that all of us had never stretched before and we were all just trying to fit in, copying each other in stretches of increasing ridiculousness and that made me smile. My plan of not wanting to stand out did not go well as, due to getting dressed in the dark at 5 o'clock in the morning, I realised with horror that I was wearing my shorts inside out.

Thankfully, runners are a helpful lot, which is why I heard the words, 'Your shorts are on inside out,' from the young woman next to me, whose leg was stretched up behind her head.

I saw Bern arriving as I emerged from adjusting my shorts in the change room, which was actually just the bushes behind the rotunda. On any other day, emerging from the bushes behind a rotunda in the botanical gardens after adjusting your shorts would get you arrested, but being amongst all these runners, no one gave me a second glance.

'Hi Bern,' I said.

'We should do some stretches,' she advised.

'I'm all stretched out, thanks,' I replied, lithely swinging my arms in large circles and nearly knocking over a pram. I suggested we should head over to the start line, and we took up a position quite a way back from the start amongst the throng of other runners who were already there.

The 20 or so minutes spent waiting for a running event to start can be quite a bizarre situation. It certainly helps when you are there with someone you know, so that at least you can have a conversation, even if that conversation is slightly awkward because you realise the hundred or so people standing within a three-metre radius of you are eavesdropping. If you are by yourself, you can pass the time checking out everyone else's brands of shoes and socks, and reading their t-shirts boasting of past running events they've entered. I did notice one bloke was bucking that trend and wearing a red Dire Straits t-shirt. A man who, like me, was favouring the old natural fibres. You can also eavesdrop on people's private conversations if they are lucky enough to be there with a friend, and foolish enough to be having a private conversation while waiting for a run to start.

There is often annoying music being played while you wait for the starting gun to go off. Race organisers must think that the runners will be inspired by having 'Eye of the Tiger' continually blasted at them early on a Sunday morning. I had no problem with rocking out to it at 2 am on a Sunday morning with the Superband, but at this particular time and place it was more annoying than providing athletic inspiration. Even worse than the loud music is the irritating master of ceremonies, usually a commercial radio DJ or local 'personality' whose job it is to rev up the crowd and interview some poor athlete associated with the event.

MC: [Booming DJ voice.] 'So, what advice have you got for all the runners out there today?'

Athlete: 'Um ... when the gun goes off ... um ... start running ... and ... um ... just have fun ...'

[Awkward pause.]

Eventually the pre-race festivities finish and we all breathe a sigh of relief when the gun goes off or the hooter sounds to signal the start of the race. For some reason you get the urge to start jumping up and down on the spot, moving your shoulders in small circles and shaking your hands out, which, if not done carefully, puts you in danger of whacking the two people behind you in the crotch. If you're standing way back from the front like I usually do for these races, everyone starts shuffling forward at this point until we are all really close together but there is no room to move so we all have to stop again for a minute or so. No one is talking now. Eventually you notice the crowd in front of you slowly start to move and then you are all kind of walking but not yet running. Then you are all walking a bit faster and some people start to do small jogging steps. Then suddenly you are all running, trying not to trip the person in front of you, or be tripped by the person behind you whose crotch you just whacked thirty seconds previously. At about this stage you cross the official start line.

During my first race this was the moment when I saw all the people around me pressing buttons on their watches. Runners must be very disorganised people and always late for something, I thought, as I noticed many of them constantly checking their watches during the run.

Before I knew it, I was literally off and running with thousands of strangers, and we were all running slightly faster than we should be – possibly due to a combination of having waited so long for the race to start and not wanting to seem slow around our peers.

No one talked, and about 1k into the race, we all took a sharp left turn into one of Melbourne's long traffic tunnels that usually are the sole territory of trucks, cars and Swedish backpackers on skateboards. As we ran down the gradual slope of the Domain tunnel, all noise was intensified around the slanting walls and it became noticeably louder the further we went. The only sounds that could be heard, though, were the pad-padding of masses of pairs of running shoes and another white-noise-like sound. Could it possibly be the cheering crowd that had turned up to support their friends and families who were running? No, it was the sound of thousands of people breathing heavily in an enclosed space, like what you would hear if you received a dirty phone call from 10,000 people.

About 10 minutes into the run, most runners had established a pace that they were happy with, though every now and then one person would come flying through the crowd, dodging and weaving like they had slept in and were trying to break the race record. The Dire Straits t-shirt man was one of these maniacs and I thought, 'Sheesh, if you have to go that fast, why don't you start further forward in the pack, you nimrod?' As this run was my first, I had no particular goal in mind in terms of time; I just wanted to finish the race.

During these types of runs people are very friendly and will often have a little chat with you. I enjoyed the feeling of being a part of the whole thing. When I am running, I see myself having the style of a sleek Kenyan athlete, gliding effortlessly along with balance, poise and a beautiful, economical stride. The reality, of course, is the complete opposite. The first time I ran in front of some shop windows and saw my reflection across the street, I nearly stopped to see if the guy across the road (me) was injured or insane and running from some imaginary monster. I was all bent over and my elbows were stuck out like I was doing some kind of sailor dance.

During fun runs you see every style of running imaginable. Long stride, short shuffle, head back, head down, arms in, arms out, hands open, thumbs stuck up (this style is known as 'The Fonz'), fists closed, dragging one foot – but enough about my style … Every body shape and size is represented and you realise that being trim and perfectly proportioned doesn't necessarily mean that you are going to be a good runner able to clock up many kilometres. After all, it's not 'how' it's 'how many'.

We surfaced from the tunnel and were greeted by a view of the leading runners speeding across a bridge *way* off in the distance. It didn't look like they were chatting with each other. Just outside the tunnel was the first drink station, loaded with small plastic cups and manned by dedicated volunteers who thrust cups of water enthusiastically at the runners. I didn't know what to do or what the drink station etiquette was but it seemed fairly straightforward – grab a cup, drink some, then throw the half-filled cup near a bin. The volunteers at these events really do a great job, but they generally get no thanks as most of the runners just grab a cup from their hands and keep going. If you want to have a little fun with them next time you find yourself at a drink station with a volunteer holding a half filled cup towards you, look at them with a serious face and quickly ask, 'Is this cup half full or half empty?'

Of course before I started in this run, I didn't know what it felt like to run the distance of 14 kilometres, and as I plodded along in silence, I asked myself all sorts of questions.

Am I going too fast? Am I going too slowly? Will I be able to keep this pace up for the whole race? Should my arms be hurting like this? I shake them out and keep running. The questions keep coming. Why is my knee hurting like that? Is that normal? Why are my nipples stinging? Is that a stitch I can feel coming on? Wow! I haven't had a stitch since primary school. I've never run further than 12 kilometres so what happens when I get past the 12-kilometre mark and each step becomes unknown territory? Maybe I am genetically able to run 12 kilometres, but one step beyond that distance causes my spleen to explode?

I eventually made it past two more drink stations and the dreaded 12-kilometre mark loomed ahead. I ran past the big sign holding my breath, though the worst thing that happened was that I nearly ran into the guy in the Dire Straits t-shirt, who was bent over vomiting into a rubbish bin. He was either suffering from exhaustion or Industrial Disease.

Bern had been very supportive throughout the run, giving me helpful little tips like 'don't drink too much water', 'run on your toes going up hill' and 'stop jumping on my back, I can't give you a piggy back ride'.

As the final kilometre approached, quite a substantial crowd had gathered along the barriers of the course and I was surprised to see and hear strangers cheering on all of the runners with gusto. You can't help but get caught up in the atmosphere and over the last few hundred metres I found myself running faster, digging deep and hurting. For the first time since the Bribie Island Festival Fun Run of 1979, nearly 30 years ago, I was running as fast as I possibly could yet I had no idea why. I was not about to come first. I had no rival that I was trying to defeat. I didn't even have a personal best time to beat. As this was my first race, Bern graciously let me cross the line in front of her.

A Mistake You Only Make Once

The giant digital clock over the finish line told me I had been running for one hour 17 minutes and 38 seconds.

We wandered among the thousands of other runners who had already finished, completed an even more complex routine of stretches, then lined up to collect a free sports drink and a showbag filled with free stuff from the event sponsors. These showbags usually contain things like free pairs of shoes, GPS watches and gold ingots – but on this day my bag only contained a sugary energy bar, a sticker for a local radio station and a voucher for a 10-per-cent-off massage. It was at about this point, as my body was returning to normal, that I noticed I was a bit sore around the chest area and realised in horror that my nipples were bleeding. Yes, it is as painful as it sounds and I thought, 'Ahh, so that's why no one wears cotton t-shirts when they do this running thing.' That's one mistake you don't make twice.

Even before the sweaty stench of $25 socks had faded, I realised that, like it or not, I was now a runner and I was happy to say it out loud and tell anyone who would listen. I felt like Sam I Am at the end of *Green Eggs and Ham*: I *do* like running here and there, I *do* like running everywhere.

I felt a sense of freedom while I ran, though I think a different freedom to the freedom the Americans were trying to sell to me when I was touring over there. Maybe you get that feeling because running is free – it costs nothing, right?

You just spring out the front door and off you go. There's no expensive joining fee like down at the gym. And swimming? That's just full of hassles. Whenever you want to go out for a run, you don't need to pack a bag and drive down to the pool and find a park and pay to get in and get changed with strangers (why is there always a nude chubby guy brushing his teeth in the change room at pools?) then find a lane that suits your swimming style and then swallow a floating used band-aid, then get out of the pool and repeat it all before you get home again. What about those rich blokes you see on a weekend morning, cycling in big packs, wearing tight clothing plastered with French and Italian brand names, riding $10,000 bikes and drinking $5 coffees at poncy beach front cafes?

Nah, running is free. All you need to buy is a decent pair of shoes and you're off! Free as a bird – one of those running birds that can't fly. You might need to get some good socks, too, to go with the decent running shoes, but that's it, shoes and some quality socks ... Maybe a couple of running tops, you know the absorbent types – long and short sleeves for different weather conditions. Then, you're away! Actually, you could probably do with some of that compression gear too ... a vest and some shorts. I've found that a light running hat is a good idea as well, and a beanie. Not just any beanie though, a special *running* beanie. I believe they are technologically designed to be good for ... erm ... running, that's why they cost 50 bucks. Better get some running gloves while you're at it; they're just like normal gloves except they're ... um ... running gloves. Get some running sunglasses, too, they're just like normal sun– You get the picture. Perhaps you could consider a GPS watch, I've found it really helps your pacing during training runs. Yeah, you should get one of those. Then you only need to buy some tubs of sports drink mix, some gels and energy bars, entrance fees to half a dozen fun runs, a drink bottle belt, a new iPod, a subscription to *Runner's World* magazine – and $2000 later you are a runner!

At least one of the drawers in my wardrobe became dedicated to running gear only. Then winter appeared, which meant a whole new level of running gear. There were long-sleeved running shirts, hooded tops, raincoats and tights. Yes, tights. All these new items arrived and took up another drawer in my wardrobe. Blokes I know who are runners all secretly love the colder months. Despite the obvious change in temperature and the dark early mornings, there is one thing about running in winter that blokes love – we get to wear tights. Not because of how they look and feel of course; what blokes love about wearing tights is the advanced sporting technology that has gone into the tights to support our glutes and leg muscles and make them perform at their athletic peak. Yeah, that sounds right ... support the leg muscles.

Of course the big question males have to ask themselves when contemplating wearing running tights is: 'Shorts or no shorts?'

If you're wearing shorts over your tights you're kind of saying, 'Yes, I'm a man who likes to run – and I've got cold legs.'

If you're wearing tights without shorts then you're basically saying, 'Yes, I'm a man who likes to run – and here's my dick and my balls.'

I'M GLAD I NEVER HAVE TO DO ONE OF THOSE *EVER* AGAIN

With my first official run out of the way, Bern wasted no time in signing us up for our next running adventure – the Great Ocean Road half marathon, in six weeks' time. Looking back at that time frame, it really wasn't long enough to prepare properly for my first 23-kilometre run. The run is between two towns along the Great Ocean Road so it's a little bit longer than the usual half marathon distance of 21.1 kilometres.

I thought, 'If I've just run 14 kilometres and I increase my long run by one k each week, I should be fine, as long as the weather stays nice.'

The day of the race rolled around and the weather was not nice.

The area of Victorian coastline between the towns of Lorne and Apollo Bay is particularly spectacular. The Great Ocean Road, which winds its way along the rugged, windswept coast, is one of the most beautiful and stunning roads in the world – if you're in a car.

On foot, in winter, it's a nightmare. The temperature at the start of the race was just over nine degrees Celsius and I am sure it got colder as the run progressed. There was a howling headwind, it rained for most of the run, and somehow it seemed like there were more uphill sections than downhill, even though we started and finished at sea level. Sure the scenery was amazing – wild waves crashing over jagged rock formations and cliffs – it's just that I felt like I was running along the deck of a storm-bound ship that was about to be wrecked upon those jagged rocks. I don't think many people were having a very good time. There was no friendly chatter as there had been during the Run for the Kids. Near the halfway point, during a slight lull in the extremity of the weather, I spotted a koala up in a tree above the road. I thought it might be a good thing to share with the people running around me and said, loudly:

'Hey, koala! Right above us, in the tree, there!' Though as my mouth was half paralysed with cold and exhaustion, it came out as, 'Huh! Kwahah! Ah hapahah undawee! Dar!'

No one said a word and I could almost hear them thinking to themselves, 'Oh great, now there's a weirdo. Why do I always get the weirdos running near me?' With each step, I could see them all slowly spreading out and moving away from me. Even Bern was backing away, unsure if I had been pushed over the edge of mental stability and it was all her fault.

We made it to the end, with the final two ks the hardest thing I had done in my life up to that point. I was completely knackered and so glad that it was over. I remember thinking, 'Well that's it, I just ran a half marathon and I never have to do one of those ever again in my life.' On the drive back out of Apollo Bay, there were quite a few sorry-looking runners arriving and I realised that those poor saps were just completing the full marathon.

'Madness,' I thought. 'How crazy are they?'

I would soon be finding out for myself just how crazy.

EIGHT SCHOOL MUMS, A FAST LESBIAN AND ME

After seeing my running reflection in the shop window and noticing my Quasimodo-like gait, I thought it might be a good idea to get some advice from a professional, as I wanted to keep this running habit going and I had heard many things about wrecked knees and hips and feet caused by years of running. I didn't want to be doing it wrong and hurting myself. So when I saw a flyer for a local running group pinned to the noticeboard at the local cake shop, I grabbed one. The flyer said to, 'Call Deirdre at Fit2Gether Running Group.' The name Fit2Gether looks like a randomly generated password, but it sounded like it was run by someone who knew what they were doing, so I gave Deirdre a call.

Fitness groups, like hairdressers and Thai restaurants, tend to go for 'punny' names. Hairdressers have names like Hairway to Heaven, Hair Fidelity and Curl Up N Dye. Some Thai restaurants I have seen include Thai Tanic, Thai-Riffic and The King and Thai. Names for businesses working in the fitness industry are no different, though they usually involve words like 'fun', 'fit' and 'life' and tend to leave out words like 'pain', 'sit-ups' and '6 am'.

The following Tuesday morning I woke up at 5.30 and ran the two kilometres from my house to the running group meeting spot at a local park. No one was there. I waited for 15 minutes before I realised I was at the wrong park, then ran aimlessly around the streets of Yarraville for a while before heading home. It was no great loss, as an eight k run before 7 am is a great way to start the day as far as I am concerned.

The following Tuesday morning, I again woke at 5.30 and ran the three kilometres from my house to the running group meeting spot, this time at the correct local park.

Meeting a group of strangers is a bit awkward at the best of times, let alone at 6 am on a Tuesday morning. At least it was dark and, as all of us had quietly crept out of our houses about five minutes previously, no one was in the mood for a social chat. Besides, we were there to run. Deirdre did the introductions, speedily rattling off everyone's names in her pleasant Irish brogue.

'Hello,' I said, instantly forgetting all their names.

The running group was a mixed bunch, comprising eight local primary school mothers, a fast lesbian and me. Each week we would generally head off as a group to various locations a few ks away to run up and down stairs, climb hills and do 800-metre sprints down sleepy suburban streets. Then we would run back to the park for sit-ups, push-ups, fall-downs and more mysterious stretches. Of course, you could be doing all these kinds of exercises by yourself, but you don't. That's why these groups are such a great thing, they get you out the door once a week. The social aspect is good, too. As we got to know each other better, there was lots of friendly banter and support, and some of us started to do our long weekend runs together.

After about four weeks I was still unsure how my running style was going. I had been reading up about it, but with the amount of differing advice available online and in magazines and books, I was still a bit confused. There are more tips for a correct running style than there are for a correct golf swing, and that's saying something.

Look ahead, land mid-foot, feet pointed straight, hands at your waist, arms at 90 degrees, relax your shoulders, lean slightly forward, maintain a neutral pelvis. That is a hell of a lot to remember when you've also got to take into account selecting a song on your iPod, dodging dog poo and trying to decide whether or not to keep jogging on the spot while waiting at traffic lights. With all that on your mind, it's a wonder you can even watch where you're going.

'Ah, yeah, sure I ran into that pole, but did you notice the neutrality of my pelvis?'

Just as most of us who play golf don't have a swing like Tiger Woods but can still get around a golf course okay, most of us can run just by putting one foot in front of the other and letting thousands of years of human evolution take its course. So one morning as we were all running back to the park for stretch-offs or leg-overs or whatever, I asked Deirdre if she thought I was running correctly.

She said, 'Looks fine to me,' rather offhandedly, and that was that.

A MARATHON? IN ANTARCTICA?

I first heard about the Ice Marathon through my friend Bernadette. For many years I have had an obsession with Antarctica and its early explorers. In the early 1990s, during one of our tours in the US, I came across the book *Endurance*, which tells the story of Sir Ernest Shackleton's doomed 1914–17 expedition when their boat was crushed by the pack ice and Sir Ernest led the men through an incredible 15-month journey across snow, ice and ocean. All 28 men survived and the story is truly one of the greatest adventures ever told. For me, that story sparked a never-ending quest for books and information on the heroic age of Antarctic exploration. As many people do, I often dreamed about being able to visit Antarctica, but the idea of doing one of those flights where you fly tantalisingly over the continent and fight to take photos through a tiny window never interested me. Nor did I relish the idea of going all the way down there to take photos of penguins from a boat. That didn't sound like the kind of Antarctic experience that would, ahem, float my boat.

A few years before the Scaredies decided to call it quits, I was walking through Izzi and Popo on my way to our office. Bern was sitting at the front counter, looking at the computer.

'Rusty!' she exclaimed. 'You have to come and see this!' I walked over and looked at the screen. It showed a site featuring vintage Italian sunglasses.

'Oh ...' I feigned interest. 'They look lovely ...'

'Not that,' she changed the screen to the homepage of the Ice Marathon. 'You know they run a marathon in Antarctica.'

A marathon in Antarctica! Wow!

My first thought was that it would be an amazing thing to do but I would never do it. When I looked at the price – US$15,000 – I knew that it would be an amazing thing to do but I would *definitely* never do it. At that stage in my life, with house payments and young children, it was surely something that I could never seriously entertain. Besides, I had a comedy duo that needed to break up first.

THAT'S IT! GET FUCKED!

About five years before the end of the Scaredies, we were up in Sydney for a corporate gig. John called my hotel room and asked if he could come up for a chat because there was something he needed to tell me.

'Uh oh,' I remember thinking.

John had been undergoing a kind of 'spiritual growth period' for a few years and I thought we might be in for another one of our 'talks'. Not that I'm afraid of talking about spirituality or emotions or honesty – it's just reality that I have a problem with.

John and I had always been able to talk openly about the group and our relationship and every six months or so we would put down the guitars and bring up something that one of us had been thinking about or was worried about and we were usually able to talk it through without getting too 'self-help brochure' about it. In all our time working together, there was not one shouting argument between us. Sure, we had our disagreements, usually when John refused to do things my way, but there were no fisticuffs, no throwing things, no storming out of a room, slamming the door and shouting, *'That's it! Get fucked!'* We liked to work more subtly than that, though in different ways. After a long afternoon of disagreements, I would dream up elaborate fantasies of starting a new group and working with somebody else, while John would go and write earnest, soul-searching folk-pop songs.

So it kind of took me by surprise in Sydney that day, when he came into my hotel room, sat down and said, 'I don't want to be in the Scaredies any more.'

It was obvious that his spiritual awakening was nearly complete and as I look back, the signs had been there for a while. He had recently moved to Brunswick and had taken to wearing a hand-knitted beanie everywhere he went. John was from the quiet, conservative suburb of North Balwyn, for God's sake! He had had quite a sheltered childhood, culturally speaking. His entire school life was spent singing in a church choir six days a week, not watching cartoons on the lounge room floor after school like most kids. When I met John he had never watched a single episode of *The Brady Bunch* and, apart from church music, his musical exposure up to that point had been ABBA, two Billy Joel albums and, oddly, Blondie's *Parallel Lines*. Over the next 20-odd years of working with him, I witnessed first-hand John's exciting journey of discovery as he experienced popular culture, music that inspired him, and alcohol. So when he started wearing that beanie I should have seen it coming.

Not that we finished up the group straightaway. I somehow convinced him to keep going for a while. My main motivation was basically fear. There was fear of change, fear of not knowing what I would do after the Scaredies finished, fear of not earning any money.

The biggest of those three thoughts was by far, 'What am I going to do with myself when the Scaredies finish?' I had been chugging along fairly nicely ever since I had moved to Melbourne 20 years before, doing exactly what I had always wanted to do. Now I was facing a healthy dose of reality and it was not sitting well with me. It's not like I had a burning desire within me to fulfil some unaccomplished dream, like some people who find themselves in their forties and out of a job. I wasn't thinking, 'Great! Now I can finally start that little mowing business that I've always dreamed about,' or 'Gee, performing and travelling the world has been lots of fun, but now I just find myself increasingly being interested in GST administration and taxation accountancy.' Actually, becoming a taxation accountant would have made the decision to finish the group much easier, I simply would have enrolled in a TAFE course for taxation accounting, joined a local squash team and stepped in front of the nearest bus.

There were plenty of things I knew that I didn't want to do, and to list them here would be tedious, not to mention offensive to parking inspectors or any members of a capella groups that may be reading this book. Even though I had convinced John to keep going with the Scaredies for a while, I knew I had to come up with some sort of plan for life beyond the Scaredies, but I didn't. Life kept on quietly and comfortably moving along while I was delaying the inevitable end of the group and my life beyond it.

It was great to do something that you absolutely love and enjoy and then have people come up to you and say things like, 'We had such a great time and gee you are fantastic.' Who wouldn't like that? There are not many jobs where you get instant feedback like you get when you are a performer. Good and bad.

How many times does a parking inspector get someone saying, 'Gee you did a great job out there today, I wish I could do what you do. You are so amazing and I just loved watching you today. You have really made my day!' It's just not going to happen. With a parking inspector they are more likely to hear, 'You're shit, mate!' and 'Get a real job, fuckwit,' which are actually things that I have had shouted out to me before, so I guess it balances out.

With the small level of fame that we experienced, I feel grateful that I can walk around happily in public without being hassled. These days the odd person will look at me a bit funny and say, 'I think I have met you before, what school did you go to, or what pub do you drink in?' Then I say, 'Did you just watch a repeat of an old *Spicks and Specks* episode? Yeah, well, that's probably it.'

Nevertheless, who would want to give all that up?

GO! WHERE ONLY HUNDREDS HAD BEEN BEFORE!

After a few more years of doing our weekly radio spots, corporate gigs and the odd festival run here and there, John once again downed his guitar in the office one day and told me that he really needed to break free from the Scaredies to pursue his own serious song-writing career. This time, no amount of logic or pleading was going to change his mind and we agreed that after a year-long farewell tour, we should end the group the following December and that would be it. No more Scared Weird Little Guys. What the hell was I going to do? I just still couldn't get my head around it. The Scaredies had been my life for the last 20 years and it was very difficult to imagine life without it.

One afternoon in a fit of 'what-am-I-gonna-do-with-my-life' panic, I tried to write down a list of possible jobs I could do that used the skills I had garnered over all the years of performing and touring.

I came up with two: commercial radio morning show sidekick and advertising executive, and I didn't really want to do either.

I knew I would not be starting again from scratch and I would probably get into something to do with entertaining and comedy, sure. I guess, with all those years of experience, I had some sort of idea about making people laugh.

A cab driver in Adelaide once said to me, in a thick European accent, 'Oh, hey, shit you are one of dose guys, right? Dose funny guys from da TV ... Oh shit mate, you guys are funny, mate. You know what you do is so hard, mate. Dat is one hard thing to do, mate, to make someone laugh mate, dat is hard. To make someone cry, now dat is easy, mate. You punch dem in da face and they cry ... Easy mate! But to make dem laugh, mate, good for you, mate.'

Before I could really move on from the Scaredies, I needed to do something, but I didn't know what. I needed to do something that was a once-in-a-lifetime experience. A challenge. A mid-life crisis, if you will, but maybe a controlled mid-life crisis that didn't have me dying my hair and buying trendy clothes and hanging out with young people.

Maybe I could buy a sports car, that's what I hear blokes going through mid-life crises do. But I didn't really like sports cars that much and the only one I could afford would be one of those model sports cars in 'Collectible' stores in large shopping centres.

I went and saw a life counsellor to talk about the mid-life issues that face men who are going through changes in their employment situation and their lives in general. The life counsellor, or barman, as they are more commonly known, had some interesting suggestions. He said there a number of things you could do to help find your new calling. I could travel the world to a far-off place. I could learn a new language. I could attempt some sort of difficult physical challenge. Do you see where I am heading with this? Through the haze of all these new possibilities, and four or five mojitos, I heard a voice saying, 'Ice marathon ... Ice marathon ...'

My head was spinning, probably because of the mojitos, but also because of the new-found goal — that I should go ... go to Antarctica! Where only ten or twenty thousand people had been before me! And run! Run a marathon ... Where actually only about 100 people had run a marathon before, so that sounded like a pretty cool thing to go and do.

I had my goal and the decision was clear. We finish the Scaredies and I immediately take off on a once-in-a-lifetime trip to the bottom of the world to run a marathon!

I talked it over with Denise and she was extremely positive about the whole idea as soon as I mentioned it. She said I should just go. We could borrow the money and put it on our mortgage. She said that I would hate to put it off until I was too old or unfit and it was the kind of thing I had to do now, while I had the opportunity. She was urging me so much I believed she thought that I might die down there and she would finally be rid of me.

'YOU SHOULD FILM IT...'

Bern suggested I make a documentary about doing the run. It was a good idea. Done well, it would make an interesting show, no doubt, and it might provide a way that I could pay for the whole thing. I did some sums and spoke to a few filmmaker friends and it got quite scary, financially speaking. To pay for a camera and soundperson, and myself, to get to Chile, then Antarctica and cover post-production would be close to $100,000. I had four months to secure the money, find a film crew, write the plot line and capture the training footage before the race. I couldn't see it happening.

Then fate took a turn, as it always does. The planning for the Scaredies final tour needed to take in the valuable time of December, exactly the time when I needed to be out of the country for three weeks. I didn't know what to do. I really wanted to go to Antarctica and do this run, but the Scaredies tour had to take precedence. I had no choice. The Ice Marathon was cancelled and the dream was over.

Or was it?

Of course it wasn't. I just had to postpone the race for until the next year, so the dream wasn't over.

Or was it?

● ● ●

Putting the race off for another year worked out well. It gave me time to finish the final tour of the Scaredies, which had now ballooned out into May of 2011. I also got to organise a proper training schedule. Another thing that transpired in a positive way was that the cost of the race had come down, and the Australian dollar had gone up. The cost of doing the Ice Marathon, which included the flights to and from Chile, all accommodation and food in Antarctica and any costs associated with the race was going to be 10,000 euros (about AUD$13,000).

That would still make it highly improbable that I could secure funding to make a full documentary.

If I couldn't afford to take a film crew with me, I thought there was no reason I couldn't do it all by myself on an iPhone. Why not? Sure I had never made a film or documentary before, but I knew how to tell a story and I had taken plenty of video footage on the phone. I had heard that some people were making full-length films on them, and many short films were now shot on phones. I knew that for a good documentary, though, the sound had to be top quality. With the rise of YouTube and Facebook, people are used to seeing vision that is not high quality. So as long as the story was told well, I reckoned I could do it by myself. I looked into applying for a grant from Film Victoria, who offer various amounts of money to people wanting to make films or docos, so I sought some more advice from some friends who work in the film world.

I called up an old mate, Bradley Howard, who I had first met in Brisbane 20 years before when he was doing sound for my mate's band. Bradley had since moved into making film and television and had directed most of the Chaser's series, as well as *Newstopia* for Shaun Micallef. I knew he had recently made a Logie-nominated documentary and he would be a good person to talk to about fundraising and grants for films. When I told Bradley about the idea of going to Antarctica, running a marathon and making a doco about it by myself, he immediately said, 'You *have* to take a camera person with you. The race is what the whole doco is about and it must be captured properly to tell the story accurately and do it justice.'

He asked when the race was, took a moment to check his diary and said, 'Hell, if you get me to Antarctica, I'll do it for nothing!' He already owned all the necessary camera and sound equipment, so suddenly the idea of making a proper story about the experience became a reality. Let's just wind back a bit there: *'If you get me to Antarctica ...'*

I did the sums. If I was to pay for Bradley to get to Antarctica, I had to cover two return Antarctic airfares – the cost of getting down there was the same if you were running the race or not.

Basically, this was going to cost me AUD$30,000. I treated it as an investment. If I could sell the documentary for a decent amount, I may break even on the whole venture, but I still had to come up with the money in the first place.

LOCK IT IN, EDDIE

The idea of just adding the money on to our mortgage wasn't sitting well with me. Someone suggested I hold a fundraising night to help secure the funds, but I didn't like the idea of that, either. It's not like I was sick, or raising money for a charity. Essentially the whole thing was a completely selfish undertaking. Not selfish in a bad way, necessarily, but it was all about me. I didn't *need* to do this run, so I wasn't going to ask my friends for money so that I could do it. I could ask my brother to lend me the money, as an 'investment'. Though if I asked my brother, it would be more like an investment/gift – he is very generous – and for this trip, it just didn't feel right for me to take charity.

How was I going to pay for it? I optimistically bought some Tattslotto tickets after I was driving along one day and saw the big sign outside the newsagency that trumpeted a $20 million Super Draw – today! People were actually lined up outside the shop to buy lotto tickets. You can buy tickets for lotto on every day of the week, and the prizes are always around the million-dollar mark. Why aren't there people lined up every day? Are they saying, 'Oh, a million dollars, I don't even get out of bed for a million, but whoa, 20 million! That's more like it.'

Many people dream about what they would do with the money that they would win on Tattslotto. I like to dream about what I would do with the money that I have spent on Tattslotto.

One afternoon my mum was over at my house visiting and we were watching her favourite quiz show, *Millionaire Hot Seat*.

I never usually watch television at that time of the day, so I never get to see *Hot Seat*, but I do enjoy a quiz show and in the past have even been a contestant on *Temptation* and *The Einstein Factor* – my special subject was bluegrass music of the 1940s. The grand total of my winnings for both shows is a pen. A very nice pen, I might add. So nice, in fact, that I never use it, because it's my 'good' pen. As I barked out the answer to one of the questions, Mum said, 'You should go on that show, you'd be very good at it,' in the way that only mums can.

I went on the website and did the quick tryout quiz and filled in the application. Two days later I received an email informing me there was to be an audition for *Millionaire Hot Seat* in two weeks' time, and that I was invited. I turned up at a suburban university lecture hall on a week night for the audition. It was quite an exclusive event – there was just me and 500 other greedy hopefuls looking for an easy way to make some quick cash. We were told to bring a folder and a pen, and I took no chances. I had a folder, two pens and four pencils, because, you know, one of the pens might run out of ink and the other one might simply stop working, as pens are sometimes inclined to do, hence the pencils, which won't run out of ink or stain your shirt, but will easily break if you drop one, which is why I had four – anyone would think I was taking this a bit seriously and really needed the cash.

Occasions like these can be quite bizarre because you turn up feeling a bit shy and nervous on the inside while trying to maintain an air of confidence and composure on the outside. I walked down the hallway towards the lecture theatre and saw a line of people holding folders and pens, so I knew I was in the correct general area. In an unfamiliar setting like this, when you are faced with a group of strangers standing in a line, you don't want to do anything to embarrass yourself, so your first reaction is to simply join the end of the line and stand there, even though all the people in the line had probably just walked in like I had and obediently stood at the back of the line, not knowing if it was the right thing to do. No one wants to show that they don't know what is going on, so we all stood there, pretending we knew what was going on, which just made the line get ridiculously long. The alternative was to bravely walk past all of the waiting people to the front of the line to see what was actually going on, thereby risking looking like a pusher-innerer – and that's just plain un-Australian. Luckily, one of the producers of the show came out and called us all to move forward to collect some contracts to read and then sign. I quickly skimmed over the first of four pages of densely written legal-sounding words and scribbled my signature. The agreement could have said anything.

> *I, the undersigned, do hereby and wholly consent to my wallet and first-born child becoming the complete and rightful property of Channel Nine and its subsidiaries; and I agree to be sold into slavery and work at the Channel Nine cafeteria for the term of my natural life. Signed, Rusty Berther.*

I assumed it was something about not being a prison escapee or on drugs and promising not to punch the host, Eddie McGuire, in the face if you actually made it on to the show.

After we had signed our lives away, we all crammed into the lecture theatre for a 30-question, multiple-choice quiz in the style of the *Hot Seat* questions from the show. After the answers were read out, half of us were sent home. Due to my skill at answering questions that I didn't know by simply watching which answer caused the most people to bend over and tick a box on the answer sheet, I made it through to the next round of the audition. We filled in yet another form here and one of the questions asked, 'What are your four strongest subjects?'

The cynical part of me thought that they asked that question so when you are on the show, they don't ask you any questions from your strong subjects, so that you don't win any money. I thought I would trick them and therefore listed my strong subjects as:

Volcanoes
The lyrics of Hall and Oates
Compost
Movies that start with the words 'Police Academy'

Someone equally cynical asked the producer about this question, and he very honestly said he didn't care if contestants went on the show and won money. He loved it when people won money because it made the show look good. All he wanted to do was make an entertaining show that won the ratings. Fair enough, I thought. He then showed us some clips from previous episodes with contestants being a bit outrageous and outgoing and telling entertaining stories. Essentially that's what they wanted from us if we wanted to go on the show. Then, one by one, we all had to talk about ourselves and tell a story on camera for a minute. I sat down, put on my best smile, and said something like, 'Hi, my name is Rusty, I have just finished 20 years in a musical comedy duo and now I am going to Antarctica to run a marathon.'

A few days later I got the call to go on the show that was taping in three weeks' time.

I turned up at the television studios in Docklands at 7.30 am with four changes of clothes, not because wardrobe had asked for it, but because I was so nervous I kept soiling myself. Actually it was because wardrobe had asked for four changes of clothes. There were roughly 30 contestants there as they film five half-hour shows in one day, and we were all herded into a waiting area where we had to fill out yet more forms and contracts. I am sure you would fill out less paperwork if you were trying to adopt a child. Channel Nine now knew more about me than my bank manager, my doctor and my wife combined. On my passport, in the bit where it says 'who to contact in case of emergency', mine just says 'Channel Nine'.

There was a line in the appearance agreement that no employees of Channel Nine or their families were allowed to appear on the show. I was a little concerned, as I had appeared on Channel Nine shows in the past, and I was also about to do a song on their upcoming AFL Grand Final breakfast show and didn't want to jeopardise my eligibility to appear on *Hot Seat*. I talked to one of the producers about it and he said it wouldn't be a problem. Apparently I wasn't as important and famous as I thought I was.

After handing in our signed contracts and receiving our Channel Nine tattoos, we were shepherded into another waiting area, which was to be our home for the day. Thirty people who didn't know each other, all a little bit excited and nervous, and all with nothing to lose; except the respect of our friends and family if one of us blew an easy question for 125 grand.

If you've never seen the show before, this is how it works: there are six contestants, sitting in order one to six, a hot seat and a host. There is a potential top prize of one million dollars. Fifteen questions are asked and only the contestant sitting in the hot seat can answer. They have the choice to answer or pass. If they answer correctly, they remain in the hot seat and the prize money increases. If they answer incorrectly, they are out and the next contestant moves into the hot seat. If they pass, the next contestant moves to the hot seat and must answer the question. To win the money, you must be sitting in the hot seat for the final question, and answer it correctly. The contestant who passes must rely on the other contestants answering correctly or incorrectly so that the prize money builds and so that he or she can be sitting in the hot seat at the end.

My God! I never realised just how complicated this game was until I tried to write out an explanation for someone who has never seen it before. You can probably gather from all this information that it was pure luck to be sitting in the hot seat for the final question. You couldn't really study for this game – you either knew the answer to a question or you had to guess the multiple-choice answer. You were just as likely to know a question worth $125,000 yet be stumped by the $1000 question.

Sitting in the waiting room, we were given our starting seat numbers and told which show we were going to be on. I was to be sitting in seat one for the second show to be taped that day.

I have done literally hundreds of television spots over the years, but I was pretty nervous that day as the other five contestants and I sat waiting for the lights to flash and the voice-over guy to say '... And here's your host ... Eddie McGuire!' He introduced the show and welcomed me to the hot seat. We made some small talk about the Scaredies finishing and how we had played a few Collingwood functions over the years. On the inside I was squirming at the mention of this and was expecting the producer to burst out any minute and say, 'Stop the show! He's played gigs for Eddie and Collingwood! Get him out of here!' But he didn't and before long I was facing the first question, for $100.

Let's face it, the early questions on *Millionaire Hot Seat* were just in there so people blessed with lower brain function and Collingwood supporters, could go 'Aww, duh ... dat's an eezy wun ...' They made the correct answer fairly obvious, so I really didn't want to get these early questions wrong. I answered the first few, which were along the lines of:

What's a flat pack most likely to contain?
A: An Elephant
B: The Eiffel Tower
C: Richard Wilkins
D: Furniture
What is the third letter of the alphabet? Is it:

Lock it in, Eddie

A: D
B: C
C: A
D: B
Me: 'Lock in C, Eddie.'
Eddie: 'Is that A or B?'
Me: 'A? It's not D, so B.'
Eddie: 'Change it to B?'
Me: 'The answer is C.'
Eddie: 'A?'
Me: 'You want a punch in the face? Oh *that's* why I signed that thing …'

I cunningly worked the prize money up to around the $1000 mark when I was faced with a slightly tricky question about Australian music. It was an audio question and I had to name a band from the late 1990s. My knowledge of popular commercial music stopped in about 1986, when I threw myself into learning everything I could about early country music, so I knew I was going to have a problem. In *Millionaire Hot Seat*, the only possible strategy you can follow is, if you are in the hot seat early and you don't know a question, you should pass. Then your fate is in the hands of your fellow contestants, who you want to answer some questions correctly to build the prize money up, but not too many or you won't have a chance to get back into the hot seat to have a crack at the money. As fate would have it, with three questions left and the prize money at $10,000, there was a nice, older chap in the hot seat and I was next in line. He answered the next question correctly and here is where we stood: the money was now at $20,000 with two questions left. He couldn't pass because it would put him out of the game with no chance of getting back into the hot seat, as there was still one bloke behind me. If he answered correctly, he stayed on to answer the final question for a shot at $50,000 and I was out of the game. If he answered incorrectly, I was into the hot seat for the final question to win $20,000. He seemed like a nice bloke, but I *really* wanted him to get this question wrong.

The question was:

Which golf tournament is also known as 'Glory's Last Shot'?

A: US Open
B: British Open
C: US PGA
D: US Masters

'Oh no,' I thought, 'old guys like golf, my chance at getting in the hot seat is gone!' I had no idea what the answer was and, thank Golf, neither did he.

He guessed D – British Open, but the correct answer was C – US PGA.

So there I was in the hot seat for the final question worth $20,000. It had been nothing but pure luck that had conspired to get me there; it could have been any one of us. All I was hoping for was a question that I immediately knew the answer to.

Eddie liked to build up the tension, stretching it out for as long as possible:

'So, Rusty, what would you do if you won $20,000?'

I wanted to say, 'Uh, I dunno, Eddie, twenty grand would buy a *lot* of pot ...' but I simply told him the truth:

'I'm going to Antarctica to run a marathon and I need this money to make a documentary about it.'

It was the first time I had ever seen Eddie lost for words, then he said: 'Uh ... wow ...'

I wanted him to say: 'You know you could buy a *lot* of pot with that much money.'

It was time for the question.

I was thinking, *'Please-let-me-know-it-please-let-me-know-it.'*

Eddie read: *'On television ...'*

'This is good,' I thought, 'I've watched a lot of television.'

Lock it in, Eddie

'... which of the following shows about an extra-terrestrial was the first made?

'A: *Mork and Mindy*

'B: *Alf*

'C: *Third Rock from the Sun*

'D: *My Favourite Martian*.'

I thought I knew the answer right away, but all that was going through my mind was, '*Don't-fuck-it-up-don't-fuck-it-up-don't-fuck-it-up.*'

The screen in front of me showed that I had 55 seconds left to answer, so I knew I could take my time.

'Well, Eddie ...' I pondered, '*Mork and Mindy* was late seventies ...' *don't-fuck-it-up-don't-fuck-it-up* ... 'and *Alf* was in the mid-eighties ...' *don't-fuck-it-up-don't-fuck-it-up* ... 'and *Third Rock from the Sun* is fairly recent ...' *don't-fuck-it-up-don't-fuck-it-up* ... 'and I do remember watching *My Favourite Martian* when I was young, and I am pretty sure it was in black and white ...' *don't-fuck-it-up-don't-fuck-it-up* ... 'so could I please lock in D: *My Favourite Martian*?'

If you watched the show, you'd have noticed that if at this point Eddie said, 'Are you sure you want to lock it in?' you were wrong and you should change your answer. This time, though, he immediately moved straight on and said, 'D is locked in. *My Favourite Martian* is correct! You've won $20,000!'

I remembered back to the audition, watching people doing their outrageous celebrations, so I jumped up, hugged Eddie and kissed him on the lips. Of course I didn't do that, I would never hug Eddie McGuire.

WHAT IF MARATHON WAS CLOSER TO ATHENS?

I am sure most of you have heard the story about the Greek bloke called Philippoussis or something like that who ran from the Greek town of Marathon all the way to Athens with the important news that the 490 BC equivalent of the new iPads had arrived or whatever. Anyway, it's a great story, and after Phil ran about 40 kilometres and then died of exhaustion, the Greeks thought it would be a top way to spend two or three hours as part of an athletics meet, and the marathon was born. There's actually quite a bit more to the story, and after a hard afternoon's research down at the local library, (okay, I admit it, it was actually Wikipedia ...) I found out some other interesting facts about the beginnings of the marathon as we know it.

- When the modern Olympic games were re-established in Athens in 1896, the legend of the running Greek bloke was relived with a 40-kilometre run from Marathon to the Olympic Stadium in Athens.
- The official marathon distance of 42.195km was established during the 1908 London Olympics, when the length of the race was extended so that the finish could happen in front of the Royal viewing box.

- Early marathon runners avoided water, instead favouring a mix of goat's milk, Schnapps and urine.

That last one may not actually be true. They really should make Wikipedia more difficult to edit. There are literally hundreds of different versions of how the marathon started but if you read between the lines we can probably accept that at some time long ago, someone ran about 40 kilometres from the town of Marathon into Athens, which then gave the marketing department of the 1896 Olympics a great way to finish off the games for that year. Incidentally, that first modern Olympic marathon was won by Spyridon Louis, a Greek postal worker, in a time of two hours, 58 minutes, 50 seconds – a fine advertisement for the quality of the Greek postal system, which obviously needed fit posties. There was speculation that, due to his skills as a postal worker, Spyridon was better able to avoid the many stray dogs that roamed the marathon course, and this contributed to his win.

The marathon has now become a standard part of every Olympic games since 1896 and marathons have exploded in popularity, with over 500 official marathons being run around the world each year.

What is it that makes humans of all shapes, sizes and speed think that it's a good idea to line up in their thousands and run that distance? Especially when the first bloke that ever did it apparently dropped down stone cold dead at the finish. Why do people run?

I have a little theory about humans that may go some way to explaining why some of us would put ourselves through such a seemingly horrible experience as a marathon. It involves hobbies and the pursuit of happiness. Most people have hobbies; things that they have an interest in that they enjoy doing, it's a natural human trait. I have noticed that most of the things that humans love to do can be traced back to the very beginnings of our early ancestors. Cooking, singing, dancing, drawing, camping, telling stories, gardening, hunting, fishing, sewing, playing or listening to music, making craft, playing sport, playing games. All of these pastimes make people happy and it's usually something they do without giving too much thought to. The dictionary meaning of the word pastime is: '*An activity that someone does regularly for enjoyment rather than work; a hobby.*' Literally it is to 'pass the time' but I think it also represents the stuff that humans love to do that is from a 'past time'.

My point is that we do these things because we have been doing them for thousands of generations, and they bring happiness and fulfillment.

That is why people run.

Though it doesn't explain golf.

It possibly explains why people like to run around a park in the morning anyway, but does it explain why so many people take part in an event where you are seen to be successful if you don't die at the end of it?

I don't know if that explains marathons, but it was my turn to try and find out.

• • •

In April of 2009, fourteen months after I began running, something clicked inside my head and I decided to run in the Melbourne Marathon in October that year.

If you are a runner, the idea of doing a marathon floats in and out of your consciousness from time to time. Before you complete one, it is the biggest thing you can do as a runner. People who are not runners will ask you if you have done one, or are thinking of doing one. ('What's a marathon ... like 14 ks or something?')

During that first year of running I certainly thought about, and immediately dismissed, the idea of running a marathon. Usually at the end of a run of, say 14 kilometres, you ask yourself, could I now go and run that distance again, and then run it over again? At the end of a run is the worst time to be entertaining thoughts like that. Upon completing the Great Ocean Road half marathon for the first time, and in the days following it, the idea of a marathon seemed, quite simply, insanity. Why on earth would you do that to yourself?

Then, after a few more months with your running going along well, the thought starts to creep back into your mind. 'Could *I* do a marathon?'

Once I had made the decision that I was going to enter the marathon (and paid the $110 fee upfront), I set about getting into a training plan. Every single time I stepped out the door and ran, I was thinking about the marathon. Having a strong vision in my mind just seemed to make everything come together a little more easily. It made me want to get up early and go for a run. I started a training diary, which listed every run I did, and that also added to the motivation of getting prepared for the marathon.

I researched marathon training plans online and borrowed a few books to see what I was in for, and I was surprised to find out that it was not as scary as I first thought, though one expert wrote that 'most people with any fitness level could walk 42 kilometres, *it's not that far*'. Not that far? Where do you live, mate? Mildura?

What I gathered from most of the information available about taking on your first marathon is that you need to have been running for about a year, and then have completed four to six months of training.

There are many different programs you could follow if you want to successfully complete a marathon, but most of them recommend a similar pattern: run on three or four days a week, with one of those runs being a long run of increasing length, usually on a weekend. The weekly long runs should start at around 12-16 kilometres and build up to at least two runs over 30 kilometres. That's pretty much it. You can choose to do all sorts of variations on that, like including cross training, sprints and speed work or a weights program, but if your goal is just to finish a marathon, it's really not that complicated.

I had a reasonable fitness base to start with and chose a beginners' program that I adjusted along the way. It was an 18-week program that went something like this:

Monday – rest

Tuesday – running group (six k run, sprints, hills, core work)

Wednesday – longer run of 10-16 kilometres

Thursday – six to eight kilometres

Friday – rest

Saturday – short easy run (five kilometres)

Sunday – long run

I did not follow this plan to the letter as some days I was travelling or busy or hungover or I simply couldn't be bothered. Therefore the long run was sometimes on a Saturday or a Monday and things would get shifted around. The main thing was to keep on track for most weeks and not get down on yourself for missing one session. As long as the long runs continued to build, I knew I was probably going to be fine.

Please note that I am not a running instructor, or an expert on marathon training programs and would not necessarily recommend that you follow what I did. You should take the advice of someone more experienced than me, though if you do decide that I am to be trusted and you think my advice is worth listening to, I have some real estate opportunities in a local swamp that I want to talk to you about.

The Scaredies were travelling interstate quite a bit during the months before the marathon, so I had the privilege of being able to experience many runs around the country. The CBDs of all capital cities in Australia, except for Sydney, have excellent running tracks along their beautiful beaches, rivers and lakes. Sydney has a nice short section through the Botanic Gardens, and they could have had an amazing running track along the harbour, but I guess someone got greedy and sold the land to people who put up pools and fences and boat sheds, I believe in order to stop runners and walkers from enjoying the harbour, so whoever was responsible for that blew it. Darwin is a bit tricky to run in too, not because of a lack of tracks – there are plenty of those – but because it's simply too fucking hot.

Thanks to Google Earth, I could map out runs before I got to a city or town, which is how I got to plan an interesting 32-kilometre run in Cleveland, an outer suburb of Brisbane on Raby Bay, about six weeks before the date of the marathon. I had noticed on the map that there was a large bushland reserve about five kilometres from where we were staying, and it seemed to have plenty of tracks to run along. I devised an intricate route, which would enable me to place drink bottles and food at various points so I could collect them as I criss-crossed through the bush tracks, and I even printed out a map to help me during the run. We actually had two shows up there at an outdoor festival, one on the Saturday night and one on Sunday afternoon, so the timing was perfect to fit in my carefully planned run.

I had all manner of energy bars and gels and small juice bottles refilled with Gatorade crammed into a small bag around my waist, along with my map, and I hit the road just after 6 am. At about 6.15 it started raining. I call it rain, but it was more like the air was filled with water. A thick, tropical deluge fell for about 45 minutes, but at least it was warm, and once you get going, rain is not so bad to run in, as long as your feet stay dry. My feet, of course, were not dry – they were soaked. They were so wet I may as well have been running in foot spas instead of shoes. There was so much water my fingers even developed the prune-like effect you get when you've stayed in a swimming pool for too long.

Nonetheless, I continued running through the deserted early-morning streets of Cleveland, on my way to the bushland reserve. 'Bushland reserve' has a bit of an ominous ring to it. It's the kind of term you only hear on news bulletins when they are doing a story about a grisly murder – '... *the man's body was found in a bushland reserve in the outer suburb of Cleveland. A police spokesperson said, "He would have been easier to identify if his feet and hands hadn't rotted away due to excessive wetness."*'

I started to think more about where I was going to run and was feeling a bit concerned, as I had told no one where I was going. John knew I was heading out, but he would be sleeping until after I was due back. I wouldn't be missed until we were introduced onstage later that afternoon and John would say, 'Hi, we're the Scared Weird Little Guys, I'm John ...' and eventually the pause would go on for too long and he would look to his right and finally realise I was not on the stage next to him, but in a shallow grave in the local bushland reserve.

I squelched my way to the secluded track that led into the reserve. Surely no murderers would be out in this weather. I checked my map and concealed a drink bottle and power bar behind a tree, as if anyone was going to steal it. A few more kilometres along the track I pulled out my map again and was quite dismayed when it disintegrated into a sloppy mush of wet paper and printer ink. No problem, I thought. From memory, the bush reserve I was running in was merely two large, slightly misshapen squares, one a trapezium and the other a parallelogram ... and I was somewhere near the easternmost side of the trapezium ... or was it a rhombus? Damn! I was lost.

Of course I could have retraced my steps, but that was no fun. I was only seven ks into a three-hour run that I had looked forward to for weeks. I could actually get completely lost for at least another two hours and still be home for breakfast. Off I slogged, through mud and trickling streams formed by the storm that had now trailed off to mere steady rain. I came to an intersection of trails, cached some more supplies and continued on. At various points I would hit the edge of the reserve and glimpse suburban houses through the trees, reminding me that I was okay and not in an episode of *Survivor: Bushland Reserve*.

I eventually reached what I thought was the far corner of the reserve, the place I could remember on the map where I would meet up with a main road that took me straight back to the hotel. I couldn't retrace my path as I had already run about 20 kilometres and didn't feel like doing that distance again, so I took to the suburban streets in what seemed to be roughly the correct direction and did another five ks or so. I wasn't panicking, but it didn't feel right. I reached a different main road and continued on, still feeling I was going in the wrong direction. Strangely, all signs of any houses had now disappeared and I was possibly on my way to the Gold Coast. I was feeling tired, hungry and thirsty, but I had given up hope of retrieving any of my cached supplies long ago, and the wet footwear was causing a couple of large blisters to form on my heels. I considered hitchhiking, but thoughts of shallow graves came back to me. Plus, I was still only at about 27 ks and I really did want at least to complete the run. Finally, about two kilometres ahead I saw a plant nursery, which I stumbled into 10 minutes later and asked the lady behind the counter if she had a street directory.

'Where ya going?' she said cheerfully.

I was in no mood for cheer.

'I just need to know where I am,' I said.

'You're in Redland Bay Road,' she laughed.

I thought that might be helpful to someone who *knows where the fuck Redland Bay Road is*!

'I don't know where that is,' I said, not cheerfully.

'Where'd ya come from?'

'I don't know, uh, the bush reserve.' My brain wasn't functioning too well.

'Ooh, you *are* lost.' She seemed to be enjoying this.

What if Marathon was Closer to Athens?

'Can … I … please … just … see … a … map?' I said through clenched teeth.

'I don't have a map,' she replied, smartly.

On the counter was a vase filled with happy-looking ceramic bumblebees that were attached to long pieces of wire so you could stick them in your garden. I imagined what she would look like with one of them sticking in her neck.

'I have a street map you can use,' came a friendly voice from behind me. It was another customer, who took me to her car and let me use the map. It took us both quite a while to establish exactly where we were, but eventually I saw there was a reasonably simple route to follow to get back to the hotel. About 40 minutes later I staggered back to my destination. I had done 34 kilometres and had been out for over three and a half hours. It was a great feeling to finally take my shoes off and look at the state of my feet, which looked like medical specimens just removed from a briny medicine jar.

● ● ●

Four other people from the running group, including Deirdre, were also training for the marathon, so we did most of our long runs together. To help familiarise ourselves with the marathon course, we would meet up at 6 am on Sundays during winter to run parts of it.

I was surprised to see that the longest run as part of my training program was 36 kilometres. Most programs do not recommend that you run the actual distance of a marathon as part of your training. I don't know whether they believe that doing 42 kilometres will hurt you and hinder your training, or that they think you should leave the last six kilometres of the marathon in uncharted territory, so you feel like you really earn it. Also recommended is that you have someone you know run the last part of the marathon with you, so they can give you support and you can have someone to swear at. Bernadette graciously agreed to be my support person and would meet me at the 37-kilometre mark.

With a few weeks to go before the race, I learned about what was to become one of my favourite parts of marathon training – carb loading. The idea of carb loading is that in the last few days before a race you rest and do little or no training at all and increase the amount of carbohydrates you eat, which will then boost the amount of glycogen in your muscles. Glycogen is basically how carbohydrates are stored in the muscles, and when you are undertaking an endurance event like a marathon, I'm told you want to make sure your muscles are jam-packed full of glycogen. Apparently most people take this as a signal to stuff as much pasta as they can into themselves for two days before a big race, but this can also have a negative effect if you eat more than you normally would and eat foods that you are not used to. I just enjoyed not running for a few days and eating so much pasta I didn't think my muscles could have taken any more glycogen.

The night before the marathon, I carefully laid out my running gear, with the race number pinned onto my shirt and all the other gear, checked and ready to go. I was taking no chances, and had invested in a new pair of $35 socks. That's $10 more quality sock power than my last pair had. It is suggested that you get as much rest as you can before the race, so I went to bed at 10 pm but woke up every hour from 1 am, finally getting up at 5 am to perform necessary ablutions, get dressed and try to eat some porridge and toast to jam some final glycogen into my muscles.

I met with the other four marathoners from the running group and we all travelled in together, sharing our nerves and goals for the day. I had chosen the goal of completing the marathon in less than four hours, which is a popular choice for beginners. The average time for finishing marathons is roughly

What if Marathon was Closer to Athens?

four hours, 27 minutes for men, and four hours, 54 minutes for women.

To come in under four hours, I needed to average five minutes 37 seconds per kilometre for the entire race, which is not too fast, but it's certainly not a slow jog either.

People who don't run will often say things like, 'Oh, I don't know how you can run so far, I would get out of breath just running 100 metres.' But running out of breath is not really an issue in a marathon, unless I guess you are trying to run it in two and a half hours. I have never puffed and panted during long runs; the lungs are fine, it's your body that usually faces the biggest struggle.

It was set to be a beautiful day, weather-wise. Clear skies and a top of 22 degrees Celsius, and I was all set for the race as we lined up among the other 5000 starters at 7 am and completed the previously mentioned routine of checking out the other runners' t-shirts boasting where they had run. My nipples were safely protected under a layer of paw paw ointment and heavy duty sticking plaster and I was wearing a bum bag containing my supplies for the next four hours; an iPod, earphones, five carbohydrate gels, spare ointment and bandaids and some pain-killers.

I had a pace band on my wrist that I had printed off the computer. It listed all the kilometres, one to 42, with the exact time I should hit each one. I also had a brand new GPS watch, which beeped after every kilometre and showed me how long the previous one had taken.

After listening to the obligatory dull interviews with some unfortunate celebrities who were doing the race, the gun went off and we were away. It is difficult to keep your pace in the early stages of these runs as it is crowded, though everyone also tends to run a bit faster than they would like due to all the excitement. I noticed I had done the first kilometre in just under five minutes, so I was ahead of schedule. It took me most of the second kilometre to work out in my head what my time would be if I ran all of the race at five minutes per kilometre (300 seconds × 42 = 12,600 ÷ 60 = 210 minutes or three hours 30 minutes, yes, I know, plus another minute for the final 195 metres).

My second kilometre was five minutes 30 – that was more like it and so continued my marathon. I soon heard a bloke running beside me ask, 'Are you Rusty?' and we had a nice conversation for the next two ks. Then I caught up to a couple of the running group girls for a couple of ks and it was time for the first drink station, which I walked through before getting back up to pace. According to my pace band, I was ahead of my four-hour goal by about a minute and a half and things were feeling good, though I really did need to pee. We were running around near a golf course at this point, so I took advantage of a clump of trees to relieve myself, along with about twenty other blokes and a couple of women. Whatever... in a marathon, you're all among friends and everybody understands what we've all been through just to get there, so if you have to have a squat amongst the bushes, no one gives a second look. After about eight kilometres, my pace band had become a smudged, indecipherable mess due to sweat permeating the sticky tape I had covered it in. This was not such a bad thing as, to keep my mind busy, I got to perform more of the complex maths equations in my head as each kilometre passed. Anything like that helps to keep your mind going over that amount of time. Imagine you have to go on a four-hour car trip by yourself. That is a lot of time to think. You can at least listen to music, as I was at this point in the run. I had prepared a long playlist of songs to listen to during the marathon, even though I usually don't like to listen to music when I run. I prefer the silence and enjoy letting my mind wander. At this point in the run, though, it was fun to listen to music for a while. I had quite a mix of artists represented, like Johnny Cash, Tom Petty, Steve Earle and Buddy Miller, through to Eminem and Pink. This took me up to about the 15 k mark, when I turned off the music and started a few conversations with people around me. It's pretty easy to start a conversation at this point in a marathon. I would just say something inane like, 'Beautiful day to be running,' or 'Is this your first marathon?' and people were happy to have a few minutes conversation to help pass the time, as it was still early in the run and yet to get really horrible.

As I passed the halfway mark, I was feeling really good. My calculations showed that I was about five minutes ahead of my four-hour goal pace and I was wondering if I might be able to break three hours 50 minutes. Oh, how that was going to change. I was still feeling okay at the 28-kilometre mark, as the course turned from St Kilda beach to head up Fitzroy Street. I was soon thinking, 'Since when has Fitzroy Street had such a steep hill on it?' It was the first inkling I had that it was about to get much harder. Heading back into the city down St Kilda Road, I passed the 30-kilometre mark with trepidation, as it is around this point that the dreaded 'wall' often rears its ugly bricks.

'Hitting the wall' is caused by basically running out of energy. All that glycogen in your muscles that you had been trying to stock up on by carb loading eventually gets depleted. Your brain runs on glycogen, just like your muscles do, and your body knows that the brain is more important than the muscles, so if you are running low on glycogen, the brain is going to get first choice ahead of the poor old muscles, who are just trying to get you to the end of the stupid race. If you continue on, the brain will eventually run low on glycogen and proceed to get all hypoglycaemic on your ass; which will also affect the way you think and you may become emotional. That is why you see people near the end of marathons stumbling, babbling and crying, and that's what I had to look forward to.

It was just after the 32-kilometre mark that I caught up to Deirdre from the running group. She was not looking good. I felt okay still and was fairly sure that my brain was not hypoglycaemic yet. I didn't really feel like chatting, though I said to her, 'How're you going Deirdre?'

She was staring straight ahead and said quietly, 'Talk to me, Rusty, tell me a story or a joke or something.' I thought this was maybe not a bad idea. Anything to pass a couple more kilometres, so I reeled off a few jokes and stories and I must say I didn't get much back from her. Talk about a tough crowd. I have played to some unresponsive audiences in my time but nothing compares to telling jokes to someone in the early stages of hitting the wall in a marathon. I eventually gave up and we drifted apart as I was now starting to feel pretty terrible myself and I think telling those stories had sapped the last bits of energy from me.

'Thanks a lot, Deirdre!' I thought. 'Way to drag me down into your energy sapping world of no energy, you energy sapper.

'Whoa,' I thought, 'where did that bout of nastiness come from?'

It was the first appearance of 'Bad Rusty', and he was about to make himself a major part of the final stage of the marathon.

I passed the 35-kilometre mark, where the course travelled up a road in the Botanic Gardens. The next two kilometres were uphill and absolutely awful. I slowed down my pace and noticed that I was still overtaking quite a few runners who had slowed to a walk or even stopped. I passed through a drink station and walked through it. I didn't feel like drinking and I didn't feel like not drinking, if you know what I am saying. I felt quite numb, so I took two cups of water and poured them over my head.

Bad Rusty said: 'Just walk, this is stupid, what are you doing?' But I overruled him and started jogging the final uphill section to where I would meet Bern. My pace had slowed right down now and I was doing almost seven-minute ks. The thought of finishing under four hours was slipping away and I couldn't have cared less.

What if Marathon was Closer to Athens?

At the 37-kilometre mark, Bernadette joined me and said, 'Hi, how are you going?'

'Fucking terrible,' said Bad Rusty.

'Just ignore him,' I said and we continued on in silence.

I was hurting all over, my arms, my neck, my feet, my hamstrings and a weird spot behind my left knee were all aching.

Bad Rusty was gaining in confidence and I could feel him taking over. He was really going for it.

'Why are you doing this? Who cares? Just walk. It doesn't matter if you break four hours. *No one cares.* Just walk! Just stop running!'

I would answer him, trying to retain some semblance of fighting spirit.

'Come on mate, you can do it. You're okay. You've done the training, you can break four hours.'

'Why are you doing this? When was this ever a good idea? You're hurting. You're not an athlete. You're in pain and that can't be good for you. What about all those people you've read about whose muscles melt and they die before the end of the race?'

Bad Rusty had a point. He was slowly convincing me to walk. He continued. 'Isn't pain there for a reason? Isn't it your body telling you that something is wrong and you should stop doing what you're doing because it's bad?'

'No. I've come this far and I still have a chance to get under four hours. You can do it, there's only four ks to go. That's just like running down to the park, doing one lap, and then running home again.'

Bad Rusty was shouting, 'But I don't wanna run down to the park, do a lap, then run home again. I don't wanna do that! I just wanna stop running!'

I countered: 'You can do this, you can push through the pain.'

'What's the point? Why push through the pain, what are you trying to prove? It doesn't matter; you're not an athlete, you're just a bloke running a stupid marathon, why push through the pain? Just walk!'

'It's going to be okay; I can see the MCG from here. That's the finish line, it's going to be over soon, just keep going.'

It is interesting to note that all of the countless marathon training programs available focus on the physical aspect of the training and there is hardly any mention of the mental battles that you are going to face. I don't really know how a training program could prepare you for your mental struggles; maybe something along the lines of this:

Week 12

Tuesday – eight kilometres easy run.

Wednesday – 40-minute fartlek with 5 × 3-minute surges.

Thursday – Travel to a dark place within your soul and have a mental battle which questions your psychological limits and emotional stability.

Friday – five kilometres easy run.

'Shut up!' said Bad Rusty.

'You shut up!' I snapped back. 'You're just a manifestation of my foggy, hypoglycaemic brain! I shan't listen to you any more! Be gone, Bad Rusty! You only exist because I didn't eat that last forkful of broccoli orecchiette last night! You're weak and you're a quitter!'

'Sheesh, there's no need to get personal,' said Bad Rusty, a little sadly.

God knows what my face looked like during this internal dialogue. Bern must have noticed something was going on and she cautiously asked how I was feeling as we were walking through the final drink station, only three kilometres from the finish.

I explained what was hurting and where and she suggested I change the way I run, get up on my toes a bit and alter my form.

What if Marathon was Closer to Athens?

We jogged off again and I changed the way I had been running and, by golly, I think it was working. With two ks to go, I was almost flying. Bad Rusty had gone away, though it wouldn't be the last time he would come out during a run. The feeling of running and using slightly different muscles was working a treat. I checked the time and I had been going for three hours and 50 minutes – I just had to maintain a good pace and my goal of breaking four hours was still achievable. I could see the MCG and with one k to go, I knew I was going to make it. Though even with Bad Rusty gone, my overwhelming thought was that I just wanted to stop running. It would be over soon, but that didn't make the last bit any easier. The final 500 metres of the race was quite bizarre. The course was planned out so that all the runners finish with a lap of Melbourne's prestigious sporting ground – the MCG. What a way to finish! I had thought when I first read it. The Melbourne Marathon Festival also takes in a half marathon, a 10 k and a five k run, and they are all planned to finish at roughly the same time, which is a nightmare for poor saps like me who are struggling through the final metres of their first marathon and find themselves suddenly surrounded by sprinting children and mothers pushing prams. It's not that I thought I was better than them because I had just done a marathon; it's just that I couldn't help thinking, 'Well, fuck off out of my way, I just want to get this thing over and done with.'

I had always imagined that when I crossed the finish line in the marathon, the main emotions I would feel would be euphoria and jubilation. After completing a lap on the hallowed turf of the MCG – one of the greatest sporting stadiums in the world – I would stand with arms raised and a joyous smile on my face, staring up at the heavens and soaking in my incredible achievement.

It was not like that at all. Upon entering the MCG, still dodging my way through the riff raff, I thought, 'Oh God, I still have to run all the way over there.' I noticed the big clock above the finish line displayed three hours something, so I picked up the pace and when I hit the line it said three hours, 59 minutes and 50 seconds. I had reached my goal but at that point I really didn't care. The overwhelming emotion I felt was that of relief; relief that I wasn't running any more. Then the thought of not having to run any more led to happiness – happiness that I didn't have to run any more. Deirdre came in just behind me with a time of 4:00:13, and we congratulated each other and met up with our other running comrades.

There was a dull feeling somewhere within me that was saying, 'I did it,' but it really wasn't until a few days later, when the pain subsided, that I could actually experience the feeling of achievement and satisfaction that comes with the completion of a goal like running a marathon. The days post marathon can be accurately summed up by Dr Smith from *Lost in Space* when he said, 'Oh, the pain ... the pain.'

Immediately following the race, after devouring any food that was unfortunate enough to come within the vicinity of my mouth, and limping back to the car, I spent some time walking in the cold ocean, then spent the day on the couch before we all went to Deirdre's house with our families to celebrate. You would think you could have a decent night's sleep following a physical exertion like a marathon, but I woke up wide-awake at 1 am, starving hungry. After six pieces of Vegemite on toast, a litre of Gatorade and half an old movie on television, I made it back to bed around three in the morning. The first day post-marathon was deceptively not too bad. My legs were feeling quite stiff and sore so I got a massage that had me screaming in pain instead of releasing gentle oohs and ahs of relaxation. The pain over the next few days unfortunately got worse before it got better. Getting in and out of bed was comically painful and going up or down stairs was virtually impossible. Mentally it was a bit difficult also. After six months of build-up, with so much of my focus aimed at the marathon, it didn't surprise me that I would be feeling a bit down. We had a family holiday on the Gold Coast booked for the week after the marathon. Daily swims in the ocean and a few casual runs along the beach were a perfect way to fully recover and also to get some of the focus off me and back on to the family.

Imagine if the town of Marathon in Greece, was only 30 kilometres away from Athens, instead of 40 kilometres. Marathons as we know them would be completely different. We'd be running them every weekend. 'Hitting the wall' would not be a metaphor that meant reaching the end of your endurance, it would merely mean to hit a wall with something.

New Zealand runner and bronze medal winner at the Rome Olympics, Barry Magee, once said, 'Anyone can run 32 kilometres, it's the next ten that count.'

Jerome Drayton, winner of the eighty-first Boston Marathon, said: 'To describe the agony of a marathon to someone who's never run it is like trying to explain colour to someone who was born blind.'

There is something about that 42-kilometre distance that makes it just out of reach for most humans. It's a fascinating thing. If a marathon was only 30 kilometres, it wouldn't have this aura of difficulty about it, and 50 kilometres would be too far. Here are some of the responses I got when I asked some marathon runners to complete the sentence, 'Marathons are ...'

'... more of an adventure than a race.'

'... sheer stupidity, but I'm still looking forward to my second.'

'... addictive.'

'... to be respected.'

'... about the challenge of making it to the start line, and the reward of making it to the finish line.'

'... like childbirth – painful and joyous.'

'... a great way to learn about yourself.'

'... a physical challenge that is mostly in the mind.'

'... 195 metres more than the meaning of life.'

'... a great equaliser. Short or tall, rich or poor, everyone's on that start line together.'

METATARSO-PHALANGEAL ARTICULATIONS ...

Postponing the Ice Marathon for a year meant that I could really build a solid training base for the run, as it was still over a year away. I hadn't started following any specific marathon-training plan yet, but there was no hurry as I had a pretty strong routine already established. The running group was continuing and I was generally doing two or three other runs a week plus a nice, slow two-hour run on most weekends.

One day I noticed a slight pain on the top of my left foot, behind the second toe. It didn't affect me while I was running, but would continue to ache a bit after I finished each run. It wasn't enough to make me limp, and mostly it was barely noticeable, so I continued to run with it. I ran in a local half marathon and I think my confidence got the better of me as I tried to run quite fast (for me), and break one hour 45 minutes. I achieved that time (1:44:50) but in the days following the race, the pain in my foot became noticeably more intense, and I decided I needed to see someone about it. The lesson here – if you're not an athlete, don't try to run fast.

I went to the nearest hospital and, after determining that it was not a psychiatric hospital, got some x-rays done on my foot. When the x-rays were ready and I first looked at them, I said,

'Excuse me, I think you may have the x-rays mixed up as this appears to be the x-ray of the flipper of a seal.' Sure, I do have webbed toes, but I was truly amazed at the shape and number of the bones in my foot, and its incredible likeness to some kind of aquatic creature. If you've never really looked at the bones in the human foot, you should, because they're amazing. There are 26 bones, 33 joints and more than 100 muscles, ligaments and tendons in each of your feet and ankles. During a 10-kilometre run, the average person takes about 8000 steps. If you break it down, that's a lot of bouncing around and jolting of all those little bones and muscles, and with all the differing running styles that we individual humans have, it's no wonder that there are so many freaky little pains and injuries that develop in our feet from time to time. The human foot is a beautifully designed piece of anatomy that has evolved over a couple of million years of walking upright and, regardless of whether you are an evolutionist or a creationist, you have to admit that the foot is pretty damn impressive.

There are differing opinions on the theory that, since the invention of shoes, the general health of human feet has declined. Runners are a group of people who obviously use their feet a lot, and rely on them being in good working order.

One trend that is gaining acceptance among the running community is barefoot running. The general idea being that if you use your feet in the way nature intended (without shoes) you will make your feet naturally stronger and you will be injured less. It makes perfect, logical sense to me, and though I don't run barefoot, I always spend parts of the day wearing no shoes, in an attempt to actually engage some of the poor little shoe-restricted ligaments and muscles that dwell within our ambulatory appendages. Going unshod is not unfamiliar to me as, growing up on an island in Queensland, I spent most of my childhood barefoot and didn't wear shoes to school until Grade 7. But this is not a book about barefoot running and I am certainly not an expert on running or feet.

Of the 26 bones in each foot, seven are called tarsal bones: the talus, calcaneus (heel bone), the lateral, intermediate and medial cuneiforms, cuboid, and navicular. All of those bones are located at the rear and top of your foot, just below and in front of your ankle. Then there are the metatarsals and phalanges (the long, finger-like toe bones). The big toe has two phalanges, and the other four toes have three phalanges each, called middle, distal and proximal.Even before I looked at all these bones in my x-rays, in my opinion my injury felt like a run-of-the-mill slight widening of the second metatarsophalangeal joint in the second toe which was causing synapsis and some soft tissue pain. It was obvious, but I could barely believe it when I took my x-rays to a specialist, and she said it looked to her like a slight widening of the second metatarsophalangeal joint in the second toe, which was causing synapsis and some soft tissue pain.

'Pfft,' I thought, 'what would she know?'

Well, a lot apparently, as after I Googled my diagnosis, I found that it was not an uncommon injury among the online running community. Boy oh boy, runners love talking about an injury online, and it is very helpful to know that other people are going through the same thing that you are. Often, it seems, due to the very specific nature of some running injuries, they get misdiagnosed or even remain undiagnosed. No matter what the obscure nature of your running injury, you can bet that someone out there has had it before you and can probably offer some assistance about treatment. I am sure if you searched on 'gradual bulging of the right kneecap after 6.25 kilometres of a 10-k run,' there would not only be an online forum and a support group, but quite probably a charity fun run raising funds for research and treatment of 'gradibulgakneeitis'.

The immediate advice I got from a podiatrist and my chiropractor was simply to stop running for a month and reassess after that length of time. That one month became two and then three months off. It is difficult to explain what it's like to have an injury that prevents you doing precisely what you want to be doing. Of course it's frustrating, but I would also throw in annoying, depressing, infuriating and challenging. One of the most difficult things for many people when starting running or any form of exercise is finding the motivation to get up, get going and be consistent. I was mentally ready and willing to get out there and run, but physically incapable of doing it. You would think that as I was coming off a great routine and having achieved the commitment to regular exercise that it would be simple just to replace the running with other activities. There was no reason I couldn't have kept doing all of my core and strength exercises and maybe some cycling or swimming while I was not able to run, and I hope some of you reading this could do that, but I couldn't. I lost motivation and felt resentment whenever I saw someone running along the street. I was taunted at every turn by things that reminded me of running. The bloke in the milk bar wearing runners – bah! The mums at the school drop-off wearing their running gear so they could go to the café looking like they had already exercised – phooey! The running magazine arriving in the post, full of pictures of fit-looking people, all happily *running* ... Aaaaggghh! Adding to my feeling of discontent was the knowledge that the Ice Marathon was looming on the horizon. A couple of months into the enforced lay-off, the Scaredies were travelling around the country on our final tour, and I gradually started to get my exercise mojo back by visiting the local pool in whatever country town we happened to be in and fluffing around for an hour or so. I won't say doing laps because I am not a great swimmer, but at least I was getting out there again, doing my own version of swimming, which was part water aerobics and part trying to not drown.

    The first run after three months off was cautious to say the least. I did three ks and my injured foot felt fine. When I finished there was still the slightest inkling that something wasn't right down there. It was just enough to make me aware of it. I ran every second day and by the end of the month I was up to a distance of eight kilometres with no major pain. I took another two weeks off, just to make sure, and now felt like I could really start to focus on the Ice Marathon preparation. With eight months to go until the race I did a 14-kilometre fun run, which was the longest distance I had run in five months. I got through it fine, but I couldn't say that everything was completely back to normal just yet. I would have to nurse this foot through the long runs of the upcoming training.

STAIRWAY TO HELL

If the road to heaven is paved with good intentions, then the road to the Ice Marathon was paved with soft sand, repetitive exercises and bad music. The training program that I adopted to prepare for this physically challenging run was a bit different to the one that I followed to do my first marathon. After reading some stories by people who had done the Antarctic run and talking to a couple of previous entrants, it sounded like the most difficult part of running in Antarctica was the soft surface, which drains your energy and tires your leg muscles more quickly than running on the road or a track. In one of the marathons they did there a few years back, they had 15 centimetres of snow a few days before the race, which caused no end of trouble for the competitors. My head filled with visions of me plodding through the snow with tennis racquets strapped to my feet.

As I didn't want my training to put too much stress on the tiny bones in my foot, I decided only to run three days per week, and never on consecutive days. I really concentrated on simply getting as fit as possible, so I started going to a gym three times a week to do 90 minutes of cardio on the days that I didn't run.

I hadn't been a member of a gym since the early 1990s and heard from my mate, Michael, about a new local gym that had started up and charged $4.50 per visit with no contract, so that sounded like a good place to start. The gym was located in an obscure area of an industrial park, between a panel beater and a commercial pastry maker, and it was well-equipped with plenty of new-looking fancy gym equipment and cardio machines – three bikes, four elliptical trainers, a rowing machine and a Stairmaster.

The Stairmaster, ingeniously named to entice anyone who wanted to master stairs, and designed by Sadist & Co. of Germany, looked like a normal set of three steps with handrails on both sides. The difference from normal stairs being that when you stood on a step, they all moved downwards and the bottom one disappeared, making you take another step while remaining at the same level. The steps then fiendishly reappeared at the top, forcing you into in a never-ending procession of stair climbing – surely many people's idea of hell. Good idea for a song though – 'Stairway to Hell'. I ignored the Stairmaster for a few weeks, but once I gathered the courage to use it (when there was no one else in the gym) I realised it gave an extremely thorough workout and was very useful to anyone who wanted to get really good at climbing stairs.

While sitting on any of the stationary bikes, due to what I can only imagine are some previous indiscretions in another life, you were forced to simultaneously watch three large television screens set up in front of you. They were tuned into the three main commercial television channels and as I was generally at the gym after 9 am, the shows on offer were the customary mindless morning shows littered with infomercials on the latest breakthroughs in bra technology and machines designed to transform your abs by getting you to ride some kind of pendulum-based mechanical bull contraption while balanced on your hands and knees. It sure seemed to be working for the steel-abbed young things in the ad. Could that really be me after only four E-Z payments of $99.95?

The televisions had an FM frequency listed over each set that you could tune into if you wanted to listen to the sound. As I didn't bring an FM tuner to the gym with me, I had to rely on the closed captioning, which conveniently provided subtitles for people in gyms on stationary bikes.

These subtitles interpreted what the person on screen was saying and sometimes they were even accurate. The half-hourly news broadcasts always offered some interesting mistakes in the subtitles, when they reported things like: '... *and that was Tony Abbott, who is* rubbing *against Kevin Rudd in the upcoming election ...*' or '... *to finish his blessing, The Pope said go in pee ...*'

A couple of hours on the cardio machines in a gym could pass fairly slowly, so you had to be inventive to pass the time. I would listen to Spanish lessons or music, sometimes I would bring along a Sudoku or a crossword – though this was a little more difficult while I was on the elliptical cross trainer – or I would just watch other people while trying not to get caught watching other people and occasionally catch other people watching me before I could watch them. Listening to music was sometimes difficult in this gym, as they would mostly play a commercial radio station belting out the 'Hits of Today and Tomorrow' SO LOUD I couldn't hear my own music on the little earphones jammed into my ears.

I would often go and see the one-armed man who ran the place while he was sitting at the front counter, and ask if he could turn the music down a bit.

'But people like it,' he would protest.

Here's an idea: how about you turn it down a bit and if people find that they can't do their workout as hard as they would like to because the latest Katy Perry song isn't making their ears bleed, then we can look at turning it up again. Also, there are only two other people in the gym at the moment; one is a skinny man in his 60s who looks like he would find André Rieu too loud, and the other is a young guy in a cut-off Nickelback t-shirt, lifting weights with an expression on his face like he is trying to pass a medicine ball. I don't think any of us are going to benefit by having to hear Danni Minogue's new single played at a volume that would make a helicopter pilot ask to have it turned down.

After a few weeks of doing just cardio exercises, I thought I should maybe do some weights to prepare my legs for the upcoming slog through the snow, so I started tentatively heading over to use some of the weight machines on the other side of the gym. It was like starting running again, as I kept expecting the experienced weight-machine users to ask to see my weight machine-licence. New technology in gym equipment had evidently come along in leaps and bounds since the early 1990s, and I was faced with 20 or 30 intricate-looking machines made of black and silver steel that looked a bit like a get-together of lame Transformers. If you've never used these pieces of equipment before, it can be quite confusing trying to work out exactly which machine does what. There's usually a seat of some sort, which is identifiable by the sweaty bum mark on it. Then there are either some handles or foam-covered extensions that hopefully, but not always, determine whether that particular machine is for the use of your arms or your legs.

To help newcomers like me, on each machine there was a little instruction plate with diagrams of what looked like a completely different piece of equipment and cryptic instructions that said things like:

> *Sit laterally, keeping thighs flush with seat (but backs of knees off the containing arm). In one movement, lower your quadriceps between knee and ear, keeping hips above ankles, yet maintaining engaged abs while lightly gripping handles. Keep deltoids fluid yet inelastic, exhaling 90 degrees, with full extension while completing soft locking. Avoid hyper-engagement.*

After a few weeks of confused pushing and pulling, Deirdre thankfully came to the rescue and devised a program for me specifically aimed at improving my running technique. Judging by the exercises she got me to do, this generally involved parts of the body that I thought didn't have much to do with running at all. There were lots of arm exercises and plenty to do with something called my 'core', including an exercise I think she got off the internet called 'planking'. I had read that a few people had died while doing the plank on hotel balconies and the like, so I was a bit reticent at first.

For those of you interested in what I actually did for my gym training, I will list it here.

Three days per week:
- Various cardio – 60 mins
- Rowing machine – 10 mins
- Skipping – 800-1000

Weight program with eight-kilogram weights:
- Split squat lunges – 10 each side
- Physio ball leg curl × 12
- Dumbbell bench press × 12
- Dumbbell squat to press × 12
- Split dumbbell curl press × 12
- Dumbbell pullover extension × 12
- Plank – two minutes
- Ball raises × 20
- Leg raises × 10
- Crab 5 × 5
- Plank – two minutes
- Repeat weight program

On alternate days I would go for runs of varying lengths, usually six to eight kilometres, and Sunday was my preferred day for long runs. I tried to do as many of those long runs on trails if I could, concentrating on time more than distance.

Judging by the results of past competitors, I knew the Ice Marathon was probably going to take me between five and a half to eight hours, so I tried to get out for around four hours at a time, having plenty of walking breaks.

Seven weeks before I was due to depart, I heard about a Melbourne man called Tristan Miller, who in 2010 had completed 52 marathons in 52 weeks in 42 countries. The 2010 Ice Marathon in December of that year was his fifty-first and penultimate marathon. He was now doing some motivational speaking and I got in contact with him to ask him about his experience in Antarctica. He was a very affable and friendly man – full of life and completely and beautifully crazy– and he agreed to meet me at a café in Melbourne. Before we met I thought, 'What on earth do you ask a bloke who has just accomplished what he has?' It was an amazing achievement, full of adventures and travel stories and illness, but finding out about the previous year's exploits was going to have to wait, as I was more interested in asking him about the specifics of Antarctica and the Ice Marathon. I had the equipment list with all the recommended clothing, but I wanted to know exactly what Tristan had worn, down to the last sock and glove. Was it really that hard physically? What were the weather conditions like for him? He usually did his marathons in about three and a half hours and it took him over five hours to complete the run in Antarctica. Wow, that surely meant I was looking at a time of over six hours. I grilled him on the clothing that he took to wear in the race and around the camp and we compared notes, as I had procured most of my kit by that stage. I was still trying to get hold of some decent boots to wear in Antarctica and Tristan generously insisted that I take the pair that he had bought for last year, a very heavy and bulky pair that should do the trick. I told him I was bidding on a good pair of boots on eBay, but he made me take his pair just in case. He asked me about my training and one thing he stressed to me about the surface in

Antarctica was that it was like running in soft sand, and that I should do a two-hour run per week along the beach. Because I am good at doing what I am told and because I was starting to get a bit scared about Antarctica and if I was actually going to be able to finish the run, I took his advice. Every Wednesday until I departed, I travelled over the Westgate Bridge and ran from Port Melbourne to Elwood along the beach and back. Running on the uneven, soft surface of a well-used beach that is full of footmarks and sticks, not to mention dog poo and syringes, made my leg muscles very sore, but I believe it was a 'good' kind of sore. The risks of running on soft sand are sprains, tendonitis or damage to my Achilles, but the worst thing that happened to me during those beach runs was getting chased by a small yappy dog, and copping a nasty case of sunburn on a typical Melbourne spring day that started in heavy rain and, 15 minutes later, switched to burning sunshine for the rest of the run.

DODGING FORKLIFTS AND FROZEN PEAS

I had heard that some of the previous participants in the Ice Marathon had, as part of their training, done some running in a giant industrial freezer to simulate the conditions of extreme cold and test out their clothing. Not one to be left out, I thought that sounded like a great idea and set about finding a giant industrial freezer. The *Yellow Pages* didn't have any listings at all under the heading of giant industrial freezers, and if you Google 'giant industrial freezer' you get links to a company that builds giant industrial freezers (duh), as well as info on the world's largest freezing trawler. It's a factory freezing ship, useful if you have to freeze tonnes of fresh fish or a thousand minke whales or whatever. Incidentally, on this page I also read about something called a 'factory squid jigger' which is either a sophisticated squid catching ship, or someone in a squid factory who jiggers squid.

Anyway, I knew that these giant industrial freezers must exist somewhere in Melbourne and, as I live in a part of the city where there are more trucks than cars, I simply drove around until I saw a semi-trailer freezer truck and followed it. Eventually it came to its final destination – a giant industrial freezer.

That was step one taken care of – locate giant industrial freezer, but what next?

I sat outside in my car trying to think of what on earth I was going to say, and to whom for that matter, that would convince someone in charge of a giant industrial freezer to let me in. I hoped that there was a possibility that maybe someone inside was an old Triple M listener, or had seen me on the telly (I had appeared on the *Sale of the Century* gift shop, for goodness sake), and how that might make them somehow bend the rules on letting a member of the public run around on ice-covered concrete on their business premises.

After a few mock conversations with myself, much to the amusement of the truck driver parked across the street, I jotted down the name of the company and headed home to contact them from the safety (and anonymity) of the telephone. After a few more mock conversations, I mustered up the courage and dialled.

'Good morning, Giant Industrial Freezers Incorporated, how may I direct your call?' shrilled the receptionist.

With all the confidence of someone who has just rehearsed what they are about to say a dozen times, I said:

'Hello, I would like to talk to someone about running around in your giant freezer.'

Pause ...

I hadn't anticipated an awkward pause like this, so I thought she obviously needed more information.

'You see, I need to simulate conditions of an Antarctic marathon.'

Pause ...

Okay, I need to bring out the big guns.

'I am making a documentary about an Antarctic marathon, my name is Rusty – I used to be in group called Scared Weird Little Guys – you may have heard of me.'

Longer pause ...

Damn! I should have kept that one up my sleeve.

She finally said: 'Umm, I guess you could talk to Gary – but he's out. Should I tell him you called? ... Randy, was it?'

'Rusty.'

'From Lano and Woodley, was it?'

'Yes, Lano and Woodley.'

Gary never called.

My giant industrial freezer dream was going absolutely nowhere when, out of the blue, a seemingly unrelated phone call started the ball rolling in a different direction.

I was contacted by a company called BFG Australia, who were interested in having Rusty and Another Guy (my new comedy group) perform for a Christmas function. I spoke on the phone to Genevieve, the woman organising the gig, to run through the details of the event and I asked all the usual questions you have to ask when booking one of these shows.

How many people will be in the audience?

How long do we have to play for?

Do we get free drinks? Etc.

'And what business are you in there at BFG Australia?' I asked, sounding like I really cared.

'Oh, we are a frozen foods storage company,' she said.

My brain snapped to attention as the words coming through the phone swirled around in my head: *Frozen ... Storage ... Free drinks ...*

'You wouldn't happen to have some kind of giant industrial freezer out there at BFG Australia, would you Genevieve?' I asked, as if it was something I asked about every gig we did.

'Of course we do, Rusty!' she laughed. 'Would you like to come out and run around in your recently acquired thermal layering system of clothing to simulate the conditions of an Antarctic marathon? I'll get Norman from our giant freezer logistics department to give you a call.'

She didn't actually say it exactly like that, but you can pretty much guess how the conversation went, and suddenly things were looking up for me, giant industrial freezer-wise.

A few days later I spoke to Norman from giant freezer logistical administration or whatever it was called. We made small talk for a while about footy and frozen food logistics and how he loved our song called 'Sonia'. Then I explained that 'Sonia' was not a Scaredies song, but actually a Lano and Woodley song.

With all that sorted, he said it would be no problem at all to come out and do some running in their giant industrial freezer.

'Just one thing,' said Norman. 'I am a little bit concerned about our old friends Health and Safety. Could you come up with a little piece of paper that we can both sign that promises you are not going to sue us if you slip over?'

'Slip over?' I said. 'Oh come on, Norman, it's only ice-covered concrete, how slippery can it be?'

Norm got a little more serious: 'Well, I know nothing bad is going to happen. I just think that we should get something signed ... you know ... in case something bad happens.'

'Sure thing, Norm!' I said. 'I'll call my lawyers and have them draft up something for us.'

Now, as we all know, 'calling my lawyers' actually means 'search the internet for free legal contracts', so I spent a rather dull morning sifting through an alarmingly large number of 'Free Legal Contract' websites. Frequently, I would locate exactly the type of contract I needed only to discover that when a lawyer's website says 'Free Legal Contract' it means anything but 'Free Legal Contract'.

Annoyingly, the proprietors of these sites had them configured so that you couldn't even use cut and paste, damn them! Ah lawyers; always one step ahead of us poor saps searching for free legal advice. The only thing worse than a lawyer not prepared to give free legal advice is one that knows how to configure a website to not allow cut and paste.

Eventually, I found a very legal-sounding, generic contract called an indemnity agreement, which I simply typed into another document from the screen – take that, lawyers! I edited it down to a paragraph, removing most of the lengthy phrases, which were filled with unnecessary legalese, and replaced them with words like 'wholly', 'Party A' and 'restitution'. Even though the agreement probably would have satisfied Norman, I thought I should have it checked out, so I called a lawyer friend to quickly look it over for me.

Remember, all I wanted to do was head over to a giant industrial freezer, put on all my layers of newly acquired Antarctic standard running gear and run a few laps. It goes without saying that I was going to be extremely careful. The last thing I wanted to do at this stage was to get injured slipping on some icy concrete and jeopardise the whole trip.

It seemed simple enough. But somehow, even lawyer friends can't keep it simple, can they?

After a few hours of looking over the agreement, my lawyer buddy called me back.

'Okay Rusty, I've had a look over your indemnity agreement and I am a little concerned at some of the wording.'

'In what way are you concerned?' I asked.

'Well, it's fine to say that you won't sue them if you slip over and injure yourself, but what if the roof caves in?'

'What?' I said.

'If something happens that's your own fault then that's fine not to sue them, but you don't want to indemnify yourself from something that's their fault.'

'Like the roof caving in,' I said. 'Look, I am sure it will be fine. I promise I will be really careful.'

'What if a box of frozen peas falls on your head?' (He actually said that.)

'Hmm ...'

'What if you're left in a vegetative state and your Estate decides to go ahead with legal proceedings on behalf of your family?'

Jesus! This was not sounding really as fun and exciting as it was a few minutes ago.

'All right, thanks mate,' I told him. 'I will have a chat to Norman from the industrial freezer place [search the internet for a more detailed form] and get back to you.'

'Okay Rusty,' he said, 'now you know I am going to have to charge you fo–'

I didn't hear the last bit of what he said as I had already hung up the phone.

Against my extensive legal advice, I decided to go ahead and do the run anyway with the simple, generic indemnity agreement.

A few days later, on a sunny Melbourne afternoon, Norman met me in the front office of BFG and, even with the signed indemnity agreement, I got the feeling he was still a little nervous. He shook my hand, looked furtively from side to side to check no one was watching us, then said in a low voice, 'Follow me.'

I felt like I was in a scene from *The Sopranos* and I was about to buy some stolen frozen goods from the back of a truck.

'Yew call dis a focken baax o' frozen focken peas, asshole?'

Norman and I had to cross a road to get to the giant industrial freezer.

'Why are you looking at the roof?' he asked.

'Oh, no reason,' I said. 'By the way, when was the last time the roof was replaced on this freezer building?'

'Funny you should ask, it was replaced about seven years ago,' he laughed. 'The extremely cold temperatures actually weaken the roof trusses.'

'Oh great,' I thought.

'Why, do you think it's going to collapse?' he laughed even harder.

I laughed along with him, though not quite as uproariously.

Norman showed me into the staff room of the giant freezer and I got changed into all my Ice Marathon gear for the first time. It felt a bit like when I was nine years old on the day I got my soccer uniform and tried it on for the first time at home. The first thing I noticed walking into minus 18 degrees Celsius was that it actually wasn't as bad as I thought it was going to be, and I don't mean to sound funny about it, but I was expecting the cold to take my breath away and hit me in the chest, making me shiver. Sure it was cold, but at times during the next hour, I could remove my gloves completely to take photos and adjust my clothing and it didn't hurt, though after about 30 seconds it would start to get a bit uncomfortable. One of the workers cleared a section of the freezer for me with a forklift so I had two rows about 20 metres long all to myself. Forget about icy concrete, one thing that would really wreck my afternoon, let alone my plans to go to Antarctica, would be getting run over by a forklift loaded with frozen goods.

My little running track in the freezer was dwarfed by towering industrial shelving, stacked 10 metres high with boxes of frozen goods like Jenny Craig diet meals, fish fingers and frozen mini-quiches. I certainly wouldn't be starving if a storm blew in and I was trapped there, unlike poor old Captain Scott when he and his unfortunate companions were confined to their tent on their way back from the South Pole with supplies running low. If only they could have reached outside the tent to grab another Jenny Craig meal from the towering stack they probably would have lived to tell the tale, though I am sure Scott's diary would have made mention of the lack of caloric content.

> *Day 132: Great God! Another meal of skinless teriyaki chicken and vegetables has left us wanting in the calorie department. I fear that too many more of these may be the end of us. RF Scott.*

With an endless supply of frozen goods, Captain Oates would never have met his downfall there, and instead of being known for his famous last words, 'I am just going outside and may be some time,' he would now be known for saying, 'I'm just going outside, anyone for another mini-quiche?'

I searched high and low, literally, for any precariously placed boxes of frozen peas that might fall on my head, but thankfully didn't see any. Before I started running, I walked around the circuit and inspected it with a fine tooth comb looking for any signs of ice or frozen patches that I might slip on, but it appeared to be quite safe. I also gave the roof a good going over and, even to my untrained eye, the trusses seemed reasonably solid.

I started jogging very slowly, doing 10 laps clockwise, then 10 in the reverse direction. I immediately had trouble with my goggles, which fogged up so I couldn't see a thing. I had brought along three pairs to try out and none of them worked well. This was going to be a problem. Not just because of the possibility of running into some boxes of fish fingers in the freezer, but if I couldn't see the ground during the run in Antarctica, it would make for a very difficult experience. I knew that the air in Antarctica was supposed to be extremely dry, which would probably help, and the air in the freezer was quite moist, judging by the amount of ice that was forming around my face in the small amount of time I had spent in there, but I would certainly have to look into new eyewear. I kept on running around in the freezer for about an hour, probably doing about eight kilometres. The other pieces of clothing that I was wearing seemed to be suitable for the temperature of minus 18 degrees. My feet were toasty warm and I hadn't sweated very much. Of course there was no wind in the freezer and all of the recommended clothing I had assembled was aimed at wind protection, so how the wind in Antarctica would affect how I felt remained unknown.

THE MOST INTRICATE ONLINE SCAM EVER?

To apply for the Ice Marathon you simply go through the website and send the race organiser Richard Donovan an email expressing your interest, then you pay a deposit and that's it.

Richard was extremely easy to deal with, answering all of my questions about possible filming difficulties and technical issues promptly, while being as helpful as possible. He went out of his way to ensure that Bradley could attend the race and make the most of his opportunities to film everything that he could. I got the impression that nothing would faze him.

An accomplished ultramarathon runner, Richard organised the first ever marathon at the North Pole in 2002 and started the Antarctic Ice Marathon in January 2006.

In February 2012, Richard attempted to break his own record to become the first person to run seven marathons on seven continents in less than five days.

Starting in Antarctica, at the Russian Novo base, he set off on a marathon several hours before a Russian cargo plane's scheduled return flight to Cape Town. After completing the first marathon in four hours 30 minutes, he flew to Cape Town, travelling by himself with just one carry-on bag. When he arrived in Cape Town, he had nine hours to disembark, leave the airport, run a marathon and return to check in for a flight to São Paulo, Brazil, where he repeated the process.

From there it was onto Miami, London, Hong Kong and finally Sydney, where he crossed the line four days, 22 hours and three minutes after he started. At each location he was met by local running experts and officials to ensure he ran the correct distance on custom courses. When he got to the finish line in Sydney, he had run 295 kilometres and flown 43,530 kilometres, and after he reached Hong Kong he couldn't keep any food or fluids down, not even water. He got desperate during the final marathon and chanced a beer during the race – 'for some carbs'. It was the first time something had stayed down in days.

The successful attempt received worldwide press coverage and Richard raised plenty of much-needed funds for his chosen charity, an organisation called GOAL, which works to alleviate the suffering of people affected by famine and drought in the Horn of Africa.

If you think Richard had it hard, think of the poor passenger seated next to him on the flight from Hong Kong to Sydney. If there's one thing worse than a hungry, thirsty Irishman reeking of body odour to sit next to on a long flight, it's a hungry, thirsty Irishman reeking of body odour who can't even keep a beer down.

Even with all the publicity surrounding his incredible feat, if Richard wasn't raising money for a charity that he strongly believed in, I got the impression that he really couldn't care less if anybody even knew about it.

And what goal could possibly top that feat? Richard would like to be the first person to actually run across Antarctica. Start at one side, go to the South Pole, and then continue on to the other side. He says he wants to do it by the end of the year.

What would Shackleton or Scott think of that? With the years of preparation and tons of supplies and dogs and manpower that it took for them just to get to Antarctica, to think it could be possible for someone to run across Antarctica is nothing less than amazing.

The Most Intricate Online Scam Ever?

Three months before the planned date of the Ice Marathon I transferred the balance of what I owed electronically. I sent Richard an email with the details and said, 'Now I just hope you are a real person and not the proprietor of one of the most intricate online scams that has ever existed.'

NOW JUST SIGN HERE ... AND HERE ... AND HERE ...

Once I was financially committed to going to Antarctica and attempting this marathon, I started receiving some of the many requisite official contracts, medical forms and information guides from Antarctic Network International, the US-based logistics company that transports and accommodates the Ice Marathon participants.

I have spoken about the complexity of the *Hot Seat Millionaire* contracts and the intricacy of trying to appease health and safety laws while running in an industrial freezer, but if you want to see really complicated legal agreements, sign up to travel to the remotest part of the world, a place that experiences some of the most extreme weather on earth, to take part in something as physically challenging as a marathon. Then, my friends, you will see some serious fucking pieces of paper.

Before they would let me on the plane, I had to read, initial and/or sign the following documents:

- Ice Marathon clothing list
- Antarctic clothing list
- Guidelines for visiting Antarctica
- Biosecurity and equipment cleaning guidelines
- Medical information form

- Personal information form
- ANI terms and conditions contract
- ANI waiver contract
- Union Glacier Camp information and conditions
- Punta Arenas information

After printing them all out, it took me the best part of a week, and about $80 worth of printing ink, to get through reading and signing them all. On a side note, how can it now be cheaper to buy an actual new printer than it is to replace all of the printing cartridges on my existing printer? What kind of rare ingredients are they using in printing ink? Panda saliva? Baby dolphin's tears?

Being responsible for the transportation of humans to such a remote and inhospitable place as Antarctica obviously comes with a massive responsibility, so I had no problem filling out all the forms in full detail, to appease whatever conditions were required to get there. I went off to see my doctor for a full medical examination and was happy to see that everything was working fine and there were no issues or medication that I needed to concern myself with. My blood pressure was a bit high and I have a family history of that. Even with my consistent running, I am usually on the borderline of recommended blood pressure levels. I comforted myself with the thought that in extremely cold temperatures, it's probably better to have a bit of extra high pressure to send the blood pumping through your veins to help keep the cold at bay. My doctor asked if I wanted to get any flu shots or, as I was travelling to South America, immunisation shots for typhoid or rabies. I laughed and said no, as I was only really in transit through South America and thought that those germs surely couldn't survive down in Antarctica.

Adventure Network International (ANI) want to make it really clear to you before you travel that they're not stuffing around when they tell you that the continent of Antarctica is a dangerous place to visit. The waiver forms include many detailed descriptions of how you can injure yourself and/or die there, including, but not limited to: frostbite, altitude sickness, excessive solar radiation, falling down crevasses, snow blindness, avalanches, slipping on ice and extreme low temperatures affecting metabolism. Added to that is the obvious remoteness and lack of full medical facilities if something serious does go wrong, plus the fact that inclement weather could hinder the ability to get you back to civilisation within a reasonable time frame.

What they are basically telling you is that it's dangerous and if you hurt yourself, it's not their fault, but they will do everything in their power to help you. Needless to say, I thoroughly investigated my options for travel insurance and spent a good deal of time combing through the fine print of travel insurance contracts (more bloody contracts) to see if running in Antarctica was covered. I was happy to find out that running is the only sport covered by travel insurance, as long as it is not a professional race, and there was no special mention of Antarctica. Regardless, I spent a long time on the phone, triple checking all the details with the insurance company representative, as all participants in the race were informed that to get emergency transportation out of Antarctica and back to Chile would cost over $200,000.

WHAT KIND OF SHOES DO YOU WEAR?

This was by far the most common question I got when people found out I was going to Antarctica to run a marathon – besides what … ? and … why? – 'What kind of shoes do you wear?' It's a good question and it was certainly the first thing that I wondered when I looked on the Ice Marathon website all those months ago. After registering, you get sent the 'recommended clothing list' and I immediately set about trying to find the appropriate gear. I soon learned that in Australia there is just not the market for the type of clothing that I was going to need, and while I found some of the undergarments and socks in local shops, most of the specialist gear was going to have to come from overseas. Thanks to the internet or 'super shopping highway' as I came to refer to it, it wasn't too difficult to track down most of the gear.

To perform a physical challenge like a marathon in Antarctica, you need to use what I call the 'Sara Lee Danish system' – layer upon layer upon layer. The layering serves to keep you warm enough, yet the clothing also has to be light enough so you can run in it. The general idea of a layering system is that you have a base layer to wick the sweat away from your body; a mid fleece layer to provide insulation; and an outer shell layer to provide protection from the wind.

Here is what was recommended to us to wear for the Ice Marathon:

Feet:
- One or two pairs of sock liners.
- One pair of wool blend socks.
- One pair of trail running shoes.
- Two tennis racquets.
  (Only kidding, we did not have to use tennis racquets.)

The shoes that I took were Under Armour Janan trail running shoes. I decided to try two pairs of wool blend socks with no sock liners.

Legs:
- A pair of mid-weight base layer tights
- A pair of outer windproof shell pants.

I took both of these to wear in the race. The windproof pants were from a hiking shop and from what I could tell were fairly common among hikers from Canada or northern Europe who go out in the winter. A middle layer for the legs was unnecessary if you were going to be running most of the time.

Torso:
- Base layer – long-sleeved fabric that can wick sweat away from the body.
  I took an Under Armour long-sleeved thermal top.
- Mid layer – long-sleeved fleece top or microstretch zip top. I decided to use the latter, which I found locally.
- Outer layer – a light windproof shell fabric jacket with zips.

When I got this ($600) jacket I thought they were joking, as it was so light and flimsy. I have worn $10 raincoats that were warmer, but who can argue with a tag that offers '... *total windproofness and maximum breathability, combining the comfort of a soft mid-layer and the water resistance of a shell in one garment*'.

When it comes to levels of 'windproofness' you can't argue with 'total'.

Hands:
- One pair of thin glove liners to fit inside mid-weight gloves.
- One pair of good quality insulated mittens.

Head and neck:
- One balaclava.
- One facemask.
- One hat or beanie.
- One neck gaiter.

I went for an all-in-one style balaclava/facemask with a hole for my nose and breathable mesh over my mouth. It also had a built in neck gaiter, which is basically a nice warm extra bit that goes around your neck. I also had a thin cotton beanie to wear over the top of my head.

Eyewear:
- Good quality ski goggles.

So that was the clothing for the race covered. Then another clothing and equipment list was sent through that listed general wear for standard Antarctic conditions, which I won't list in full here. The three-layer system came into play again and the clothing involved lots of warm, expensive-sounding words like Polartec, Goretex, fleece, and thermal. Knee-high winter boots rated to minus 60 degrees Celsius were also required. As these boots were all over $250 retail, with postage costs of $50, I tried desperately for months to secure a used pair on eBay from some northern Canadian hunter or Skidoo rider from Kirkland Lake, but I was unsuccessful. Then Tristan Miller came to the rescue by giving me his boots, even though I told him that I was in the middle of bidding on eBay for a virtually new pair of super-extra-ultra Canadian boots rated to minus 100 degrees. I ended up getting them from Tasmania for the grand total of $22. Sure they were two sizes too big for me, but that meant I could wear lots of pairs of the cozy woollen socks that my mum had knitted for me, plus they weren't as bulky as the ones Tristan gave me, which would help with my packing. Other items on the list were sunscreen (SPF 50 because of that big freaking hole in the ozone layer that is smack bang over Antarctica), lip balm, sunglasses and a one-litre plastic water bottle (with a wide opening) to use as a pee bottle, but more on that later.

The protection and maintenance of Antarctica as a pristine environment is something that the ANI takes very seriously. So seriously that it has its own three-page information sheet informing impending visitors to Antarctica about the importance of not bringing any foreign seeds, sand, diseases or raw chicken into the continent. It also warns that while you are in Antarctica, do not feed any animals, take all your rubbish with you and be careful not to remove or stand in guano, seal feces or placenta, which crushed any hopes I had of adding to my extensive seal placenta collection.

THE EVIL BEYOND THE DOOR

With less than two weeks to go before departing for the Antarctic, all my training, preparation and planning was proceeding as well as could have been expected.

For the previous two months, I had stopped drinking alcohol and was maintaining a disciplined diet to maximise the training and lose some weight to prevent me from sinking into the snow any further than I had to.

Then something happened that threatened to blow the whole trip and undo all the hard work that I had done up to that point. I was in Brisbane having just performed with my new group 'Rusty and Another Guy' at the Steve Irwin Foundation charity gala. You can imagine I was on quite a high, adrenaline still pumping through my veins after slaying a room full of drunken corporate types, buzzed to the gills on banquet wine and the thrill of seeing Bindi Irwin in person.

I was back in the hotel and it was quite late, around 1 am. The only noise inside the room was the low volume of the television. I was flicking the channels between a Spanish *fútbol* match, a B-grade horror flick called *The Evil Beyond*, and an infomercial featuring a man shouting at me to convert my door into a gym.

I was startled from my semi-conscious, rambling thoughts by a knock at the door.

This was it. The moment I had been dreading for two months had finally arrived. I gulped, closed my eyes and took a deep breath. I had to be brave and face what was waiting for me on the other side of the door. No! I thought. I can't go through with it ... Why now? Why me?

The knocking came again, this time a little harder and more impatiently and a voice followed the knock this time. A clear, calm voice that belied its more sinister intentions ...

'Room service.'

All that hard training, all those long kilometres and hours at the gym, all that discipline gone ...

If there is a person out there who can resist an invitation to free room service, they are a rare breed indeed. I am definitely not that person.

Of course it wasn't a real blowout of my training and it was going to take more than one serve of late night room service nachos to undo everything up to that point so I thought, let the carb loading begin!

NO ENTIENDO

To get to Antarctica and the Ice Marathon, I first had to get to Chile in South America to meet up with the other competitors and catch our plane down to the Great White South. I thought this would be a good motivation to learn to speak Spanish. Remember that John and I had first dabbled in learning a bit of Spanish back in the mid-1990s, when we would put our language learning cassettes in the rental car stereo as we drove around the USA.

I had visited Mexico a couple of times and used a bit of the language there, and I maintained a few of the basics, but I was essentially starting all over again.

I researched Spanish language learning online and realised that language learning cassettes, of course, had been largely replaced by podcasts. I found one called *Coffee Break Spanish*, hosted by, oddly enough, two Scottish presenters. I downloaded a few episodes onto my iPod and whenever I was out on a long run, or down at the gym, I would try to learn Spanish as spoken by two Scots. I could often be seen, early on a Sunday morning, running the streets of Williamstown or down a lonely country road, repeating phrases like '*¿Dónde está el baño?*' (Where is the toilet?) loudly to myself.

I enjoyed the challenge of committing new words to memory and I also enjoyed speaking the new phrases in a Spanish accent. For years as part of my job I had had to do the odd accent, so I believed that I would be more understandable if I spoke with the correct inflection. My Spanish accent ended up sounding like a cross between Speedy Gonzalez and Antonio Banderas.

The podcasts were good to learn from, but to really get the hang of a new language, it helps if you can practise with a native speaker. A friend who owns a local restaurant had recently employed an Ecuadorian girl, Carolina, who was now living in Melbourne with her husband, Javier. When we were introduced in the restaurant one night, I thought it was a perfect time to practise some Spanish, and said in my rehearsed lingo:

'*Voy a Chile en Noviembre y voy a Antarctica correr un maratón.*' Which means, not surprisingly, 'I am going to Chile in November and am going to Antarctica to run a marathon.'

Carolina then answered in Spanish, which to me sounded like;

'*Chulalararaldaladalmanavonablahblahblah?*'

As most people who have travelled to another country and learned a few words of a new language would attest, it's one thing to ask a question like 'Where is the train station?' and another thing completely to have any hope of understanding the answer to that question.

So I got to practise using Spanish each time we went to the restaurant, giving orders for every person at the table, and I also met up with Carolina at a café some afternoons to learn some basic conversational Spanish. So by the time I departed for Chile, I felt like I was well prepared to put my new language skills into practise.

PACKING EXPECTATIONS ... AND A UKULELE

The day of departure finally arrived.

I awoke early, not because I had been nervously tossing and turning all night, but because my flight left at 6 am, though I didn't sleep well. Questions kept going over and over in my mind. Am I ready? Have I forgotten anything? Could I have done more training? I kept having dreams about running on snow and ice. You know that dream where you are at school with no clothes on and everyone's laughing? My dream involved being in Antarctica in minus 20 degrees with no clothes on but no one's laughing. There's no one else there but me, and I'm crying. Not because of the cold, but because I am worried that my shrunken, frozen penis will appear on camera. Why did I agree to make a movie about this?

I had packed and repacked three times while trying to solve the age-old question of one bag or two. After using puzzle skills that would make a jigsaw champion jealous, I managed to fit everything perfectly into one bag. I had all of the specialist gear needed to run in the Antarctic: boots, shoes, socks, hats, gloves and a jar of Vegemite. Then, the day before departure, I got a call from the mad marathon man Tristan Miller. He asked if I still needed his boots, because his French mate, Clement, was also going to Antarctica to do the Ice Marathon and he needed some boots and could I take them over for him? I said sure, no problem, and thus I was taking two, loosely packed, bags. This turned out to be a blessing in disguise as I could now pack my ukulele in the second bag. My mum always said you'll get invited to parties if you have something to play. I wasn't quite sure how this rule fitted into the upcoming trip, as in the unlikely event that there was a party while I was in Antarctica, it was quite likely that I would crack an invite to it with or without a ukulele. Nonetheless, I quite liked the idea of taking a ukulele to a place where few, if any, ukuleles had been before.

That brings up an interesting question: am I doing this whole thing to try and do something that not many people have done before? I have to say that was not one of the reasons I found myself packing for a marathon in Antarctica.

If I wanted to be the first in the world to do something, then I would have done the race wearing a penguin suit or something like that. Besides, I had already organised a Mexican wave of flash bulbs at the MCG, and I don't reckon anyone has ever done that before, so I didn't feel like I had anything to prove to set me apart from the rest of the world. So why was I doing the Ice Marathon?

Was it really just because I had finished up performing in a comedy group for the last 20 years?

Who knows?

That couldn't be the only reason. All that I knew was that when the Scaredies finished after all that time, I needed to do something to put a full stop after it and help me move on to the next part of my life, and this insane idea of running a marathon in Antarctica came along at the right time.

Maybe it was just convenient that I liked running and I found out that there was a marathon in Antarctica, a place I had been obsessed with for two decades, and I could combine those two facts into a physical and mental challenge that was somewhere exotic.

THE FLIGHT

Regardless of what my motivation was, I was certainly about to depart on the journey of a lifetime. After the obligatory goodbyes and a few get togethers with family and well-wishing friends, I was looking forward to getting away from Melbourne, spending some time by myself and commencing my big adventure.

I usually liked to be a bit low-key about sharing news of impending exciting experiences. Many years in the entertainment industry had taught me that you should never believe you are going to be doing something until you are actually in the act of doing it. I have been involved in so many situations where the Scaredies had been promised amazing gigs in exotic places and television shows and high-paying advertising campaigns and much of the time they fell through. Even though it was difficult sometimes, I learned it's best to keep incredibly exciting sounding events to yourself until they happen. It's just as exciting sharing your news about stuff after it has actually occurred, and then, only if it comes up in conversation. What's that old proverb about a bar of gold in your pocket is still a bar of gold.

Contrary to this hard-won wisdom, I hadn't been keeping quiet about this upcoming trip to Antarctica at all. In fact just the opposite. I could hardly help it, though. I had just finished up with the Scaredies, and most people I spoke to were aware of that, so the obvious question I got asked was, 'So, Rusty, now that the Scaredies have finished, what are you up to?' I could hardly just say, 'Oh, a bit of this and a bit of that.' I couldn't help myself, because it's not often you get to say, 'Well, I'm just about to head off to Antarctica to run a marathon.' And when you do say something like that, you can't just leave it there and say, 'And what about you?' No, out come all the questions about shoes and clothing and jokes about penguins and polar bears and tennis racquets on your feet.

Not helping in my quest to keep a bit of a lid on it was the fact that I was still doing the odd radio spot here and there, so suddenly I found myself a little out of my depth as the go-to expert on marathons and Antarctica. As it was the 100-year anniversary of Amundsen and Scott reaching the South Pole, and 100 years since Sir Douglas Mawson had departed from Hobart to lead the Australian Antarctic Expedition, stories about Antarctica were appearing in the media virtually daily. During all the years of doing press spots for the Scaredies, I never minded talking about shows and tours and doing songs or jokes or whatever, but I had never felt very comfortable just talking about myself and that's what I was now doing, a lot. I thought more than once that I better actually complete this bloody thing, or I am going to look like a right tool.

I departed at 6 am on a Thursday morning and went straight to Sydney to catch the flight to Santiago, Chile. From there it was on to Punta Arenas, located at the very southern tip of South America, to meet up with the rest of the participants before heading to our final destination – the Union Glacier Camp in Antarctica.

Sydney was where I met up with Bradley, the documentary maker, who had come down from his home in Brisbane. He had made the trip down to Melbourne quite a few times in the last few months to capture footage for the documentary of me running, talking to doctors and experts, running, having ice-baths and running. I asked him if we should get some of the obligatory travel documentary shots of me doing things like checking in, finding my seat and sleeping on the plane. He is

The Flight

very good, Bradley, he knows what he wants and he refused to do any of those shots.

'That's bullshit!' he barked, 'I'm not going to have this doco full of those typical staged airport shots!' before making me walk around a corner seven times, looking for a place to sit and read a book.

I was well supplied with things to do to pass the time on the flight. Having done over 800 flights with the Scaredies, I now suffer from fear-of-having-nothing-to-do-on-a-plane-itis, and even for a one-hour flight I will be stocked to the gills with various knick knacks and puzzles to keep me occupied. I found my seat and immediately started unpacking my arsenal of attention engaging articles. I had my iPhone, an iPad, two books, three samurai Sudokus, my Spanish lesson notes and a cryptic crossword and as soon as we were underway, I ignored all of them and started playing battleships against Bradley on the in-flight entertainment system.

My legs were uncomfortable as I was wearing knee-high compression socks. Man those things are tight. But, with all the flying I was about to do, the last thing I wanted to get before the run was a case of that Deep Throat Veinbrosis or whatever it's called.

We stopped off in Auckland for two hours on the way over, and to pass the time Bradley had me walk through the airport with a thoughtful look on my face, to show some of the deeper feelings that I was experiencing regarding the Ice Marathon. I wish I was a better actor, because as soon as I started thinking about doing this Antarctic run, my expression changed from thoughtful to worried and concerned. Even though the training had all gone to plan and my long runs had been ... well ... long, I had been having some doubts about being able to complete the Ice Marathon. Two weeks previously I had watched an Italian documentary on the 2010 race and some of the footage was extreme to say the least. Even though the voice over was in

Italian, you could tell that the competitors were having a very bad time, not only from the pained looks on their faces, but also from the dramatic music and title of the show – *'Planeta Extrema – ¡questa é roba seria!* or something like that.

With shots of the wind-blown glacier that the race is run on and the drama of the winning runner crossing the line and bursting into tears, then revealing his blistered and frost-bitten feet, this run looked seriously difficult and I began to question why I even thought that it might ever be a good idea, and that wasn't even Bad Rusty talking. Bradley got me to talk about this on camera. He loved this kind of stuff and had a little mantra that he kept quoting whenever something went wrong. He would say, 'Obstacles create drama, Rusty, obstacles create drama.'

YOU EAT SHOE POLISH?

The flight to Santiago was mostly uneventful, except for the part where I strangled the whining child sitting across from me, though that may have been a dream, it's hard to tell, I can only recall tossing and turning for hours in a haze of whining and whinging sounds. Actually I felt sorry for the poor little chap, or sorry for his mother at least. As for the constantly coughing woman seated directly in front of me, I had no sympathy for her. I don't know how she achieved this, but she somehow managed to cough directly on to me while facing the window. It was unsettling, as I had come too far and invested too much to fall victim to a foreign germ at this point.

In a flat country like Australia, we are content to use the word 'mountain' to describe virtually any grassy hill with cows on it. So when you fly into Chile and are immediately confronted with the panoramic, mountainous vista of the Andes, it is something quite memorable indeed. I was staring dreamily out of the window at row upon row of jagged, snow-covered peaks when I was interrupted by the flight attendant serving breakfast. About time, I thought. I was hungrier than a Uruguayan rugby team.

Santiago, the capital of Chile, is located in a valley that is surrounded by many impressive Andean peaks, which serve to trap all of the smog and pollution. According to a 2003 World

Health Organisation study, Santiago is over twice as smog-ridden as Los Angeles, which means you get some serious smog views as you fly in to the Aeropuerto de Santiago. I had been awake for a few hours now and had taken the chance to do some last-minute cramming of Spanish words and phrases. This was going to be useful as Bradley and I now faced a 13-hour stopover before our scheduled flight to Punta Arenas, which was departing at 1.30 the following morning. After getting off the plane, I immediately had an opportunity to test out my Spanish-speaking skills by trying to determine where we had to go to catch our internal flight. I saw a helpful-looking Chilean man standing underneath an information sign and said loudly into his face, 'Excuse-a me-a, where-a do-a we go-a to catch-a another-a flight-a?'

Of course I didn't say that. I had a phrase ready that I had prepared earlier, thanks to the translator app in my phone. I simply typed in the words *Where do we go to catch another flight?*' and the magic Spanish fairy in the phone gave me the Spanish words to say. Then I simply put on my best Speedy Gonzalez accent and said:

'¿Dónde vamos a coger otro vuelo?'

'Just through those doors, sir, but first you have to pay your Chilean entrance fee,' he answered in perfect English. Way to shoot down the confidence of the Australian guy trying to practise his Spanish for the first time, mate. I headed dejectedly over to pay our fee and Bradley said: 'Don't feel so bad, look at it this way, maybe he is just trying to practise his English.'

We paid our US$100 each to enter Chile, and got an extremely cool-looking stamp in our passports. It was nice to see that the officials in Chile still love a noisy stamping ritual whenever they get the chance.

We moved on to the baggage claim area where we waited and waited as we watched hundreds of bags being collected before we even sighted any of ours.

You Eat Shoe Polish?

Bradley was nervous and sweating. He assured me it was because he had many thousands of dollars worth of expensive camera equipment that he didn't want to lose, and not because of the blocks of hashish that were strapped to his body.

I said: 'Are you worried about losing all of your camera gear, Brad? Remember, obstacles create drama.'

'Not that type of fucking drama!' he snapped.

Upon not seeing our bags come out immediately, I must admit my nerves were also getting a little twitchy, and just as my head filled with thoughts of trying to replace all of the specialist running gear it had taken months to assemble with tracksuit pants and hoodie tops from the local market, I realised we were waiting at the wrong baggage carousel and all of our luggage was patiently circling not far from where we were standing. Then we just had to pass through customs and we were on our way. I filled out the little piece of paper that you always have to when you are entering another country, which asks important information like whether you have been to a farm recently, have any foodstuffs or are carrying $10,000. I ticked no to all the boxes and put my bags through the x-ray machine. The surly Chilean customs officer looked at me and motioned me over to search my bags.

'Oh shit,' I thought, 'the Vegemite!' Does that even qualify as a foodstuff?

'What's this?' he said, pointing to the Vegemite.

'Shoe polish,' I said, performing a rubbing motion while pointing to my shoes.

'*Bueno*, you can go.'

I had done plenty of research into any possible taxi or money exchange scams that other travellers to Chile had experienced, so as soon as we exited the baggage area, I was not surprised to be confronted by up to 10 'taxi' drivers promising to take us downtown and help change our money. Luckily the word 'no' means the same in English and Spanish and we soon broke through the pack. Immediately a friendly, diminutive Chilean man wearing a shirt and tie approached us and asked, 'Punta Arenas?'

I nodded. How did he know that?

'Follow me, my friend,' he said, smiling. 'I take you to the check in.' He spoke English quite well, and Bradley and I obediently followed, but I smelled a rat.

'Are you from airline?' I asked in broken English, thinking for some reason he would understand me better.

He smiled again. 'I help you check in your bags to Punta Arenas.'

He sure did have a nice smile.

'Who do you work for?' I asked again, a little less suspiciously, thinking that the management of the Santiago airport might employ some friendly little Chilean blokes to help tourists when they arrive.

'I look after you, my friends,' again with the smile. 'Where are you from?' he asked.

'*Somos Australianos.*' We are Australians, I ventured, trying some Spanish.

'*¿Tiene canguro en bolsa?*' Do you have a kangaroo in your bag? he said in Spanish, laughing. It was a major breakthrough for me and my Spanish speaking. I said something in Spanish, he answered in Spanish, and I understood him!

I asked him his name: '*¿Cómo se llama?*'

'Jorge,' he replied, which is George in Spanish, but he pronounced it like he was coughing up a hairball.

Jorge did actually seem genuine now and even though we realised he was obviously not from the airline and just working for tips, he was very helpful and led us up to the check in counter where he began to converse in Spanish with the attendant. Of course they don't open for check in until three hours before the flight leaves, and we had another 12 hours before that was happening, so Jorge led us back down to baggage storage so we could free ourselves of our bags and head downtown for a look around. Jorge stayed with us and helped us store our bags, talking quickly in Spanish with the baggage attendant. I really hoped they weren't going to rip us off. Surely not, I thought, as Jorge was a nice bloke and he took a particular shine to Bradley, who, understandably, was concerned about leaving all his camera gear in a luggage storage room in Chile, and was speaking extra loudly to the men so that he was understood, though he did refrain from putting an extra 'a' syllable at the end of every word.

I paid Jorge with a 5000-peso note, and after he quickly walked away smiling, I was hit with a pang of panic, thinking I had just given him 100 Australian dollars, then I realised it was only 10 dollars and it was worth it to experience my first conversation in Spanish with a Chilean.

Bradley and I negotiated the fare into the downtown area with a taxi driver and as we pulled away from the airport, Bradley swore he saw Jorge merrily loading all of our luggage into his car.

We caught the cab into the centre of Santiago for a little adventure and went to some markets and had a look at the Plaza de Armas, the main square in the middle of the city. We had read about, and been warned by Jorge, to be aware of pickpockets while walking around Santiago and not to wear flashy jewellery, so Bradley reluctantly had to remove his diamond earrings and necklace. We were careful, but didn't experience anything even remotely confronting or challenging during our six or so hours in the city.

The Plaza de Armas is surrounded by some beautiful buildings in the style of colonial architecture and it's a good place for people watching, as it contains a vibrant collection of stall holders, artists, tourists, chess players, children playing in fountains, street performers, lovers, stray dogs and families. I watched a street-performing duo who had a large crowd gathered around them. The act seemed to virtually be just two oddly shaped guys conversing with each other. (The scared weird Chilean guys?) The larger one was wearing jeans with no shirt and the other, smaller guy was barefoot, dressed in a suit, and standing on a wooden box. They were seemingly having an argument, in Spanish, and they were getting big laughs. I was fascinated. I could recognise about every fifth word, and by the time my brain worked out what that word was in English, 10 more words had gone by, though the rhythm and pauses of the jokes sounded familiar.

Bradley dragged me away to get some 'ambling tourist' shots, then we walked up Santa Lucía Hill, a medium-sized hill near the centre of town adorned with ornate facades, stone stairways and fountains. At the top there is an excellent lookout that offers spectacular, though smoggy, views of the city and surrounding mountains. I loved reading the graffiti that was scrawled into the concrete walls. It was mostly the familiar names-of-young-lovers-expressing-their-commitment-to-each-other that you would see on any lookout in Australia, except the names were different.

Raoul ama Lupe
Carmela ti amo – Fernando
Tito y Renata para siempre
Jorge loves Bradley

Of course if it was a lookout in Australia, there would be the obligatory cock-and-balls scrawled in there somewhere and, encouragingly, I didn't see one anywhere. The graffiti scrawling young lovers of Chile obviously had class.

We made it back to the airport with about seven hours to kill before the flight to Punta Arenas. Bradley and I both breathed a sigh of relief to find all of our luggage was still intact at the storage area, then we trundled off to try to talk our way into one of the airport lounges.

No amount of interesting sounding accents and/or charm was going to convince the girl at the LAN lounge desk to let us in for free, but we did get in after paying US$25 each. It was worth it for a long hot shower and guaranteed free wi-fi, snacks and beverages for the next seven hours. Even if the wi-fi was awfully slow, I devoured at least $25 worth of cheese empanadas and Chilean beer and enjoyed *The Simpsons* dubbed into Spanish, followed by *Who Wants to be a Millionaire?*, again in Spanish. We had no idea what was going on but joined in with the Chilean businessmen in the lounge shouting out the answers and scoffing when the contestants got a question wrong.

I had decided to break a self-imposed three-month alcohol ban. Like free room service, I just can't resist a fridge full of free cold beers, especially if there are piping hot mini empanadas to go with them. With all the training I had completed, it was going to take a lot of empanadas and beer to undo all that work, so I thought, *'¡Viva cerveza!'*

We went out for a little wander at one point and noticed some chanting and whistling going on near the exit from the customs area. There were camera crews and journalists and a crowd of about 150 people, mostly men, all dressed in blue, red and white, some of them holding banners and flags. It was not hard to work out they were all waiting for a local football team to arrive. I spoke to one of the journalists in half Spanish/English, and him to me in half English/Spanish, and found out the team about to emerge from customs was Universidad de Chile, one of the most successful and popular teams in the Primera Division in Chile, having won the championship four times in the last 10 years.

I noticed their logo was an owl, which piqued my interest as my seven-year-old daughter was obsessed by owls. I immediately went and bought a Universidad de Chile cap and cheered with the rest of the crowd as the team triumphantly exited the airport and boarded a waiting bus. Now I had a new Chilean sports team to follow, Los Buhos – the owls. That bit of excitement passed about 15 minutes and I was really ready to get to Punta Arenas and have a rest. It had been a long day.

PUNTA ARENAS

Eventually we dragged ourselves away from the airport lounge, stumbled up to the departure gate like zombies, and caught the four-hour flight to Punta Arenas, arriving at around 5 am on Friday morning. The half-hour taxi trip in from the airport gave time for more internal reflection as the sun was just rising spectacularly over the Strait of Magellan, making me realise that I was now closer than I had ever been to my final destination of Antarctica.

The check in staff of the Hotel Diego De Almagro graciously let us have our room early and Bradley and I both collapsed to get some sleep after 36 hours of travel.

Our itinerary noted that we were some of the first participants in the Ice Marathon to arrive in this southern Chilean town of Punta Arenas, which I believe is a Spanish name that comes from *punta*, which means 'kick', and *arenas*, which means 'balls'.

Punta Arenas is on the Strait of Magellan, it has a population of about 100,000 people and quite a few stray dogs. There are no really tall buildings. There's a hill, and the houses spread out from the hill down to the water, where there is a port. There is a town square, and some shops. That's pretty much it. It's kind of like Geelong. The next time you read about some half-arsed council blabbing on about how they have the tallest ladder or the largest parking garage in the southern hemisphere, don't be so impressed, because all they are really up against is Punta Arenas.

It was Friday and the first official meet and greet with all the runners was going to be on Sunday night. If the weather held up, we were due to fly to Union Glacier first thing Tuesday morning and run the marathon on Wednesday November 30. That was less than a week until the biggest physical challenge of my life, but until then we had four days to kill. Now, what would I do if had to spend four days in Geelong? This was going to be harder than I thought. At least we had a few days to acclimatise and maybe get over some jet lag.

I woke in the middle of the afternoon – not exactly the best way to start getting over jet lag. I really felt like going out for a run to get the muscles moving and to see if I remembered how. The weather in Punta Arenas at this time of year averaged about 10 degrees Celsius during the day, so I pulled on some running tights – for warmth, not because I like wearing them, okay? I also wore a long-sleeved top, just the one pair of woollen socks with my planned marathon shoes and then I headed out for an easy 10-k run.

I was a bit groggy in the head as I stepped out of the hotel into a bracing wind and promptly nearly got run over by a car. 'Note to self,' I thought, 'they drive on the other side of the road here.' Another note to self – do not get hit by a car. I imagined the hundreds of people I would have to face when I got home from my big trip.

'So, how was Antarctica?'

'Um, I didn't get there ... mumble ... Got hit by a car in Chile ... mumble mumble ...'

I started off down the path along the beachfront, into a fairly stiff breeze, my sore foot was hurting, the wind was cold and uncomfortable and I was getting a headache.

'What are you doing here?' said Bad Rusty.

'What are *you* doing here?' I said. 'It's going to be fine, the wind and the cold will be good practice for Antarctica.'

'Why aren't you wearing gloves? It's cold,' whined Bad Rusty, 'and what about our sore foot?'

'The foot is just sore from all the time we've spent in planes over the past two days, it's going to be fine.'

Like many runs that start off awfully, after two or three ks I got warmed up and things fell into place and I started to feel pretty good. My foot was feeling better and the deep breaths and blood pumping around my body reminded me of the things that I love about running. With my confidence back, I turned off the beach road and headed north into a fairly suburban-looking part of Punta Arenas. The houses were mostly a simple, Spanish-looking design set right up on the footpath, with a window either side of an ornate door. Made of weatherboard or concrete and sometimes covered in tin, they were often painted in bright colours like red, green, orange and yellow; a style that I just loved, and it was really nice to be running in such a different-looking place. I was getting a few second glances from some of the locals, obviously because the running tights were showing off my muscular pins.

Then I realised that in South America, where the men are proudly macho, they probably hadn't seen many blokes poncing around wearing tights. I continued on.

As mentioned, Punta Arenas had many stray dogs roaming the streets. The stray dogs used to be quite a problem until a few years ago when the council undertook a 'stray dog relocation program', which I believe involved lots of poisoned meat and some guns. Later I spoke to a fellow named Carlos at the tourist office and he told me that before the 'relocation' the beachfront was virtually a no go zone with hundreds of stray dogs ruling the area. At the time of my visit there were a few dozen or so dogs lazing around the town square, and a number of random individuals and little packs roaming the back streets, and nobody seemed to mind too much.

Unlike the stray dogs I had seen in countries like Mexico or Indonesia, where they all looked quite similar, the stray dogs here possibly hadn't cross bred so much and still retained some semblances of distinctive dog breeds. There would be a Labrador next to a small white fluffy dog and a corgi-looking pooch.

Now, I like dogs. It's because of a dog that I run, but I was not going to pat any of these strays, even though they were quite docile-looking and hardly gave you a second glance. I certainly didn't want to pick up any disease that was going to ruin my chances of being let into Antarctica.

Maybe the dogs weren't used to seeing many people running, or maybe it was the tights, I don't know, but as I approached a harmless-looking small white dog on the footpath, he stood up and started growling at me. I slowed to a walk and we faced off.

'It's okay, little fella,' I said. 'I'm a friend, I'm not going to hurt you.' He obviously couldn't speak English, as the growling intensified. My mind raced, what were the damn Spanish words for 'good' and 'dog'? I shouted, *'Bueno perro, bueno perro,'* a few times to no avail and then thought, 'What do I do now? Do I back off? Do I walk past, smiling? Do I run?' Surely I could outrun this little guy. Visions of me limping up the street with the dog latched onto my Achilles didn't deter me as I sprinted past him and continued on up the street. He took after me in pursuit. Oh shit, I could hear the clacking of his claws on the concrete footpath just a few metres behind me, but after about 10 seconds, the clack-clacking gradually got fainter and I let out a sigh of relief.

Then I heard the heavy clack-clacking of his larger, angrier friend getting louder and gaining on me. Jesus, why didn't I get those rabies shots? I picked up the pace but the situation was getting desperate, so I decided to go for the old 'shout at and dominate the canine' routine. I stopped and turned around, waving my arms and shouting '*Geddoutofidyamongrel!*' in my best outback cattleman's voice, only to realise that both dogs had already stopped about 20 metres back up the road, so I was shouting at an empty footpath. How ridiculous the scene must have looked: a gringo in tights running crazily from a small white dog, who was then joined by a larger dog, then, when both dogs had stopped, the gringo turned and maniacally shouted an indecipherable Australian phrase at nothing.

If the blood had been pumping through my veins before this happened, my blood pressure would have been going through the roof at this point. I began a slow jog back to the hotel, dodging any dogs I saw, but when I was about a block away from my destination, a pack of about seven dogs rounded the corner and headed straight towards me. Where is a slab of poisoned meat and a gun when you really need it?

Again, this pack of dogs were all different shapes and sizes. There were a couple of Labrador types, a big ridgeback, a mangy-looking poodle, a few small hairy dogs with matted coats, and the leader was a large German shepherd.

They looked like a pack of badass, Chilean Hairy Maclary dogs.

If you are unfamiliar with Hairy Maclary, it's a rather excellent series of children's books about a pack of mismatched dogs in a small town. All of the dogs have a cute little rhyming description that is repeated every time you see the dog. There is Hairy Maclary from Donaldson's Dairy, Bottomley Potts all covered in spots, Bitzer Moloney all skinny and bony, Muffin McLay like a bundle of hay, etc.

Now I found myself confronted with the Chilean version of the Hairy Maclary dogs:

Pedro von Shabby, all mangy and scabby,
Diego Valdez, he's covered in fleas,
Scratchy Marrón, if you see him, don't run,
Jose Gonzalez, probably got rabies.

I felt like I was a tourist in South Central Los Angeles facing an approaching gang of hoods.

'Just keep walking,' I said to myself, 'don't make eye contact, you don't want any trouble here. Whatever you do, don't display any fear, I think they can smell that.' I pulled into a doorway and the gang trotted past, happily unaware.

That night Bradley and I were informed that a representative from ANI, the logistics company, was coming to the hotel to inspect all of our clothing, presumably to ensure that when we froze to death in Antarctica, they could claim it wasn't their fault, though I am sure that I had already signed at least two contracts that stated that very fact. We laid out all our clothes in the shape of ourselves on the bed; I had one shape for running gear and one shape for general wear around camp.

A nice young Canadian fellow named Brian (again, the Canadian Brians) came up to our room to do the inspection and my running gear passed the test with flying colours, though while inspecting my general gear he asked where my long johns, mid-layer fleece pants and windproof snow pants were. Before he arrived I had hidden them, replacing them all with just a small pair of running shorts, oh how I crack me up sometimes . . .

I said: 'Yeah, you see Brian, I really don't like to feel constricted around my legs and just prefer the freedom of running shorts. I am sure I will be fine, though.'

We looked at each other stony faced for about 10 seconds before I revealed my hilarious joke, which went over about as well as a severe bout of frostbite.

'We can't joke about these things, Rusty,' he said, though he was smiling. 'And, Mr Smart Aleck, I can see you don't have a mid layer for your legs anyway.'

While reading the clothing list back in Australia, I had decided that it must be some kind of mistake and that surely you couldn't need to wear *three* pairs of pants in Antarctica.

It was not a mistake, so I was sent out the next morning with a piece of paper that had 'mid-layer fleece pants' written on it and apparently if I said that to someone in the appropriate shop they would know what I was talking about. I was thinking that because I was at the southern end of South America, it was not going to be easy to find shops that sold specialist Antarctic gear. But, as Punta Arenas was the departure point for many cruises and flights to the great white south, and it was also popular with hikers and sightseers who came from all over the world to see the spectacular glaciers and penguin colonies of Patagonia, there were actually five or six specialist camping and hiking stores that offered all the equipment you could need to climb a mountain or hike over a glacier – sold at the extremely inflated prices of shops that were located at the southern end of South America.

While walking around Punta Arenas, you constantly saw middle-aged couples on shore leave from a cruise ship wearing identical North Face Goretex vests or jackets with extremely sturdy-looking matching hiking boots.

I was wearing my new Universidad de Chile cap and was feeling like a real local when I walked in to the first hiking supply shop. The bloke working in the store was obviously not a fan of the Owls and said that he wouldn't serve me until I took off the cap, and that I should follow a rival football team called Colo Colo. I laughed and thought he was joking but he was not. I had just inadvertently stumbled smack bang into one of the fiercest rivalries in sport. This was bigger than Rangers versus Celtic or Carlton versus Collingwood. Hell, this was bigger than Yamaha versus Skidoo in the world of snowmobiles, though I didn't really feel like taking this guy on in a brawl, but I did take note of the location of the nearest chair, in case it got ugly. He repeated, this time a little more seriously, that I needed to take the cap off before he could serve me, and I started to feel stubborn about it. Why should I take the cap off? I had been supporting Universidad de Chile for nearly 24 hours goddammit and I wasn't going to be told what to do by any stinking Colo Colo fan, that's for sure.

'I'm not taking the cap off,' I said, and I think he respected that decision, because he served me, though I wasn't exactly expecting a huge discount off the price of the pants. Five minutes later I was the new owner of what can only be described as the best $120 pair of fleecy tracksuit pants I have ever bought.

I don't want to sound too harsh about Punta Arenas. Before going to Antarctica, I had read a few books about other travellers heading there and most of them stopped off in Punta Arenas. Many of the stories and images they share of the town tend to be a bit derogatory, describing the rubbish and stray dogs and isolation of a remote town, so I was prepared to be disappointed by Punta Arenas, but I was not. I enjoyed my time there.

MEETING THE OTHER RUNNERS

The next day Richard Donovan arrived, along with the official race photographer, Mike King, and the official cameraman, Dave Painter, both from the UK and both experts in their field. They asked if Bradley and I would like to come out for a quiet drink, along with a few of the other runners who had already arrived. There was a tall Czech named Ladislav, who had recently run a marathon in Iceland. There was Sarah, a German lawyer from Chicago, and a wiry, 68-year-old American called Brent, who had already run over 180 marathons and was headed to Antarctica to attempt the 100-kilometre ultramarathon that was to be held the day after our measly 42-kilometre regular marathon.

We met in the foyer of the hotel and walked up the road to a large inviting bar that served pizza and sandwiches, or as they say in Spanish, *'pizza y sandwiches'*. We ordered pints of Chilean beer all round, though I wasn't expecting a big night out as I thought the runners would be into preserving the sanctity of their finely tuned bodies. I couldn't have been more mistaken as, six pints later, we rolled out of there after 2 am and hooted and hollered our way back to our hotel, at least I think it was our hotel.

I got chatting with Ladislav the Czech, after we dragged him away from the bar where he had been deep in conversation with a local *señorita* for the last two hours. I said, 'You seem to be taking to the locals quite well, you obviously speak Spanish?'

'No,' he replied in his matter of fact Eastern European manner. 'I can only speak Czech, Italian, French, English, German and a little Russian, but we got by okay.' He was very excited by the thought of going to Antarctica, and was using this trip as a springboard into running a marathon on every continent. Throughout the course of the next week, I was to learn that this is a common goal among the people running in the Ice Marathon. I hadn't really thought about this concept before. Through my travels with the Scaredies, I had been lucky enough to visit all the continents except Africa, and never thought that I could have been ticking off a marathon in each country I visited.

Heading off to every continent to run a marathon so you could tick them off your list sounds a little crazy, not to mention expensive.

Who are these people who want to run the Ice Marathon? Surely they all must be rich white people with nothing better to do. As I met more of the racers, I discovered that their backgrounds and their reasons for doing this race differed greatly.

Sarah, for example, the German lawyer based in Chicago, had been to Antarctica twice before and after this trip would have completed a marathon on every continent three times and would be the first female to achieve this feat. She was also a member of the Grand Slam Club, which is made up of people who have run a recognised marathon on all seven continents, as well as completing the North Pole Marathon in the Arctic. Currently just over 50 people have accomplished this feat and are members of the Grand Slam Club.

By the next day, all of the runners had arrived in Punta Arenas and we all went out for a social get-together at a local bar. There were 35 of us making the trip down to Antarctica and

Meeting the Other Runners

we had come from 15 different countries, listed here in order of importance – I mean alphabetically: Argentina, Australia, Belgium, Canada, Czech Republic, France, Germany, Great Britain, India, Ireland, Netherlands, New Zealand, Philippines, Poland and the USA. All 35 of us walked down the street into the cold wind blowing off the Strait of Magellan. You could feel the nervous excitement of a group of humans, about to embark on a long-planned adventure together, meeting each other for the first time. It was a very diverse group, yet we had a few things in common – running, obviously, and that formed the opening of most of the conversations that night.

'So, how many marathons have you done?' was a common introductory question, and one that in a normal situation, would be rare to confidently ask someone you'd never met before.

We had all experienced the unique reactions from friends, family and strangers when they found out for the first time that you were off, firstly to Antarctica, and secondly to do something as insane as attempt a marathon there. That gave us an instant feeling that we were among comrades and I never felt at any time that there were any real feelings of competitiveness between us. Just the fact that we were going there to attempt the Ice Marathon was enough of a challenge for most of us.

I'd already met Ladislav, Brent and Sarah, and now it was time to meet some of the others.

There was Alvin Matthews, a tanned, chisel featured Californian professional dam builder (!) who was working in Canberra overseeing the construction of a dam. He had only been running for six years, starting just seven months after breaking his back in a motorcycle accident. He had run marathons on the Great Wall of China, Berlin and Boston, and the Ice Marathon was going to be continent number six for Alvin.

Don Kern was from Michigan and was on a marathon streak of running a marathon every month for the past nine years. He had completed 229 marathons and was attempting to break the world record for completing official marathons on seven continents in the shortest period of time. He had tried twice before but failed to break the 30-day existing record. If he completed the Ice Marathon as scheduled, he would set a new record of around 25 days.

Clement Thevenet was Tristan Miller's mate to whom I dutifully delivered the snow boots. Clement was a Frenchman who worked for a Swiss bank in Luxembourg and was a recent convert to ultramarathons. If a gazelle took a human form, it would look like Clement. His slight but muscular frame and focused eyes made him look like he could run forever.

Yvonne Brown was a diminutive, dark-haired dynamo originally from Northern Ireland, who was a detective inspector in the London Metropolitan Police. Yvonne tragically had lost her young son to neuroblastoma, a rare form of cancer, in 2009 and she was running the Ice Marathon to raise funds for three other young British children who were also suffering from the disease. Yvonne was a casual runner who was asked if she wanted to do a marathon while she was in the US when her son was getting treatment. She ran it in three hours and 30 minutes.

When I met Matthew von Ertfelda, a dark-haired American from Washington DC with a square jaw and an intense gaze, I had a feeling that he looked a little familiar, as if I had met him before somewhere. I liked him immediately, as he was quick-witted and up for a laugh, but he had a serious, intellectual tone to him as well. He had been on all sorts of adventures around the world including a 35-day trek through the wilds of New Guinea and hiking the Darien Gap – the swampy wilderness that links North and South America.

Rebecca Frechette was a 26-year-old, sporty looking blonde from Massachusetts who worked in marketing. She had never run more than five kilometres before she tackled the Boston

Meeting the Other Runners

Marathon in April 2011. She then decided it would be a good idea to keep on running and attempted to complete the seven marathons on seven continents in the next seven months, culminating in the Ice Marathon. Rebecca said she knew that the physical challenge would be almost as tough as the financial problems posed by all of that international travel and associated costs. She said she kept working whenever she could and lived frugally, but still had had to go into some serious debt to accomplish her goal.

There were many more great folks that I met on that first night and we all got to know each other quite well over the next week. Most of us stayed around chatting until we were kicked out of the bar and made our way back to the hotel in dribs and drabs, where Richard, our illustrious leader, Brent, and the British camera artists Mike and Dave continued on well into the night.

THE SAFETY BRIEFING: KEEP IT BRIEF, MATE

On the Monday morning, 24 hours before our scheduled departure, we had a special information session and safety briefing in a meeting room of the hotel. At the rear of the room there was a table with tea and coffee and a couple of plates of generic biscuits, which I didn't think were a good choice for a room of carb-loading runners. Whatever. They tasted good with a cup of tea. In the middle of the room there were rows of chairs set up facing a slide projector and screen. We were either going to learn about Antarctica or be offered some dodgy timeshare holiday apartments. Most people had helped themselves to biscuits and hot drinks and were standing around in small groups quietly chatting when a tall, gruff Australian named Bruce marched in and told us all to sit down. He worked for ANI, the logistics company and had been appointed to take the briefing and talk at us until we all questioned just why the hell we had signed up for this trip.

The briefing was brief in name only and consisted mostly of Bruce describing numerous shots of the Union Glacier camp toilets and mechanics' hut, and then calling for the next slide to be shown. The reason he spent so much time telling us about the toilets was that going to the toilet in Antarctica is a major undertaking. Apart from the difficulty of walking in there and having to remove 12 layers of clothes and three pairs of gloves before you can even start going about your business, the whole process was slightly different. As Antarctica is a pristine environment, you cannot leave anything there. Anything. It's not a case of simply digging a hole in the snow, filling it up and then digging another hole. All waste must be bagged up and flown back to Chile to be disposed of there. Liquids and solids must be separated, so for blokes wanting to do a bowel movement, it was a case of using the urinal, then moving over to the toilet to complete the process. For females it was a little more complicated, as you can imagine, as it involved two separate toilets and let's just say that things aren't always necessarily that easy to control, especially if it involves shuffling around a frozen wooden floor, mid process, with three pairs of pants around your ankles. So Bruce had to spend quite a bit of time telling us about all of the toileting possibilities we were going to face and how to deal with them. He then stressed and stressed again the importance of hygiene in remote and confined areas like an Antarctic camp. If a bout of gastro was introduced into close living conditions like those on the Union Glacier, it could be disastrous and everyone needed to wash and disinfect their hands before and after virtually every activity.

He perked up when he began to explain in great detail what happens to your skin upon prolonged exposure to extremely cold temperatures.

Of course this section of the talk was accompanied by many slides depicting the frostbitten fingers, toes and crotches of various poor saps who had been trapped on mountains or spent the night down crevasses in Antarctica. He cheerily mentioned that we shouldn't venture too far from the camp, as it was located on a giant glacier filled with unseen crevasses. At this point someone asked if this was the same glacier we would be running the marathon on. Bruce said yes. I thought as long as

The Safety Briefing: Keep It Brief, Mate

the planned marathon course didn't go up any mountains or down crevasses, we probably wouldn't experience the kinds of horrific frostbites that were shown in the slides.

Or would we?

Due to the heating of the hotel being way too warm and the fact that I was still suffering from jet lag, I was constantly fighting falling asleep, despite Bruce's loud voice. It was difficult to concentrate and I was falling in and out of consciousness. This was not good, as I really didn't want to get into trouble with grumpy old Bruce, and I especially didn't want to miss some vital piece of safety information. I pictured myself at the bottom of an icy, freezing crevasse with Bruce standing at the top smugly shouting down to me, 'I think somebody wasn't listening to the safety briefing, were they?'

Bruce finished up by saying that while it was important that we understand the dangers of where we were going, his job was really to ensure that we had a good time and a friendly experience ... any questions?

I decided that, in the name of friendliness, I should ask Bruce a stupid question.

'While we are in Antarctica, will we need a password to access wi-fi?'

Bruce answered me seriously (no wi-fi) and I realised he probably got questions like that all the time. Then someone asked if their mobile phone would work there, and I understood that I was working with professionals here, so I shut up.

WHAT DOES MYSTERY TASTE LIKE?

The rest of the day was spent wandering around the town, as Bradley needed to buy an extra bag to take with him. We were told to head out to a large department store on the edge of town, and that the best way to travel there was by *colectivo*. *Colectivos* were just normal cars that followed a specific route, like a bus. You hailed them on the street and you paid the driver directly (300 pesos, about 60 cents Australian) for each journey. It really was just like getting into an unroadworthy car with no seatbelts, driven by a stranger who you couldn't understand and who drove with complete disregard for the road rules. It was everything that your parents told you never to do, so it was quite fun in a dangerous kind of a way. When you got near to your destination, you just shouted, '*Para, por favor,*' (Please stop) and off you went.

We got dropped off at an enormous, shed-like superstore called Sanchez and Sanchez, which was like a Chilean Kmart crossed with Bunnings that also sold booze. Bradley got his bag and I got a few bottles of the Chilean national drink, Pisco. It's a brandy-like alcoholic drink made from grapes. I asked someone why it's called Pisco and he said after three or four, go for a wee and see what colour it makes your Pisco. Speaking of bad Spanish jokes, we spent the ride home making up routines for an act called 'Sanchez and Sanchez – Chile's Finest Comedy

Duo'. See them perform their renowned 'Where's my taco?' routine. Who could forget their hit song 'One-eyed Señorita'? And who doesn't love it when Sanchez says 'Holy Guacamole!' (Raucous laughter ...)

We got dropped off back in town and ran into a few of the other runners in the supermarket, who were stocking up on last-minute supplies, which generally involved some kind of alcoholic beverages from their home countries. We had been informed that the weather at Union Glacier was clear and that we would be departing at 7 am the following morning. I hadn't eaten since breakfast and was getting quite hungry. I had been very careful to avoid eating anything from the street vendors, so I bought from the supermarket a packet of almonds, some rice crackers and a bag of corn chips with the interesting name of '*Misterio*' flavour. In Spanish *misterio*, unsurprisingly, means 'mystery' and I just couldn't resist buying it. It was an interesting marketing idea – that someone would buy a food product with an unknown flavour, though with corn chips it's not like it was going to be a huge surprise, right? You could probably guess that it would be some sort of salty, cheesy flavour. *Misterio* flavoured chicken, on the other hand, might not sell as well.

Bradley and I spent the afternoon packing all our gear to go to Antarctica, leaving out our 'camp' wear, as they referred to it. When we arrived and stepped off the plane at the Union Glacier, it was going to be minus 20 degrees and windy, so we would be travelling there wearing our full kit.

I got hungry again, so I cracked open the *Misterio* corn chips, thinking that I could buy another packet to take home later on. It is difficult to describe what they tasted like.

They were salty, that's for sure. There was definitely some cheesiness going on, as well as chilli, maybe paprika, plus some unidentifiable spices. I felt like a contestant on Masterchef doing a taste test. Hmm ... is that a hint of lime in there? ... Are those pine nuts I can taste?... Whatever it was, the chips tasted a bit weird and I didn't finish the packet.

After a bit of a rest, Bradley and I trotted off to our favourite Chilean restaurant to meet up with Matthew from DC. It was our third time there and the staff greeted us warmly as we walked in, met Matt, and found a table. I was getting more confident with my Spanish, though I had a minor hiccup when trying to order a pineapple juice for Bradley. I wanted to say, 'My friend would like a pineapple juice,' so I said:

'*Mi amigo quisiera jugo de pene.*' The waitress stared at Bradley with a shocked look and laughed.

I had actually said, 'My friend would like penis juice,' mixing up the word *pene* (penis) for *pina* (pineapple). Come on, that must happen all the time, surely? Why would the inventors of the Spanish language make the words for penis and pineapple so similar? That's just asking for trouble.

Anyway we all had a hearty laugh about it and got on with dinner. This was two days out from the marathon and we had entered prime carb-loading time. From now until the race, it was all rice, pasta and bread to pump that glycogen into our muscles and hopefully keep the brain from becoming hypoglycaemic. I just had to use that word again, now that I have learnt how to spell it.

Matthew was an interesting dude and we were in the middle of swapping stories when he mentioned, as an aside, that he was once on this television show called *Survivor* and had we heard of it? Had we heard of it? It's only, like, my faaaavourite show, lol. Sorry, I was a bit overcome there. Denise and I absolutely loved *Survivor* and had watched every series of it. That's why Matthew looked familiar. He was the runner-up on *Survivor Amazon* – the sixth season of *Survivor*, filmed in 2003. During that season, he was portrayed as the bad guy and edited to seem a bit crazy. He ended up losing to one of the annoying, skinny models. I quizzed him for about two hours on everything you never get to hear about, like the audition process, the food and how many crew and cameras are around during the filming of the show and do they tell the contestants what to do or say. I was absolutely fascinated by his stories.

About halfway through my dinner of rice with salmon and tomatoes, I suddenly felt not hungry and a bit of sweat broke out on my brow. 'I'll be fine,' I thought, and we walked back to the hotel devising a new reality television show – *'We took sixteen stray dogs and gave them to sixteen strangers to see if they could train this motley collection of mutts off the street and turn them into dog show superstars. Get ready for* ... *'My Fair Doggy'. Each week a dog is voted off ...'*

Fun times, indeed ...

We got back to the hotel and Bradley got me to talk to camera about my feelings about the impending adventure. We settled down around 11 pm and an hour later I awoke with a searing pain in my stomach. It was that familiar feeling of having something inside you that wants to get out, fast. I rushed to bathroom and threw up with such force I started feeling dizzy. Then the other end of me got busy, before I had to do some more violent puking. I felt like I could pass out, so I had to lie down on the floor. This was bad. I couldn't stop thinking, 'Not now, please, not now. Why tonight? Why me?'

I couldn't believe that after all the planning and all the training that this was actually happening. If it was an injury that caused me to miss the run, it would have been disappointing but possibly easier to understand. But illness? And only hours away from our departure. This was cruel. I was lying there, delirious and sweating on a hotel bathroom floor at the bottom-most point of South America and my Antarctic dream was over.

Or was it?

Of course it was over. I was lying there with my face pressed against the cool floor tiles, as it was the only thing that made me feel less than horrendous. Spinning colours of all descriptions were floating through the blackness behind my eyelids. Fluids were desperately trying to leave my body through every means possible. There was no way that they would let me catch the plane and enter the camp, and even in the remote chance that I was allowed to travel to Antarctica, how was I supposed to run a marathon in some of the most difficult conditions you could face?

This was really, really bad. I felt shattered physically and emotionally. I eventually crawled back to bed then awoke after another hour to repeat the cycle of vomiting so violently I had to stop and lie on the floor to hallucinate and cool my face, then sit on the toilet using my bum as a sprinkler. My body desperately wanted whatever it was that was inside me to get the hell out as soon as possible. I wasn't only throwing up my past few meals – I was trying to get rid of meals from years ago. I didn't know what the culprit was that was causing this nightmare and I tried to recall everything I had eaten in the past day. Nothing I saw after it came back up looked familiar. Wait a minute. Are those pine nuts I can taste? Not the fucking *Misterios*! Or should I say the '*Dysenterios*'. After four of these vomit/hallucinate/spray cycles, I checked the clock – it was 4 am. Three hours until we left. This was like a horrible nightmare coming to life. Three hours! I was never going to make it. There was only one thing to do and that was to pray for bad weather. Then the plane would be delayed and I would have time to hopefully recover a bit. I went back to bed again and dozed until the next attack of the *Misterio*.

I didn't want to wake Bradley, though the noises I had been making could have woken a sleeping cameraman, which eventually they did. During my next foray to the bathroom, I heard a tentative, muffled voice from the other side of the bathroom door.

'Are you okay, mate?' Bradley asked.

I opened the door and said, 'I feel like shit. I just don't know if I can go through with this, we leave in two hours.'

'Obstacles create drama,' he said, turning his camera on, but I was in no mood for that.

'Yes, obstacles create drama,' I replied, 'and a camera shoved up your arse creates pain. Turn it off.'

The next trip to the bathroom gave a little bit of hope, as there was simply nothing left to throw up. I was just going through the horrible noises and convulsions associated with dry retching. I was concerned about getting dehydrated because the sprinkler end of me was still going at it full blast. If I was going to attempt to run, I at least needed to keep some fluids down. I suddenly realised what this was. This was the opposite of carb loading. This was carb unloading. My concerns about running the race had evaporated and I needed to concentrate on just getting to Antarctica. Even if I couldn't run the marathon as I had intended, if I could just get myself there and still be alive, I was going to drag myself around the course on my hands and knees. I could not let this stop me.

The phone rang at precisely 7 am. It was Richard and he simply said, 'Fog has moved in to the Union Glacier, go back to bed, I'll call you in two hours with an update.'

Oh the sweet feeling of relief that the words 'fog has moved in' brought to me. I got some sleep and was woken by the phone ringing again, just after 9 am.

Again Richard said: 'The fog is still around, don't go anywhere and I will call with another update at noon.'

I don't know what I would have done if he had said to pack up, we're ready to go. It would have been virtually impossible for me, but at that moment the continuing delay came as more good news to me. I was hoping for as much bad weather as Antarctica could come up with.

I sent Bradley out for supplies – a packet of plain crackers and as much Gatorade as he could carry. Any water that I was drinking was still coming straight back up. I wondered what kind of badass bug exists in your stomach that makes water inedible.

What Does Mystery Taste Like?

For those of you who are still interested, I was still very 'loose' when it came to the subject of stools, not that I want to go on about it, but at that point in time, it was quite important to me. For the next three hours I sipped on Gatorade, which either came back up or went straight through me. I couldn't face eating even a plain cracker just yet, so it was a case of waiting for the next phone call, which came at noon to inform us of yet another three-hour delay. I decided to get out of the hotel and visit a pharmacy to see what drugs they could offer me to help.

First I had to check my electronic Spanish translator to find out exactly what I should say. I recalled that one of the Spanish podcasts I had listened to dealt with exactly what I was about to do, and at the time I heard it, I remember hoping that I would never be in that situation. But there I was, learning the phrase 'I need something for *'vómitos y diarrea'* and I don't believe any translation is necessary for you there. I went to the pharmacy and explained to the man behind the counter all about my *vómitos y diarrea*. He gave me some tablets and drops, though with my Spanish, he may well have been giving me tablets and drops that *caused* not cured *vómitos y diarrea*. I made it back to the hotel just in time for my next visit to *el baño*. The 3 o'clock update brought another postponement and it was during this delay that I felt the first sign that there might be light at the end of the tunnel, so to speak, as I stopped vomiting, but still couldn't eat anything.

Finally, at 7 pm, twelve hours after our original departure time, we got the call to check out of the hotel and board the bus to the airport.

I struggled into all of my layers of clothes and felt very overdressed, as my body temperature was higher than normal so it could fight the dreaded *Misterio* germs that had infiltrated my body. I felt extremely drained of energy as I clomped down to the foyer in my two-sizes-too-big snow boots, three pairs of pants and parka. I was still wondering how I could possibly run a marathon the next day. I told no one that I had been ill and sure, maybe I was risking introducing a previously unheard of germ into Antarctica, but I was extra careful to not accidentally shake hands or tongue kiss anyone and I quietly kept to myself.

IGOR IS NOT A DIRTY WORD

The 20-minute bus trip to the airport was fairly uneventful, as was our disembarking into the completely empty terminal of the rather smallish Punta Arenas airport. It felt good to be outside the hotel room and doing something to keep my mind occupied rather than just sitting around and watching movies dubbed into Spanish. Our passports were taken by one of the excellent and helpful ANI staff and we walked through the unmanned security screening area and into a gate lounge. It looked like my Vegemite was going to be safely smuggled into Antarctica. We were informed that as the toilet facilities on the plane were rather 'primitive', this would be our last chance to use real toilets, as we knew them, until our return from Antarctica. I took this advice seriously and proceeded to use the facilities three times over the next half hour, though I had to do it subtly, remaining as inconspicuous as possible. I didn't want anyone noticing my multiple bathroom trips and asking me any suspicious questions regarding my health and then suddenly shouting, *'Infected! He's infected!'* and lights would flash and sirens would sound and a team of experts in biohazard suits would appear from nowhere, tackle me to the ground and force me to remain in Chile while everyone else went to do the race. Thoughts turned to home again and having to explain myself to everybody.

'So, how was Antarctica?'

'Um, I didn't get there ... mumble ... got diarrhoea ... mumble ... *Misterio* chips ... mumble ...'

I just needed to get on that plane and I would be past the point of no return.

After about 45 minutes of waiting I was feeling nervous, then we finally got the call that told us we were ready for boarding and we trundled back out to the bus for the 100-metre ride to our plane. It was an impressive sight indeed.

The plane, or should I say jet, that was used to transport people and supplies to the Union Glacier was called an Ilyushin IL-76. It was a former Soviet military four-engine jet, which was originally designed for delivering heavy machinery to remote areas of the USSR. It was the perfect choice to ferry goods and equipment for the four and a half hour flight from Chile to the Union Glacier, as it was made for mid range distance flights and was able to land and take off from unmade runways.

I don't know when our jet was made, probably sometime in the 1980s when Russia was riding high on the success of the 'Moscow' song. Our bus pulled alongside the aircraft and we got off one by one to enter the jet. There was no customs and immigration procedure to speak of, unless you count standing in a shallow tray of disinfectant for ten seconds.

'Yeah,' I thought, 'kill those germs on my feet, but you guys have got no idea what kind of evil is lurking within my bowels at this moment.'

I climbed up the metal staircase and entered the Ilyushin. It was surprisingly spacious inside, probably five metres from floor to ceiling and easily that far across. There was seating in the front section for about fifty people and the space behind the seats was loaded with a shipping container and many pallets stacked high with fuel drums and other supplies. I couldn't see beyond that but I'm told the Ilyushin usually makes a round trip from Punta Arenas to Union Glacier every three days, depending on the weather, and supplies all sorts of food and equipment to the camp, as well as cargo that will be transported on to the South Pole base and other Antarctic stations.

The interior is certainly built for practicality and not comfort. The ceiling was a tangled mass of pipes and tubing and insulation with straps and cargo hoists hanging randomly above the seats. On the walls beside the seats there were a couple of inflatable life rafts and many signs written in Russian, as well as miscellaneous cupboards and heavy duty boxes crammed with who knows what. Directly in front of the seats was a giant, sombre-looking Russian crewmember, who sat unmoving while suspiciously staring at us taking our seats. He looked very typically Russian with his heavy brow and stern expression and if his name was not Igor, it was surely Ivan. He was seated at a small bench surrounded by dials, gauges and buttons of all shapes and sizes and I am not sure exactly what his purpose was. He could have been the navigator or the bombardier for all I knew.

Most of us had entered the plane, settled in and were seated in what I can say were the most uncomfortable seats I had ever sat in. They were uneven and lumpy and the padding seemed to be a combination of old foam and potatoes. I was so thrown out from the illness I had only brought on to the plane a book, my iPod, a magazine and two crosswords, which I crammed into the seat pocket in front of me. I also took the opportunity to have a dose of my *'vómitos y diarrea'* medicine. Despite having been so sick and not eating anything for the past 24 hours, it was still very exciting to be on the plane and about to depart.

The door that we had entered through was still open while a few of the crew were busy doing last-minute arrangements before take-off. 'Cross-checking' and the like, I imagine. Igor came around handing out packs of orange lollies and I thought, 'how nice, thanks Igor', but they were actually earplugs and I thought it must get loud in here when they start the eng– *Oh my God they've started the engines!* With the door still open! We've all been in a commercial jet before, when the engines have started up and you are safely locked away behind layers of metal and insulation and soundproofing. Even then you can tell it's loud. I've heard jet planes flying a kilometre or two overhead, and I can tell that they are really loud. So when a couple of jet engines start up and you are sitting a few metres from them, whoa! It doesn't even describe it accurately to say it's *really loud*, but that's exactly what it was. It was louder than Loudy McLoud, the loudest guy in Loudville, when he turns his loudspeakers up *really loud*. With the door shut and earplugs firmly plugged, the noise became bearable and we taxied out to the runway and took off.

From the very first moment I heard about the Ice Marathon, I had visions of flying into the continent of Antarctica and seeing the spectacular scenery unfold beneath me. I pictured how the unending miles of scattered pack ice and towering icebergs would open into endless stunning vistas of mountains and snow covered glaciers. I couldn't wait to experience it for myself, but it was not going to happen today, as the Ilyushin had no windows. I couldn't believe it. There were actually two saucer-sized pieces of perspex, one on each of the doors, but they had ice crystals forming over them as soon as we took off.

The in-flight service was about to start so I settled back to watch a movie and gaze at the spunky Russian flight attendants who were about to lavish me with free drinks and a hot meal, when I realised I had been dozing and it was actually just Igor, who brusquely tossed me a tube of Russian potato chips called Starvski or something like that. For a moment, being inside a Russian military transport jet made me feel like I was a spy on a secret mission during the Cold War, and in one swift movement I threw the chips in Igor's face, reached up and broke his neck, then grabbed a life raft and parachuted down to safety, when I realised I was hallucinating again.

I read the warning on the back of my *vómitos* drops and was not surprised to see that it said, 'May cause drowsiness, hot flushes and scenes from Cold War spy novels.'

It was getting late now, after 10 pm, and most people took the chance to grab some sleep. I was feeling very uncomfortable wearing so much clothing and added to that was the fact that Igor had the heating in the interior of the plane absolutely pumping. It was like a sauna in there, so I said, 'Yo, Igor ... what's up with the heat y'all? How 'bout we make it a little less tropical and a little more popsicle, dawg.'

Igor ignored me. I think he might have been sleeping with his eyes open.

I kept sipping drinks of water and Gatorade and was able to nibble on half a dry cracker that stayed down. Some carbs at last, I thought to myself, and was at least able to crack a smile. I knew I was on the way back to feeling better, I certainly couldn't be feeling any worse than I had during the previous 24 hours. I couldn't help but feel disappointed, though, and a bit jealous of everyone else with their 'health' and their 'carbs'. Regardless, I had been dealt a hand and now I had to play it, like it or not. About halfway through the flight, I took my chance with the much-maligned Ilyushin toiletski. It wasn't so bad, kind of like a bush toilet but without the redback spiders. It was midnight now, but it was completely light outside, so on the way back to my seat I looked out of the tiny window on the door, to see if I could spot any land. I saw ice! I got excited then realised that because the windows were so old and scratched, I couldn't tell if I was looking at Antarctica or merely some frozen condensation on the outside of the icy window (I think it was the latter). Speaking of icy, as I was standing there I could feel the cool gaze of Igor staring into my back, so I returned to my seat and tried to doze.

I awoke to a change in the engine sound, which meant we were making our descent into the Union Glacier. I was so thirsty!

Scared Weird Frozen Guy

It felt like I had been keeping a chunk of rock salt on my tongue for the past few hours. I guzzled some water and sports drink, noticing the sensation as the liquid ran down my gullet and into my completely empty stomach. I ate another half a cracker with no major protestations from my internal organs and thought that was a good sign.

WOW!

The Union Glacier camp is located at the foot of the Ellsworth Mountain range in Antarctica. We had just flown over Tierra del Fuego and the Drake Passage, across the Antarctic Circle, and were now about to land on a naturally occurring blue ice runway at the southernmost part of the mountain range – located about 80 degrees south and 700 metres above sea level.

I wondered just how did a two kilometre long blue-ice runway naturally occur. The answer was that at the western end of the Union Glacier, the wind came screaming down off the polar plateau and simply blasted the freshly fallen snow away, leaving a rock hard, ancient surface of ice.

Of course the runway needed to be cleared and maintained throughout the summer season when the camp was operational. ANI ran the Union Glacier camp from November through to January and it was the only non-government-run facility in Antarctica. Apart from hosting the Ice Marathon each December, the camp was also a launching place for many mountaineering expeditions, scientific teams, or just sightseers who wanted to visit the interior of the continent. As during our stay it was also the centenary of humans getting to the South Pole, the camp was busier than usual and was filled with all types of adventurers who were attempting to ski, march or drive to the Pole in time for the official celebrations.

Thankfully it didn't seem very windy as we made our approach to the runway. I was anticipating a bumpy landing, but I could barely notice the wheels touching down and it really was one of the smoothest, and longest, landings I have ever experienced. We seemed to taxi for ages and you could hear the excited chatter and feel the anticipation coming from everybody in the plane, except Igor. Finally the door opened and we experienced our first Antarctic rays of ozone-layer-free sunshine beaming brilliantly into the cabin. It was 2.30 am.

I was the last one off the plane, as Bradley told me he wanted to capture a shot of me coming out of the plane, so I obediently obeyed. It was okay, as I had to collect my hand luggage, which was jammed next to the container behind the seats. I had placed my two pairs of gloves in there, thinking that I wouldn't need my mittens for the trip to camp, so I pulled them on in anticipation of the cold temperature. Finally it was my turn to enter Antarctica.

Wow!

I stepped out of the door onto the metal stepladder and said, 'Wow!' about eight times. I had seen enough documentaries and read enough books to know that it was going to be spectacular, but wow! The runway was situated at one end of the expansive Union Glacier, which was about 10 kilometres across, so we were surrounded on most sides by rocky, snow-capped mountains and the smaller glaciers that feed into the larger Union Glacier. The sky was a brilliant azure blue with just a few beautifully wispy cirrus clouds, and the sun was perched just above the horizon, as it was for the entire time we were there.

Antarctica was beautiful. It was like seeing what things on earth were like 10 million years ago … or when Jesus invented them five thousand years ago … whatever you believe. I certainly thanked Christ that I was wearing a mid layer of fleecy tracksuit pants, because I am not exaggerating when I say it was fairly fucking cold.

There was a decent wind blowing down the glacier and we were informed that the temperature was about minus 20 degrees

Celsius. The runway was situated about eight kilometres from the camp, so arriving passengers must wait for transport to the camp in a cramped but cosy 'passenger terminal' which was really just a box with a couple of windows and a door. As I was the last person off the plane and had stopped to take a few photos, I didn't even try to get into the shelter. It was cold all right; my hands were hurting and I would have loved a third pair of gloves, but after my horrible recent experiences, I felt so happy just to be standing there in Antarctica that I was going to embrace the cold and enjoy the scenery, goddammit.

Also, if I was standing outside the terminal, I could get onto the first transport vehicle to the camp, and I was ready to try to get some rest. It was close to 3 am by now and the marathon was scheduled to go ahead in eight hours' time. I hoped they could postpone it by at least a day to give a poor, sick little Aussie boy a chance.

Bradley and I got in the first truck to camp with about seven of the other runners. It took a good 20 minutes to make the eight-kilometre trip and the friendly driver told us that part of the 'road' to camp that we were driving on formed some of the marathon track, so we all keenly checked out the surface to see if it looked as difficult as we had heard. It was impossible to tell what the surface was like from the truck as it just looked like snow to me. Snow was all we walked, stood or ran on for the entire time we were there. It *was* a glacier after all, so we didn't touch any ground or even a rock. The air in Antarctica is extremely dry and the temperature is obviously very cold, so the snow was never slushy and was more like sand. It was difficult to form a snowball or build a snowman, which disappointed Bradley greatly.

We got our first glimpse of the Union Glacier camp only when we were a couple of kilometres away from it. The glacier was on a slight slope and the few buildings that made up the camp were not tall. There really wasn't much to this remote Antarctic outpost. The first thing you saw was the tall communications antenna, which was conveniently located right next to the communications hut, which was staffed around the clock. It remained in constant contact with the outside world and other places in Antarctica using satellite phone and VHF radio and provided weather information to flight crews and climbing expeditions.

Next to that was a small medical hut that had a doctor and a medic on call at all times. The main part of the camp consisted merely of three tents, all with the half-cylinder shape of a Nissen hut. They were about 20 metres in length, had wooden floors and consisted of a double-layered tent material over an aluminium frame. The middle tent was fairly sparse and was used for lectures, information sessions or for watching movies. The other two were dining tents, one for staff and expeditioners, and the other for visitors like us. This was where we spent most of our time. This tent had a kitchen at one end and basic tables and chairs to seat about 50 people. When meals were not being served you could sit in here and write or read or play games. You could always help yourself to snacks or hot drinks of every imaginable kind. The food that was served to us during our stay was nothing less than amazing. Fresh bread was baked every day and a delicious and diverse array of salads, vegetable and meat dishes was presented at every meal, catering to all tastes and dietary requirements. As 35 runners were descending upon them for the duration of the Ice Marathon, the Union Glacier kitchen was well aware of the preferred foods and picky diets of these carb-loading eating machines, so suitable menus were designed to keep everyone happy. Fresh food from Chile was flown in on each Ilyushin flight so there was no lack of variety and I was confidently assured that there was little or no chance of anyone developing scurvy.

The rest of the camp was simply the toilets, which I have already explained, the mechanics' workshop that dealt with the large number of snowmobiles, sleds, tractors, transport vehicles and groomers required to clear the runway and groom the roads, and last of all was the accommodation area. This consisted of about 30 two-person, double-walled dome tents, based on a design used by Ernest Shackleton's *Endurance* expedition. Each tent had a wooden floor; two camp beds with mattresses, one at either end of the tent; and a small table. They were quite roomy and comfortable and you could stand up in them – well, I could stand up in them, anyway. As the 24-hour sunlight naturally heated the tents, the interior was usually a fairly comfy 0 degrees Celsius. We slept in super-mega-ultra polar sleeping bags, at least that's what Bradley and I called them, and I found them very cosy. There were no shower or bathing facilities at the camp, though they did provide a washcloth and plastic basins that you could fill with a bit of hot water to wash with. Those with braver souls also had the opportunity to have a 'snow bath' which is exactly what it sounds – rolling around and rubbing snow all over yourself.

We arrived in camp after the trip from the runway and stumbled off the truck. I stood there for a few seconds, feeling a bit dazed and overcome. This was caused by a combination of the stunning scenery, the fact that it was 3 am and the realisation that I was standing at the bottom of the world, in Antarctica. I also hadn't eaten anything since the meal with Matthew two nights ago, but there was something else I couldn't recognise that was adding to the overwhelming feeling I was experiencing. We were given a little welcome talk by one of the amiable and excellent staff of the camp, explaining what was where and where not to walk. Again it was stressed to us about leaving no trace that we had been here, as in litter and cigarette butts, and that we must always use the toilets – it wasn't like camping in the bush, where you could relieve yourself out behind your tent or by a tree.

A few minutes later we walked over to retrieve our bags from a large sled that had been towed from the plane. Sometimes when you are picking up bags from a luggage carousel at an airport, you get a bad feeling that your bags haven't made it, and until you see at least one piece of your luggage, there is a gnawing, unsettling feeling that they are not going to arrive. After helping to unload all the bags off the sled, I had that feeling – times a hundred, and I didn't exactly see a 'Baggage Services' desk anywhere where I could shout at some sap wearing a Qantas vest. I thought of the worst case scenario, but surely there's no way that one bag, my bag, could have fallen off the sled on the way from the plane and plunged down a bottomless crevasse, surely.

Of course it didn't, and just when I had visions of doing the marathon in borrowed tights and my oversized snow boots, another smaller sled arrived with my bag on it. Bradley and I went to our tent and unpacked a few things. My ukulele had made it okay, but I was concerned with it becoming frozen, so it lived in my sleeping bag while I wasn't using it. We had been told there was some food that had been prepared for the freshly arrived marathon group, so I took a deep breath and went to face some carbs.

The kitchen had laid out some bread and condiments, a lentil stew and some mashed potato that smelled absolutely delicious. I thought that was a good sign as I did feel hungry and my mouth was watering. I was taking no chances, though, so I scooped a small dollop of mashed potato onto a plate and gave my body its first proper food in nearly 36 hours.

After a bout of sickness empties your body, you're understandably tentative about putting food back into it, and this mashed potato tasted soooo creamy and good, but I stopped after a couple of spoonfuls, just to let everyone down there in my stomach dust off the cobwebs and get to know each other again.

I retired to the tent to get some sleep, which required an eye mask and earplugs, as the crunching sound of even one person walking across the snow sounded very loud as it cut through the silence. The silence! That's what added to the strange feelings I experienced when I stepped off the truck for the first time.

After a surprisingly refreshing five-hour sleep, I exited the tent in the morning and stood there re-admiring the 360-degree view. That's when I really noticed the complete and overwhelming silence of Antarctica. There was little or no wind blowing and as there were no trees or animals or cars driving in the distance, there was a total absence of peripheral noise. Wherever you are reading this right now, stop and listen for a few seconds. It may seem quiet, but there will be sounds all around you. It might be the voices or sounds of your neighbours or the low hum of distant traffic. The wind blowing through leaves, birds chirping, water flowing in a river or the ocean or the barely perceptible whine of various electrical appliances. There is always something making noise. I have been in recording studios before, in a padded and soundproofed room where you can't hear anything and there is no sound, but the silence in Antarctica was different to that. You were standing outside for a start. Your ears were not blocked and you could see for miles in every direction, but there was a complete and utter lack of sound. It was quite overwhelming and I now understood the phrase 'the silence was deafening' much better having experienced deafening silence.

Once we had all arrived in camp and had a bit of a rest, most of the Ice Marathon participants had risen and were enjoying a lavish breakfast in the dining tent. The time zone used at Union Glacier was identical to Chilean time, so it wasn't such a shock to the system for most of us. Chilean time was 11 hours different to Melbourne time, though, so my personal time clock had been virtually reversed and five hours was the longest stretch of sleep I had been able to procure so far.

As the mashed potato had agreed with me, and had not come gurgling up or squirting out, I was a bit more adventurous that morning and had a piece of toast with Vegemite and some scrambled egg and I felt normality slowly returning. More good news came with the decision that the marathon would not be held that day. The powers that be decided that it would be best to give us all a full day to acclimatise and if the weather was favourable, start the race at 11 the following morning. This was exactly what I wanted to hear and I was filled with a positive feeling that I had turned the corner with my sickness and was going to be fine for the race if I could get some more good food into me.

My bum had other ideas though, as I was still suffering from the runs, or 'Chile belly' as Bradley called it, which was restricting my ability to absorb the fluids that I needed to run the marathon.

After a couple of complicated trips to the toilet, where let's just say the separation of solids and fluids wasn't really going to plan, I went over to see the doctor for some assistance, because I love talking to complete strangers about the minute details of my bowel movements.

'Does it stink?' the doctor asked.

'Does what stink?' I replied.

'The movement,' he said matter of factly.

'Are you asking me does my shit stink?' I said.

I may have been accused in the past of thinking that my shit didn't stink, but I can categorically tell you, sir, that today, my shit does indeed, stink.

He gave me two options. He said: 'We can either give you something to block you up, or you can stop eating completely to get the bug out of your stomach.'

Bug, I thought? In my stomach? In Antarctica? Visions of the movie *The Thing* entered my head and during the conversation, I started to shake uncontrollably, split in half and then enveloped the innocent doctor in a disgusting, tentacled globule of throbbing, alien mass.

'Why are you smiling?' he asked.

'Oh nothing,' I replied. 'I'm just thinking about lunch.'

I decided to take the tablets that would block me up, as I really needed to start eating some food.

After lunch, Richard had organised for everyone to go on a little run on part of the marathon course. This was to give us all a chance to test out the running gear we had brought for the run tomorrow, and also to get a bit of a feeling for the surface. I decided not to take part, as I would need every ounce of energy for the marathon. Instead, I tried on all of my gear and Bradley got me to do some shots of light running around just outside the camp. All of the clothing felt good even though I hadn't worn it since I did the run in the industrial freezer. The temperature around camp was roughly minus 18 degrees Celsius and there was hardly any wind, so it was virtually identical to the conditions that I had faced in the giant freezer, except that I was running on snow and not concrete, there were no boxes of frozen goods and the chance of me being hit by a forklift had decreased somewhat. The sun was shining brightly on its circular journey around the entire horizon. On a clear day the sun was always visible, except for a couple of hours around 4 am, when it dipped behind one of the mountains. It got considerably colder during that time, but mostly it didn't feel too uncomfortable when the sun was shining. The rest of the day was spent walking around the camp or socialising and reading in the dining tent. I enjoyed some of the delectable salads and pasta on offer for dinner, but still ate sparingly. The 'blocking up' tablets seemed to be working, but I didn't want two kilos of pasta to suddenly 'unblock' during the marathon. I still had some concerns in the back of my mind about the ability of my body to complete a physical challenge like this given my inability to eat proper food over the previous two days.

I got a reasonable night's sleep, only waking up once to use my very useful 'pee bottle', instead of getting dressed and crunching over to the toilets. It's a fine art, using a pee bottle in the middle of the night. You don't want to be so wide-awake that you can't go back to sleep easily after you've finished, so I would just half open one eye. Conversely, you really don't want to be so sleepy that your aim suffers and you spill pee all over yourself and your sleeping bag. That would not be good. You also need to label your pee bottle *very clearly* and not store it close to your water bottle. Bradley learned that lesson the hard way, though he said it is something that you would never do twice.

MID ICE CRISIS

I woke at 5.30 am on the day of the marathon feeling the most normal I had felt since arriving in South America seven days previously. This was the first time since I had been sick that I had a positive feeling about the race. The weather was on our side. The sky was clear, the air was calm and the temperature in camp was a cool minus 15 degrees Celsius, though the start of the race was eight kilometres away, in the centre of the glacier, and that always had some wind, which would add an amount of chill to the air.

I got up to have a walk around, because breakfast didn't start until 7 am, four hours before the race.

On the far side of the camp I ran into Emer Dooley, a Professor at the University of Washington in Seattle, and Alison Hamlett, the editor of *Triathletes World* magazine in the UK. They were two of the nine female competitors in this year's race, and were also up early and having a pre-race, nerve-settling walk around the camp. Both of them were experienced marathon runners yet Emer was thinking, 'What have I gotten myself into?'

Alison, who had completed 19 marathons, said she was, understandably, 'Feeling more nervous about this marathon, because so much about this race is out of the ordinary. The temperature, the journey to get there, the severity of the environment and danger of injury and the insignificant feeling caused by our remote and isolated location surrounded by vast, immense tracts of ice and rock.' Being a writer, she used way more adjectives than were necessary, so I have paraphrased her here.

It was almost time for breakfast and I was feeling hungry. The two other marathons that I had done started at 7 am, so if you wanted to eat something decent before those runs, you had to get up really, really early, and even then you would still have the feeling of something sitting in your stomach. With this run starting at 11 am, I had the chance to have a good-sized breakfast and not have it sitting there making me feel all stodgy at the start of the race. At least that's what I thought at the time.

The servery in the dining tent was loaded with the largest selection of delicious-looking, carb-friendly foods a hungry marathoner was ever likely to see. There were cereals, toast, porridge, pasta, pancakes, bananas and mashed potato as well as eggs and fruit juices. I had a banana and some porridge, a pancake with honey and some toast with butter and Vegemite. Take that, glycogen-starved muscles! About two hours later, I knew I had overdone it. Butter doesn't sit well with me at the best of times, but it's just such a perfect accompaniment to Vegemite. Every minute or so my poor stomach was releasing up a Vegemite, banana and butter flavoured burp to remind me to take it easy – it had been a tough few days.

After breakfast, everyone gathered in the dining tent for our final briefing. We were told that the Ice Marathon course would be run over a 25-kilometre loop. To achieve the full 42.195 kilometre distance of a marathon, the starting line was situated eight kilometres away, so we would run 17 kilometres around the loop to the camp and then complete another 25-kilometre lap. There were aid stations with food, drink and toilet facilities located at the nine-kilometre mark, at the camp, (17 kilometres) and at the starting line (25 kilometres) then of course we took in one final stop during the final lap at the first station (34 kilometres). Large plastic bins had been provided so all of the runners could place any special food, drinks or clothing items they needed to be taken to the aid stations so they could be accessed during the race. The supplies that I had waiting for me around the course were a combination of carbohydrate gels and energy bars. I had a complete change of socks at the 25-kilometre station and I ran with a 1.5 litre hydration pack filled with Endura sports drink strapped to my back. It looked like a small backpack and was often used by cyclists or runners on long distance events. It had a thin rubber hose that came out of the pack, over your shoulder and had a mouthpiece that hung near your mouth, making it easy to drink while on the move.

At 10.30 am all of the runners gathered outside the dining tent to await our transport out to the starting line. It was simultaneously exciting and nerve-wracking getting dressed into my specialist clothing for the race.

I had butterflies in my stomach, though the butterflies were being quickly killed by the noxious gases that were being created by the varied mix of foods that I had eaten since ingesting the blocking up tablets given to me by the doctor.

As the sun was out and the temperature looked like it was not going to be too severe, I didn't wear the mid layer on my torso – just the base layer long-sleeved top and my light, windproof jacket. I was also wearing my two pairs of woollen socks, Under Armour trail shoes, heavy duty running tights and windproof pants, thin gloves and mittens, my all-in-one balaclava, neck gaiter and face mask, a light cotton beanie and my ski goggles.

My pockets were loaded with extra food and a good luck toy owl that my daughter, Mary-Lou, had given me. I also put on my parka for the trip out to the starting line, as we were all being towed there standing on top of an open-topped sled that looked very much like a rail truck used for transporting cattle.

We were crammed together on top of the sled for the 15-minute journey to the start, and more than one person commented that we looked (and felt) like victims being taken away to our impending doom.

My observation about the weather being not too severe was premature, as my feet were freezing cold and I was gradually losing the feeling in my toes, one by one. Many of the other runners had the same experience and we all banged our feet together or against the railing at the side of the sled, trying to get some blood flowing back into them.

The start line was merely a banner announcing 'Ice Marathon 2011' to anyone who had forgotten where we were or what we were about to do.

The start was actually a bit of a non-event. We jumped off the sled, took our parkas off and walked to the start line. I just had time for a nervous, pre-race wee at the makeshift toilet behind a small tent that was set up, before we gathered together for a group photo underneath the banner. I only had two toes left that I could feel and was hoping that beginning to run would bring the feeling back into my feet. About 10 seconds after the photo was finished, I heard someone saying 'Three, two, one,' then a siren went off and we were all running.

Oh my God, I thought. It's really happening. Am I really going to be running for the next eight hours? I wasn't sure that I was in the right headspace to be setting out on a marathon, but there was nothing that I could do but get the hell on with it. I found myself in the middle of the pack of runners and it soon became clear that some were treating this like a real race, some were keeping to themselves and some, like me, were just happy to be there and were going to take as long as it took to finish.

The pack quickly spread out to a single file as we all tried establish a pace that was suited to our individual abilities. The main thing that I noticed about the first few hundred metres of the course was the uneven surface. Three days previously, the track had been groomed with some kind of snow related grooming machine. In the days since the grooming, the wind had blown drifts of snow over sections of the track, so you would be running for five metres on a reasonable surface then suddenly sink down past your ankles for the next five metres. This made it very difficult to establish a solid rhythm, which is the essence of running a long distance event. This deeper snow also served to drain your energy faster than running on a hard surface.

Emer later said: 'I was running in Alison Hamlett's footsteps and she weighs about five kilos. She was bopping along on the ice and I was punching through on every step. All I could think was that I was going to die of exhaustion before we even got going.'

Alison was more philosophical: 'I wondered if I'd started too fast! With such a huge challenge ahead, everyone had talked about how important setting a conservative pace would be, but once the race began, I let my enthusiasm get the better of me. I remember thinking that I couldn't quite believe I was running in the same pristine, perfect environment that Scott and Amundsen raced through 100 years before. And I thought, "Bloody hell, what a gorgeous day to be running a marathon at the end of the earth!"'

Alvin Matthews had started fast and quickly thought: 'Man, this is going to be way harder than I thought.'

Clement, the Frenchman, or 'Le Gazelle' as he was now known, said: 'The ground was quite soft. Every footstep had to be light in order not to crack into the snow and lose velocity. I was very concentrated on myself, my body, my feelings, especially my heart beat. There were so many new parameters compared to a usual race that can induce an increase of your heart beat, it was necessary to find a good running pace that would entitle me to give my best without burning out!'

Clement obviously found his pace right away, as he immediately took an early lead, ahead of Matthew and Yvonne, who was happy that her toes had started to thaw out after the sled trip out to the start. She described her early strategy thus:

'I was thinking it must be easier to be nearer the front so

you would be running in frozen snow, not snow that had been trampled on by all the runners, so I concentrated on trying to run on the footprints of the two guys in front of me [Clement and Matthew] – that seems a crazy idea now.'

I was thinking along the same lines as Christopher Duff, a softly spoken American accountant who lived in Tokyo, and Yvonne – that by running in other people's footprints you would be less likely to sink into the snow. This theory didn't always work, though, as sometimes the first footprint had merely weakened the surface crust and your own foot would sink down into the softer snow beneath.

I usually found it helped to run a race if I gave myself a goal time to run it in, and to break the race into sections or single kilometres, and so fill it up with mini-targets to hit along the way.

Months before the race, I wondered what time I should aim for in the Ice Marathon. I did some extensive research looking at past runners' finishing times, which were all up on the website, to try and work out just how long it might take me. I had completed two 'normal' marathons, and both times I had finished pretty much smack bang on four hours. By searching on the names of past finishers in the Ice Marathon, plus the word 'marathon,' it was fairly easy to find other marathon times for them so I could compare my times to theirs.

The standing race record was set in 2010 by Brazilian runner Bernardo Fonseca in a time of four hours and 20 minutes, and he usually ran a marathon in around three hours 15 minutes, so I knew I was going to have to add quite a bit of time onto four hours.

Those who normally ran a marathon around the four-hour mark, like me, had finished the Ice Marathon in a time anywhere between five and a half to seven hours, so that's what I was reasonably expecting for myself. Whether or not those runners had experienced the illness that I had just gone through was undocumented, and therefore unknown. Before I got sick, I was thinking I would like to finish in under six hours, but now I was honestly just so happy and relieved to be running the first few metres of the race that I had lowered my expectations and would be happy to come in under eight hours.

After two or three kilometres I had regained the feeling in all of my toes and most people had established their pace and the space between the runners was quickly expanding. Clement was still in the lead, followed by Matthew and Alvin with a group of about six runners close behind. I was still around the middle of the field, a few hundred metres back. I overtook one of the other runners for the first time around this point. It was Sarah Ames, the Chicago lawyer, and we had been running not far from one another since the start. I said a quick hello, but she was all concentration. She recalled:

'I was thinking that this is going to be bit harder of a run than I thought and I will have to pace myself. I was also trying to learn which parts of the trail were firmer and to keep looking out for those areas, so I was concentrating on where my feet were landing.'

I was trying to do the same thing. In parts of the course, right at the side of the track, there was sometimes a thin wedge of flatter snow, possibly where a part of the grooming machine or a sled had previously travelled on the course, and this tended to be a little more solid and dependable than the middle of the track, so when it was visible, I tried to run on that. I remember thinking that I was glad I had done the runs along the beach as it often felt similar to the soft, uneven surface of the sand. If I were to do this race again, or offer any advice to people who were going to run it, I would suggest doing one two-hour run per week on soft sand as part of your training.

After three or four more kilometres, the line of runners was very stretched out and I could see the leading runners as small figures way off in the distance.

With all the concentrating on where to put my feet, I kept having to remind myself of the stunning location and I would sometimes slow down to have a look around and just shake my head in disbelief. If I thought the silence in the camp was deafening, out here in the middle of the glacier with no one near me, it was mind-bogglingly quiet.

The sound of my feet crunching in the snow seemed so loud and, as I wasn't listening to any music, it was the only sound I heard during the race apart from the times I was at the food stations.

Around the six kilometre-point in the race we were running almost directly into the sun, and it was getting quite warm. I had to remove my balaclava, and ran the rest of the race just wearing the light cotton beanie on my head. I also took my gloves and mittens off and handed them to Bradley, who had procured the use of a snowmobile and a driver for the entire race. He was busy driving alongside me taking footage, then racing ahead and setting up arty shots of me running past. I thought it was useful to have him nearby and I could at least use him to carry some of my excess clothing.

I had Ladislav running a few hundred metres in front of me and I believed Sarah was about the same distance behind me. It was very difficult to judge distances in Antarctica due to the lack of landmarks and the way that the light reflected, or refracted, or whatever it did, to make the upcoming food station look so near, yet so far away.

I spotted a dot in the distance, which I knew must be the tent of the aid station, but it was tricky trying to work out if it was 400 metres or two kilometres away.

I arrived there and was feeling pretty good at this point. I obviously had a good fitness base from the training and it had only been nine kilometres, so I should have been feeling good at that stage.

There was a table set up with an array of foods like bananas, chocolate, cookies and some lollies. There was water and a hot orange drink that was rather delicious.

Mid Ice Crisis

Some of the staff of the Union Glacier camp were manning the aid stations and they offered a cheerful face and a friendly word just when you needed it.

There was tent set up if you wanted to warm up, though at this point I think most of us were feeling quite warm. I went over behind a snow wall that had been built to house the 'toilet' which was a can with a seat on it, I had quick wee and thankfully there were no rumblings from my stomach that needed to be tended to. The 'blocking up' tablets had evidently done their job well.

Alvin later said this about his experience at the first aid station:

'Urinating in an outdoor "toilet" was quite a challenge and a bit scary, for lack of a better word. "He" didn't seem to want to come out of all the protective layers and I wasn't keen on leaving him exposed for long, due to the risk of the ever-present frost nip/bite we had been warned about.'

After I had been at the aid station for a few minutes, the cold started working its way through the light clothing I was wearing so I started off again on the next eight-kilometre leg towards the camp. The first leg had been one straight line that finished on the far corner of the course and I was now headed in a different direction and welcomed a new view of a different mountain. Hooray! Something different to look at! The sun was now directly at my back and I immediately felt colder on this section of the course. Many other runners also had difficulties trying to balance their clothing and the temperature.

Emer said: 'I couldn't believe how quickly the conditions changed. I was totally unprepared for having to strip down on one section of the course and then having to immediately cover up as I changed direction and faced away from the sun. My hands were almost instantly flash frozen once they were in the shade.'

Rebecca noted: 'I seemed to get rather hot when I was running and would take off my gloves and facemask, then 10 minutes later if I slowed down I would be cold. It was challenging trying to find the balance between comfort and cold.'

At the 12-kilometre mark, I was making fairly good time – just over seven minutes per kilometre – which put me on track to finish in about five hours. Wow, I thought, even if I slow down quite a bit later on, I could be looking at five and a half hours. At this point, when I tried to get a drink from the tube leading from my backpack, no liquid came through the tube and I realised that it had frozen solid. I had to stop and shove the tube back into the pack, against my back, so that the warmth of my body could thaw it out. I battled this frustrating problem for the rest of the race and as the run progressed and I got more exhausted, I was easily irritated by small annoyances. This second section of the race was slightly uphill, which slowed down my pace a bit. I topped the rise and as I approached the next corner, which was a 90-degree turn that headed back towards the camp and the second food station, I saw the plodding shape of a runner ahead that I thought must have been Ladislav. He was just rounding the corner.

'Ah,' I thought, 'I will use him as a target to overtake, as he is now only a few hundred metres away.' Ten minutes later I still hadn't even reached the corner. That's how misleading the perception of distance was, even on a sunny, clear day.

I overtook Ladislav just before reaching the second aid station at the camp. I took my time at this station and walked over to my tent to change my long-sleeved base layer top, which had got quite damp with sweat. I also got a slight feeling that I may have to unblock some of the breakfast, so I visited the toilets, but nothing was unblocking just yet. I wasn't feeling very hungry, so I just swallowed a gel and had a few sips of the hot orange drink, which didn't taste quite as delicious as it did the first time. I had spent about eight minutes there in total, so I took off again, still thinking about achieving some sort of good time. This next section of the race was the most enjoyable for me. There were eight kilometres until the next food station, and the surface along here was by far the most stable, as it was more sheltered than the rest of the course and didn't have many of the nasty drifts of soft snow that we had already run through on the far side of the course.

At the 21-kilometre halfway mark I passed Ladislav again, as he had started out from the last food station before me, and I was feeling okay. I had been running for exactly two hours and 45 minutes and if I kept the same pace, I would be on track for a very respectable time of five and a half hours. Maybe the Chile Belly wasn't going to affect me as I worried it would. Passing the halfway point helped me mentally as I felt that every step from now on was one step closer to the finish line and I remember thinking at that point, if I can just get to the 32-kilometre mark, I know that I am going to finish the marathon.

The third aid station approached and now I was 25 kilometres down, 17 to go. I sat down for a break in the tent, took off my sodden socks and changed into the dry pairs that I had waiting for me. The old socks weren't just wet from sweat. When my feet sank into the deeper snow, some of the loose snow would stay around at the top of my socks and be melted by my body heat, which added to the dampness. As I sat there taking a bit of a break, I wondered how the rest of the runners were going.

When Alvin had arrived at the third aid station, he was told that he was the third male runner in, and the fourth overall behind Le Gazelle, Matthew and Yvonne, who was absolutely gunning it.

'It suddenly turned into a race for me,' Alvin said, 'as I saw an opportunity for my first ever podium (or even top 10) finish. From that point, I pushed myself to my limits, physically and mentally. I was obsessed with catching the guy ahead, Matthew, and not getting caught by anyone from behind. This is the first race that I talked to God ... I made a bunch of promises to him (that I can't remember now) if I could just finish in the top three.'

I wonder how Alvin is doing with those promises to God now? I mean, I wanted to do well in the race too, Alvin, but I wasn't prepared to sell my soul.

By this point Le Gazelle (Clement) had pulled far ahead of the other runners.

Clement noted: 'I thought I could speed up a little bit on the second lap, but since the surface had been smashed by all the runners during the first lap, it took a very big great effort to maintain my speed.'

As I left the station for the second-last leg, I tried to eat a power bar from my pocket, but it was frozen solid. These bars were difficult to eat at the best of times due to their dense texture, so the best I could do was to suck on a corner of the bar for a while to weaken it and eventually snap some off. This was not such a bad thing, as it helped to pass about three ks. I was at roughly the 29-kilometre mark when it all started to go a bit horrible.

I was now on the same section of track that we had started the race on and the surface was much worse now, as Clement had found out on his second lap. As well as the extra footprints that had chopped up the surface, it was also a bit warmer as well, and the snow was softer. The middle section of this nine-kilometre, perfectly straight segment of the course was uphill and I hadn't really noticed that on the first lap. My legs were starting to feel very heavy and it was so taxing to be sinking into the surface and not being able to get any purchase to push off.

The marathon course was marked by little orange flags, 25 metres apart, which served to help the runners stay on the track if the conditions were foggy. I now used these flags to do a run/walk combination to get to the top of the rise that I was slowly climbing. I would run for three flags and then walk to the next one, repeating this cycle for about ten minutes, until I crested the hill and spotted the final aid station in the distance. It seemed quite close, but may have been 85 kilometres away for all that I could tell. I stopped here for a little look around at the scenery again and continued to be amazed, but I also felt very alone. There was a tiny speck of a runner way behind me, and in front of me I could see another speck approaching the aid station. The closest other humans to us here at Union Glacier were at the South Pole, 800 kilometres away.

My legs were still hurting and I could feel that I was getting low on energy, but with the slight downhill slope and the visual attraction of the aid station pulling me towards it, I ran all the way and arrived there to the encouraging smiles of the staff who were manning the station.

I can't speak highly enough of the wonderful people who were working there at the Union Glacier camp. They went above and beyond the call of their regular duties to help the runners complete this insane event. The person required to work for a season in the Antarctic must be competent and able to work as part of a team. Being friendly and cheerful sure helped too, and in my experience, every member of the staff was nothing less than exceptional and they made the entire stay an enjoyable experience.

My experience at this point, however, was far from enjoyable, though at last I had a strong feeling inside me that I was going to at least complete the race, even if I had to crawl. There were only eight kilometres to go.

It had taken me almost an hour and 15 minutes to cover the previous nine kilometres. I had been out on the course for four hours and 30 minutes, so I thought that five and a half hours was an achievable time and I should at least break six hours. During my time covering that previous leg, the winner of the race had crossed the finish line.

It was Le Gazelle! Clement Thevenet had smashed the previous Ice Marathon record, finishing in a time of three hours 47 minutes and seven seconds. It was an incredible effort by Clement, who said after he finished he felt so happy it was over, and just wanted to share the news with his loved ones, though it had been the hardest marathon he had run.

A few months previously, Clement had run the gruelling Marathon des Sables (marathon of the sands), which is a six-day 251-kilometre ultramarathon through the Sahara Desert, where you must carry all of your food and personal supplies with you. If Clement found the Ice Marathon difficult then what hope was there for the rest of us?

The next runner over the line, nearly 40 minutes later, was Yvonne Brown. It was an inspirational run from Yvonne, who said after the race that once she passed the first 10 kilometres, she actually found it easier than she thought it was going to be.

There's something to be said for lowering your expectations I guess.

Alvin's temporary conversion to religion must have worked, as he reeled in the distance between himself and Matthew during the final eight-kilometre stretch, battling serious cramps in the final two kilometres and finished with a time of four hours 38 minutes, just ahead of Emer (four hours, 41 minutes) and Alison (four hours 46 minutes) – a brilliant effort from these women, both excellent runners and lovely humans.

Matthew was in next with time four hours 52 minutes. When I asked him later why he dropped off so much towards the end, he said he was saving himself, because he planned to run in the 100-kilometre ultramarathon the next day! I didn't believe him.

Back at the final aid station, I had seen Christopher running off and I planned to leave quite quickly to get the final eight kilometres over and done with and maybe even catch up to him. As soon as I had stopped running when I arrived at the aid station, I felt an intense pain in my stomach. I poured myself a cup of the hot orange drink and took a few sips. I did not feel good. I thought the 'great unblocking' was about to occur so I went to sit on the makeshift toilet that was set up there, but nothing happened, just a bit of wind, and it was not the wind blowing down the glacier, if you get my drift. I walked around a bit and tried jumping up and down, which made me burp a few times, but something hurty was happening inside me and I was not sure what it was. I didn't want to stand, or sit, or lie down, or eat, or drink, or go to the toilet and I certainly didn't feel like running eight ks, that's for sure.

'Well, this is a fine mess you've gotten us into,' said Bad Rusty.

'Oh hello there,' I thought. 'I wondered when you might be making an appearance.'

'Can you tell me again, when was this thing ever a good idea?'

'Oh come on, we got sick,' I protested.

'Yes, I was going to say something about those *Misterios* back in Punta Arenas,' said Bad Rusty.

'You should've warned me,' I said.

'Would-a, could-a, should-a,' taunted Bad Rusty. 'Let's just stop and get a ride back to camp on a snowmobile. It will be good for the book.'

'No way,' I said. 'It's only eight ks, I'm going, and you're coming with me.'

'What the hell is causing that stomach pain?'

'I've got no idea,' I said. 'Probably something to do with not eating for so long, then adding a rather large concoction of different foods to my delicate stomach and now the exit has been blocked and all hell is about to break loose. Let's get out of here, it will be over soon.'

'Lead on you mad bastard, let's do this!'

Even Bad Rusty understood what we had to do here. There was to be no giving up, no whinging and no whining. Look where I was, for crying out loud. I was in Antarctica looking at mountains and glaciers that only a few hundred humans had ever seen, let alone run amongst. If this last bit of the marathon was going to be a painful, horrible and unenjoyable experience, then it was at least going to be a painful, horrible and unenjoyable experience with spectacular views.

As Douglas Mawson said in *Home of the Blizzard*, 'The ferocity of the wind was strong on the glacier, but we continued on nonetheless …'

I said goodbye to the crew who were manning the station, let off a good luck fart and started the final leg of the marathon.

The pain in my stomach was awful and unfortunately it was not relieved by the constant burping and farting that I was releasing into the clean, untouched air of Antarctica. Apart from the pain I was feeling, at this point I also felt strong with the knowledge that no matter what happened from now on, I was actually going to finish the race. I thought a lot about my family and friends and well-wishers and, after the illness I had suffered and being faced with the possibility of not being able to take part in the race at all, a few waves of relief washed over me, which helped the pain I was in. Then I would be jolted back to reality.

With each step I took I felt the pain throb in my stomach. It was like I was a one-man band who has his feet connected to a bass drum and cymbal but rather than hitting a drum with each step, the bass drum pedal would whack me in the gut instead. The musical accompaniment to my torturous one-man band set-up was provided by the tuneful tooting emanating from my backdoor trumpet.

My hands got extremely cold at this point as the sun was at my back and I cursed myself for having handed my gloves and mittens to Bradley earlier in the race, then I cursed Bradley for not being around.

With four kilometres to go, I returned to the run/walk combo again, using the flags as markers and at one stage got a strong message from my internal organs that the time to unblock had arrived. I realised I had no choice and I was going to have to break the rules of the Antarctic Environmental Treaty and make a deposit of my own that would remain buried and frozen on the Union Glacier until it eventually made its way to the ocean in about 10,000 years time.

I imagined some ultra-modern scienticians from the future finding my frozen doodie and exclaiming: 'My God! Are those pine nuts in there?'

There was no one around (!) so I went off the track a bit, kicked a hole in the snow, dropped my dacks and proceeded to let off what I can confidently say was the loudest, longest and most relieving fart I have ever had the pleasure of experiencing. I think it may have actually triggered a few avalanches on far-off mountains. There was nothing more than wind released so the Antarctic Treaty had been preserved. My renewed energy kept me going for the next kilometre even though I was barely able to keep willing my legs to keep moving. My hip joints in particular were very sore. I knew that I was going to finish the race but I no longer cared about a time. If I picked up my pace and didn't stop again, I would just break six hours, but at this point Bad Rusty and I both agreed that we didn't really give a toss about time – we just wanted it to be over. We also both agreed that this was a once-in-a-lifetime experience that we would never want to do again (with apologies to Tim Vine).

Spending six hours doing something that's really fun is generally too long and you're going to get sick of it eventually, so after all this time out on the course even the spectacular sights were now wearing a bit thin.

I rounded the final corner and began climbing the slight slope that would take me back into camp to the finish line. I had given up any chance of catching up to Christopher. He later told me that he used me as motivation to keep running the final leg. Oh yeah, Christopher, beat the poor sick guy why don't you. My musical wind symphony returned, as did the pain in my stomach, which was now threatening to add cramp into the mix.

For the second-last kilometre I continued the walk/run combo and decided that I had to run the final one k into the camp. Not for any reasons of integrity, but simply because there were quite a few people around the camp and I didn't want to be seen walking in to the finish line. I had been running for six hours, two minutes and 12 seconds when I crossed the line.

Like the previous marathons I had done, there was no moment of euphoria upon finishing the Ice Marathon. Sure I was smiling as I was cheered over the final metres by probably five per cent of the entire population of Antarctica. Oh, the feeling of relief!

Sweet, sweet relief to know that it was over. This time I actually did raise my arms, put my face to the sky with closed eyes and exhaled deeply.

I had a medal placed around my neck, then I lay down on the ground on my back and let out a small victory fart.

Immediately after the finish, I didn't really know what to do with myself. I would have murdered a hot shower at that point, but of course there were none. The next hour or so is a bit of a blur. I remember hobbling over to the dining tent and drinking a cup of water, then filling up a thermos with hot water to take to my tent to wash up a bit. I really should have tried to eat some food to start the recovery process, but the pain in my stomach was too great to even consider food. I got to the tent and changed into fresh clothes, which did feel good. I didn't know if I should walk around or stand or sit or lie down. Anything I did offered no improvement on how I felt. I started shivering uncontrollably so I got into my sleeping bag. That's it, I thought, get off my feet for a while. I wondered if I should go and see the doctor. What if I just shake and die in the tent? No one would find me for ages. I started to warm up once I was in the sleeping bag but still couldn't stop shivering. I tried to eat a muesli bar, which disintegrated at the first bite as it was so cold.

I drank some sports drink then spent about two minutes just shivering, swearing and cursing at random things. The brunt of my filthy tirade was, in no particular order: my aching stomach, the cold, the muesli bar, marathons, Bradley, my clothes, the door of the tent, which was not fully zipped up, shivering, lack of hot showers and probably a few other things that I can't recall now. I eventually fell into a sleepy kind of daze. I dreamed I was running a marathon but was hopelessly underprepared and at the first drink station I changed my shoes into heavy Blundstone boots and then I couldn't find my phone, which threw me into a terrible state of panic.

That was actually a true dream, I don't know what it means and really, it's a bit cruel to share the contents of your dreams with other people, despite how incredibly realistic and amazing they seem to you; people don't want to hear what your dreams were about, so sorry for that.

I woke up after about 45 minutes and couldn't believe that I had stopped shivering, the pain in my stomach had lessened and I was starting to feel slightly human again. Hunger also made an appearance, so I vacuumed out my sleeping bag of all remaining muesli bar crumbs and thought about joining the other finished runners in the dining tent.

My legs were surprisingly workable and when I shuffled into the tent I was welcomed with many encouraging cheers. There were warm congratulations all round and nobody asked or mentioned anything about what time anybody had run. It wasn't about that. Now, it was all about celebration.

There was plenty of delicious food available and over the next six or so hours, tired bodies and sore muscles were soon forgotten as we grazed and drank and chatted and laughed and relived the race, swapping stories with the other runners and hearing about their own experiences. Many people now brought out the supplies they had stocked up on the day before we left Punta Arenas. There was Bailey's and Irish whiskey, champagne, Chilean wine and beer, mescal and Pisco. The kitchen served only a small amount of alcohol with meals as they did not want anyone passing out in the snow on the way back to their tent. My ukulele came out for a bit of a sing later on and as each of the other runners who were yet to finish approached the finish line, there would be a shout of 'runner approaching' and we would all head out to cheer them over the line.

The next day was overcast and noticeably colder than anything we had yet experienced – around minus 25 degrees. My legs felt much better that day, though my hips were still quite sore. I think the combination of the extreme cold and the fact that I took two hours longer than my other marathons possibly contributed to a faster recovery overall. Ice baths are a common post-event treatment for athletes and are known to assist in the recovery of fatigued muscles. I was also much fitter than I was when I ran the other marathons, so that probably also affected my recovery, so by the end of the next day I was walking without too much difficulty.

At around 9 am, less than 24 hours since the marathon had started, six more brave, mad runners lined up for the running of the 7th Antarctic Ultramarathon, to be run over four laps of the marathon course for a total of 100 kilometres. Well, five of them were going to attempt that distance anyway. While we were still in Punta Arenas I had asked Richard Donovan if he would be running the 100-kilometre event, and he replied in his cheerful Irish brogue:

'Well, I haven't really been able to train as much as I would like, but I'm thinking of running 100 *miles* down there this year, as no one's ever done that before.'

So while the other guys were doing their mere 100-kilometre ultramarathons, Richard would continue on and do a 160-kilometre uber-super-mega-ultra marathon, or whatever you want to call it.

Mid Ice Crisis

I was surprised to see that Clement Thevenet was lining up for the ultramarathon. Obviously winning the marathon in record time the previous day had been a mere hors d'oeuvre for 'Le Gazelle'. Also standing at the start was our old mate, Survivor Matthew, who said he just wanted to do a 25-kilometre lap to keep the others company and then see how he felt. Awful, I suspected, but that didn't deter Matthew.

Off they trotted and over the next 24 hours the rest of us would be roused by the familiar call of 'runner approaching' and we would scramble away from our books or Scrabble games to cheer the runners on.

Matthew came in from his 25-kilometre lap looking a bit worse for wear, and fell into his tent for a nap. Three hours later someone said that he had woken up and gone out for another lap 'to see how it felt'.

As the temperature was colder, there was no sun and a very cool wind had sprung up on the far side of the course, it made conditions for the ultramarathoners much more difficult than we marathoners enjoyed (!) the previous day. They were all running their own races by now and I saw Matthew after he completed 50 kilometres. He was trying to be chipper but he looked absolutely spent. Despite this, after a hot drink and some food, he decided to do one more lap.

Was I surprised when Clement came bounding in after 100 kilometres to claim first place and another race record? Yes and no. He didn't look too bad, but he later described to me the final part of the ultramarathon:

'The last 15 k of the 100-k race was very difficult, a real life experience. The temperatures had dropped, I was facing the wind and my face was frozen. I was feeling lonely, far from the base camp and other runners. Stopping and even walking would have become dangerous; I have to admit that I then got stressed! I was exaggerating my arm movements in order to warm me up a little bit. I was singing AC/DC songs like "Hard as a Rock" to get motivated and desperately looking for the tent of the last checkpoint.

'Once I reached that last checkpoint, the path was then protected from the wind, I knew that I was safe and nearly done with the race. Just five kilometres to go after 95 kilometres – *bonheur*!'

I had gone to bed and missed the other runners coming in. The next morning I heard that Matthew had returned to camp after completing 75 kilometres and thought that he was so close to finishing an ultramarathon he had to go out and do one more 25-kilometre lap, otherwise he would always wonder what it was like to have done a 100-kilometre run in those conditions. He learned that Antarctica is not a place to be messed with, eventually staggering to the finish line suffering from hypothermia and almost collapsing. He was taken straight to the medical tent where he remained for the duration of our stay on a saline drip, eventually making a full recovery by the time we got back to Punta Arenas.

That night I put the ukulele to good use and did a short performance in the dining tent for the other runners and any staff who happened to be there. I sang a couple of Scaredies songs and a specially prepared song about the Ice Marathon I had written that afternoon that basically made fun of some of the other competitors and the event – all good natured of course.

And what of poor old mad Richard Donovan, who was attempting the first ever 100-mile run in Antarctica? He continued running through the night and successfully crossed the finish line the next morning. He had been going for just on 24 hours. Call him what you may – crazy, insane, courageous, inspiring – whatever you think, there is no doubt it was an incredible achievement.

'ARE YOU ONE OF THIS MEN?'

The following day we packed up, said our thank-yous and goodbyes to the staff and to the Union Glacier camp and caught the Ilyushin back to the civilisation of Punta Arenas. It was a different experience doing that flight while not being ill, though Igor still had the heater pumping for the duration of the flight. I spent a fair amount of time trying to look out of the tiny window and am happy to say that I did get to see some large white shapes that I took to be icebergs as we crossed from the beautiful southern continent over the Bellingshausen Sea on our way back to South America.

That night most of us went out for a huge celebratory dinner in a local restaurant. The Pisco Sours and the light hearted conversation were flowing freely.

At one point during the night, while I was on my way to the bathroom, one of the young Chilean waitresses stopped me and asked, in broken English: 'Excuse me, are you from Australia?'

'Yes,' I replied.

She showed me some words written on a napkin.

'Are you one of this men?' The napkin had the words Scared Weird Little Guys written on it. That was a surprise, but I was suspicious.

'Did one of those people at the table tell you to say that?'

'No,' she smiled. 'My friend and I watch you on the YouTube.'

I got recognised in Chile! There I was on a trip to represent the change in my life from Scared Weird Little Guy to who knows what and at the completion of my adventure, I got a little reminder that I am still just who I am and nothing will change that.

Just goes to prove what a small world this is. I was sitting there with 24 other people in a restaurant at the bottom of the world and we had all just shared an incredible experience that we will never forget and it's very likely that I will never see any of them ever again.

The day after the Ice Marathon I was having a little walk around the camp by myself and a feeling of satisfaction and achievement came over me. Some words also popped into my head.

'I can do anything.'

I don't mean that in a self-help, positive-thinking-seminar, Amway-convention kind of a way. It wasn't like that at all. This was just a deep, calm feeling of 'I can do anything,' and it felt pretty darn good.

Did this adventure scratch the itch that I needed scratched? Who can say? Well, I can say, I guess, so if you are asking, which you're not – it's a rhetorical question ... Or is it? Where was I?

Yes, I think that choosing an adventure like this, one that needed such serious mental and physical commitment has definitely helped me find closure on such an all-encompassing part of my life.

So now what? What's the next big adventure? I don't know yet, but until then, I'm just going out for a run – and I may be some time.

7TH ANTARCTIC ICE MARATHON AND 100K, DECEMBER 2011: RESULTS

MEN'S MARATHON
1. Clement Thevenet (FRA) 3:47:07 hours
2. Alvin Matthews (USA) 4:38:19 hours
3. Matthew Von Ertfelda (USA) 4:52:58 hours
4. Simon Abrahams (GBR) 4:56:49 hours
4. Joey McBreary (USA) 4:56:49 hours
6. Krzysztof Szachna (POL) 5:02:50 hours
7. Dave Kennedy (USA) 5:06:42 hours
8. Errol Damelin (GBR) 5:14:30 hours
9. Taco Jongman (NED) 5:23:00 hours
10. Doug Carrell (USA) 5:44:26 hours
11. Christopher Duff (USA) 5:53:58 hours
12. Rusty Berther (AUS) 6:02:12 hours
13. Ray Miller (USA) 6:16:29 hours
14. Riet Van de Velde (BEL) 6:28:31 hours
15. Ladislav Simek (CZE) 6:29:52 hours
16. Michael Parrott (CAN) 6:39:06 hours
17. Michael Bartl (GER) 6:51:46 hours
18. Jeremy Cashen (NZL) 7:28:10 hours

19. Tom Cashen (NZL) 7:28:11 hours
20. Mark Kooijman (PHI) 7:31:18 hours
21. Don Kern (USA) 7:53:38 hours
22. Sebastian Armenault (ARG) 8:09:41 hours
23. Anand Anantharaman (IND) 8:45:40 hours

* George Nichols (USA) ran a marathon on 2 December in 8:30:12 hrs

WOMEN'S MARATHON
1. Yvonne Brown (GBR) 4:26:10 hours
2. Emer Dooley (IRL) 4:41:30 hours
3. Alison Hamlett (GBR) 4:46:39 hours
4. Elizabeth Chapman (GBR) 5:43:57 hours
5. Sarah Ames (GER) 6:35:58 hours
6. Mala Honnatti (IND) 7:11:26 hours
7. Sophie Woo (NED) 7:31:18 hours
8. Rebecca Frechette (USA) 8:43:50 hours
9. Linh Huynh (CAN) 8:44:53 hours

* Bonnie Bailey (USA) ran a marathon on 2 December in 8:30:12 hrs

ANTARCTIC 100 KILOMETRES
1. Clement Thevenet (FRA) 12:09:06 hours
2. Marc de Keyser (BEL) 12:14:18 hours
3. Dave Deany (AUS) 13:48:14 hours
4. Brent Weigner (USA) 15:41:04 hours
5. Matthew Von Ertfelda (USA) 20:03:42 hours

100-MILE POLAR CENTENARY RUN
1. Richard Donovan (IRL) 24:35:02 hours

WHITE CONTINENT HALF-MARATHON
1. Chad Bruce (CAN) 2:30:32 hours
2. Matt Kirby (GBR) 3:01:01 hours

THANKS

I have changed some people's names in this book, either to protect them, protect me, because I couldn't remember them, or because I thought of a funnier name than their real one. I also changed some of the names of venues, towns, hospitals and bands for the same reasons.

Firstly, I would like to thank my wife, Denise, and my children Hank and Mary-Lou. Denise supported me and believed in this idea from the very beginning, sometimes more than I did. Without her encouragement and patience I would never have been able to finish this book.

Bernadette Wyer for her inspiration, encouragement and incredible generosity. Bern was originally going to do the Ice Marathon with me, but ended up pulling out six months before the race. It was Bern who first told me about the existence of a marathon in Antarctica and she was the one who first suggested the idea of making a documentary about the trip.

Bradley Howard 'my friend!' for being an excellent travel companion and fun roommate as well as a top camera guy.

Deirdre Cooney for helping mould me into an elite running machine and for good conversation on those long runs.

Caitlin, Penny, Pip, Susan, Dale and all the members of the Fit2Gether running classes for sharing some of the training runs and providing inspiration at 6 am on cold winter mornings.

Julia Taylor, thanks for believing that I had a book in me and that the stories of the Scaredies were worth telling.

Linda Funnell, thanks for caring about the book as much as I did.

Thanks to Poppy Grijalbo, John O'Brien and all at The Five Mile Press.

Thanks to Richard Donovan, Matthew von Ertfelda, Clement Thevenet, Alvin Matthews, Yvonne Brown, Christopher Duff, Emer Dooley, Alison Hamlett, Sarah Ames, Brent Weigner, Linh Huynh, Rebecca Frechette, Dave Kennedy, Ladislav Simek, Don Kern and all of the other participants of the 2011 Ice Marathon for being so generous in sharing their individual experiences. Sorry I couldn't mention you all.

Mike King for his excellent photos and kind permission to let me share some of them in this book, and Dave Painter for his wonderful camera work.

Thanks to the staff of the Union Glacier Camp and all at Adventure Network International.

Stephanie Taylor and Rachel Shephard for helping me with the Antarctic maps, and to Bruce, who actually wasn't that bad.

Igor, may you never crack a smile.

Greg, Phil and Sean from the Corky's, without you guys there would be no Scaredies.

Rob Lees for legal advice.

Carolina Cabezas – *Gracias a mi amiga para practicar español y sí, hablan rápido en Chile.*

Other people I would like to thank, in no particular order, are: Harry Silman and all at Izzi and Popo, Michael Ward, Mark Cutler, Colin Lane, Frank Woodley, Dave O'Neil, Shaun Micallef, Craig Godard, Simon Rogers, Russell Fletcher, Andrew Goodone, Judith Lucy, Dom from Motorino for the goggles, Gillian Farrow, Noelene Gorman, Sherry Plant, Jason Berther, Mark Doherty at Asics, James and Jenny Kiely, Tristan Miller, Tony Wilson, Michael Lynch, Marilen Tabacco and all at Smart Artists.

Finally I would like to give a special thanks to John Fleming. This book wouldn't have happened without many of the people mentioned here but it really wouldn't have happened without John. We shared so many incredible and amazing experiences together; meeting so many great people and doing some crazy shows all over the world – some a little scary and some a little weird. Thanks for the shows, the laughs, the stories, the hard work, the stirring conversations on long trips, and the companionship. I truly hope you find what you're looking for and if you ever want to get back together to do some gigs, I know some fans in Southern Chile who would come and see us.